6.19

HAWAII'S RELIGIONS

HAWAII'S RELIGIONS

by John F. Mulholland

Charles E. Tuttle Company
RUTLAND, VERMONT & TOKYO, JAPAN

Representatives

FOR CONTINENTAL EUROPE
Boxerbooks, Inc., Zurich
FOR THE BRITISH ISLES
Prentice-Hall International, Inc., London
FOR AUSTRALASIA
Paul Flesch & Co., Pty. Ltd., Melbourne
FOR CANADA
M. G. Hurtig Ltd., Edmonton

Published by the Charles E. Tuttle Company, Inc.
of Rutland, Vermont & Tokyo, Japan
with editorial offices at
Suido 1-chome, 2-6, Bunkyo-ku, Tokyo

Library of Congress Catalog Card No. 76–104197
Standard Book No. 8048 0710-8

First printing, 1970

PRINTED IN JAPAN

Table of Contents

List of Illustrations

Preface

Hawaii's Religions was first published in 1961 by the Kamehameha Schools Press as a booklet entitled *Religion in Hawaii*. It was not for commercial distribution but designed for use by ninth grade students at the Kamehameha Schools. It also provided information desired by the Library of Hawaii and the Hawaii State Department of Education. In this revised edition some introductory material, such as the brief statements on the nature of a particular faith, has been included especially for the students who will use the book as a textbook; but the book as a whole is written for general use, and it is hoped that it will also serve as a historical handbook.

From 1961 to 1968 a sustained effort was made to secure all facts about, and note all changes in, Hawaii's religions. Dr. Harley Ziegler of the Hawaii School of Religion prepared a section on religion for the 1956 *Thrum's Hawaiian Annual,* and this provided an outline; but the great changes in Hawaii made it necessary to check every statement of the past. Probably eighty per cent of the churches, temples, shrines, and chapels now existing have been established, relocated, or rebuilt since 1950.

9

The romanization of Japanese words is not consistent in Hawaii, here one spelling being used and there another. Throughout this book I have used the Hepburn system, which means that the spelling is Kannon, Hompa Honganji, and so forth, not Kwannon and Honpa Hongwanji.

Gratitude goes to all who have provided information. Most religious groups were very cooperative, but details were often confused and little effort had been made to keep historical information. The revision of this book was made during the summer of 1968 in preparation for a unit in a social studies course. I am grateful to my colleague Mr. Richard Greer for the invitation to present this material to the students of his classes. Mr. Greer is editor of the *Hawaiian Historical Journal*. *Mahalo nui loa* to Mrs. Glen Wakamatsu, secretary for the Religious Education Department of the Kamehameha Schools, for manuscript preparation.

I wish to acknowledge the kindness of publishers who have granted permissions to quote from their books. Appreciation is also due to Mr. Abraham Waimau of Kauai; Miss Mary Petrie of the Kamehameha Schools' staff; Mr. Fritz Abplanalp of Carmel, California; artist Jean Charlot, formerly of the University of Hawaii; and Erica Karawina (Mrs. Sidney Hsiao), artist working in stained glass. The line drawings are reproductions by Hide Doki of photographs and works by artists in Hawaii.

1. Religion in Ancient Hawaii

The religion of ancient Hawaii was similar to the religion of the rest of Polynesia. Like all religions the Polynesian religion had a theology or mythology, it had a ritual, and it prescribed a code of conduct.

First, the mythology possessed the classic quality of having many gods and heroes. Wakea, the sky father, and Papa, the earth mother, were the source of all things, including the gods. The name Io exists in New Zealand and Hawaii as a high god, as an ultimate source. However, Dr. Kenneth Emory found that "the New Zealand cult of Io had developed after Christian teaching had introduced the idea of one god."[1] Iolani, the hawk-god of Hawaii, was an *aumakua* (family god) of chiefly families, and any attempt to regard Io as the supreme god came late in Hawaiian history.

THE GREAT GODS

For the Hawaiians there were four main gods: Kane, the creator-god; Lono, the god of storm and rain and hence of fertility; Ku, the god who assisted in strenuous activities, especially war; and Kanaloa, god of the sea and of death. A fountain with the names of the four gods is at the Ala Moana Shopping Center. Kane was the creator of the sea, yet Lono rode the storms which came from the sea and Kanaloa is spoken of as the god of the squid that lived in the sea; thus their authority did not have definite limits. In fact, Kanaloa had such an inferior position in Hawaii that Martha Beckwith mentioned a "tendency by Hawaiian antiquarians to equate Kanaloa with the Christian devil."[2]

Sir Peter Buck, in his lectures at Yale on anthropology and religion, said: "In the Tahitian narratives the gods of Ra'iatea descended upon Tahiti and waged war against the god Tane. The principal invading god was 'Oro, the son of Ta'aroa [Hawaiian Kanaloa]. In the end Tane was defeated. The Temples of 'Oro were established in Tahiti."[3]

Sir Peter also stated that Cook Island traditions mention an influx from Tahiti of worshipers of Tane.

There is a possibility that some of those fleeing from Tahiti came to Hawaii, and as loyal supporters of Tane (Hawaiian Kane) reduced the importance of Kanaloa. This faint historical possibility became the basis of the first portion of James Michener's novel *Hawaii*.

Even if some worshipers of Tane fled from Tahiti to Hawaii, their influence on Hawaiian religion was far less than that of Paao. As reported by Samuel Kamakau,[4] Paao was a priest in Samoa. Paao's little son was accused of eating stolen fruit. Paao sacrificed him, but when his stomach was cut open, no fruit was found. Paao deter-

2. From a drawing by Abraham Waiamau.
There is a star, And beneath the star, There is a land.
ANCIENT POLYNESIAN CHANT

mined to leave Samoa and sailed out to sea. The journey was one of hardship, and he was adrift for weeks. With food and water exhausted, Paao arrived at Puna. He built the *heiau* (enclosed area for religious ceremonies) of Wahaula in Puna and the heiau of Mookini at Upolu Point. Both these heiaus existed until the abolishment of ancient Hawaiian worship in 1819. The *kahuna nui* (chief priest) Hewahewa, who led in the overthrow of the old religion, was a lineal descendant of Paao. The form of religion that existed when Captain Cook arrived was regarded as the religion established by Paao.

The great gods of Hawaii had many attributes and functions. In the case of each god a particular manifestation of one of its functions came to be regarded as a separate being. Lono of the rain clouds was spoken of as virtually a different being from Lono of the Makahiki, that is, of the celebration of harvest when war was forbidden. A chant to Ku was chanted as though there were a number of different gods, each having a particular attribute of Ku. Kukailimoku was the war god of the kings. On the island of Hawaii, Kamehameha was appointed custodian. The Bishop Museum preserves as one of its greatest treasures this particular war god. The manifestation of Kukailimoku is made of feather work over wicker with shell eyes and dog teeth. In every battle fought by Kamehameha, the first enemy slain was sacrificed before this god.

THE OTHER GODS

There were also lesser gods: nature gods like the shark

god, and gods for special purposes, such as canoe building and hula dancing. The most famous of these is Pele, goddess of the volcano. Because these lesser gods were associated with definite places, forces, or beings, many Hawaiians still treat certain places and forces with great respect.

A considerable oral literature developed about the Hawaiian deities. The "Kumulipo" is one of the most majestic literary achievements of any primitive people. The Pele-Hiiaka cycle of stories are worthy of a course in Hawaiian literature. The cultural excellence of the entire Hawaiian heritage makes people of many diverse religious convictions unite in preserving Hawaiian culture. The energetic builder of Ulu Mau Village is Jewish, the builders of the Polynesian Cultural Center are Mormons, and the woman who remembered and recorded the chants of her grandmother is a member of the Seventh-day Adventists. Dr. Abraham Akaka and the members of Kawaiahao Church belong to the United Church of Christ. Monsignor Charles Kekumano is Chancellor of the Roman Catholic Diocese. All of these seek to preserve Hawaiian culture.

The lesser gods merged with aumakua. Pele might be the aumakua of one family and the shark god the aumakua of another family. Aumakua might be some remembrance of an ancestor, or a carved figure or nature object.

There were other spirits or beings not subject to mortal restrictions. *Unihipili* were spirits of the dead, usually a dead child, that might enter another person. *Kapua* is the name given to a being who could change form. The shark boy, who could become either a shark or a human, is well known in Hawaii. Merging with these stories of gods and spirits are those of great heroes like Maui, with the strong-man exaggerations common to folklore.

RELIGIOUS CONCEPTS

Power was the key that tied all of these religious ideas together. The word for power is *mana.* Mana is that which distinguishes Polynesian religion from animism, which believes that spirits live in certain objects, and from polytheism, which has many gods. Everything has mana, and this mana can go from one thing to another. The mana of the gods can come into men or into objects. The carved figure of a god is not an idol, but by ritual the mana of the gods could be in the carved figure. Hence, ritual was very important.

Mana could also be preserved and protected. This was done by means of prohibitions, that is, by *kapu,* and by ritual. The kapu system had two purposes. Kapu protected the mana of a certain place or individual, and it also kept the mana from harming anyone. The taking of certain fish at certain seasons was kapu so as to protect the mana of the fish to reproduce itself. The kapu protected the mana of a chief so that he would have power with the gods or as a leader in war. The kapu became such a burden in Hawaii that even the chiefs wanted it abolished, so it disappeared quickly.

But it was different with ritual. The priest (kahuna) used a ritual (which also came to be called kahuna) to direct mana. The overthrow of the ancient religion abolished the office of priest, but belief in the power of ritual did not disappear. The word kahuna continued to be used to designate ritual, although the priesthood and heiaus no longer existed.

Mr. David Bray, Sr., whose powerful chants in the ancient manner are authentic ties with old Hawaii, makes an interesting distinction that shows why belief in kahuna (ritual) survived. The ancient form of ritual, including human sacrifice, was termed the heavy kahuna. With the coming of Christianity, the heavy kahuna was replaced by the light kahuna, which is simply rituals and chants. Often these chants are Christian. Hawaiian Christian ministers often bless a home or consecrate a new project with a Christian ritual using the ancient symbols of salt water or *maile* leis. An understanding of this light kahuna brings an appreciation of how a devout Christian woman sought to save her home and her church at Koae by providing an offering to Pele.

Another way in which ancient Hawaiian religious values survive is in an almost unvoiced recognition of mana in certain individuals. If you would understand what mana can mean in the present day, listen to an old Hawaiian speak of the pastor of Kawaiahao Church as her *kahu* (shepherd), or see the leadership which Monsignor Charles Kekumano exercises among the Catholics of Hawaiian ancestry.

Ancient Hawaiian life, which was not separate from religion, developed *aloha*. Some of the spirit of aloha was due to the circumstances of living. In northern climates people had to preserve fruit and grain for the winter. In

Hawaii a big catch of fish required cooperation and could only be shared. In Europe a man's home became his castle when it was the shelter by which he survived the winter. In Hawaii there was no word for home. From this common life of sharing came aloha.

The meaning of aloha is that we are united with affection in our common life. This heritage of ancient Hawaii becomes powerful in a Christian context. Consider this quotation from the statehood sermon by Dr. Abraham Akaka:

> One of the first sentences I learned from my mother in my childhood was this from Holy Scriptures, "Aloha Ke Akua." In other words, "Aloha is God" [God is Love]. Aloha is the power of God seeking to unite what is separated in the world—the power which unites heart with heart, soul with soul, life with life, culture with culture, race with race, nation with nation. It is the power that reunites a man with himself when he has become separated from the God within.[5]

So it is impossible to consider religion in Hawaii as beginning with the arrival of various missionaries. The religious values of ancient Hawaii still provide strength for religion today.

THE OVERTHROWING OF THE KAPU

Historically, the form of ancient Hawaiian religion ceased in 1819 after the death of Kamehameha I. Kamehameha had a number of wives, of whom Queen Kaahumanu exerted the strongest leadership, although Queen

Keopuolani had the highest rank. Kamehameha had
designated his son Liholiho as king and Queen Kaahumanu as co-ruler. Queen Keopuolani, the mother of
Liholiho, was the person of highest kapu in the kingdom.
She broke the kapu by eating with her son Kauikeaouli.
When Liholiho saw his mother eating with his younger
brother in defiance of the kapu, he joined them; this
meant the end of the elaborate social and religious system
which had been Hawaii's. Hewahewa, the kahuna nui,
or high priest, promptly joined the alii and led in the
destruction of the heiaus and their temple images.

There was some opposition, and finally a battle was
fought in which the defenders of the ancient faith were
defeated. The meaning of the ceremonies in the heiaus
was gone, and the caste system by which the alii were set
apart in various levels was overthrown; but the belief in
mana, as it existed in a ritual or as demonstrated by an
outstanding leader, remained. The new which was to come
received its meaning in terms of the old. In a little pamphlet Mr. John Dominis Holt expresses his pride in being
a Hawaiian, pointing out that "the people had thrived
and multiplied in spite of the kapu ritual, the greedy
aristocracy and their feudal way of life."[6]

SURVIVAL OF POLYNESIAN IDEAS

As observance of ancient Hawaiian religion ceased, the
temples and sacred places were abandoned. The Hawaiian
people ignored but continued to fear the ancient shrines
of their former religion. The heiaus had always been kapu
and the sense of a kapu place continued. At times other

racial groups decided that this fear of the old heiaus was a superstition that could be disregarded and stones from the heiaus were used for building purposes. Disasters, great or small, were associated with the violation of kapu places. A bold Catholic priest built a church on the Puu Kohala Heiau at Kawaihae. The Hawaiians refused for the most part to go to the church, and it was rebuilt at another location.

Even in modern times, this belief in ancient kapu provides folklore explanation of disasters. The collapse of the first dry dock at Pearl Harbor was attributed to the shark god. The Maunalei Sugar Plantation on Lanai failed when the irrigation wells became brackish, and the explanation for this was that the plantation had used stones of the Kahea Heiau in building a railroad. In the building of the Wilson Tunnel on Oahu, the preliminary engineering survey did not reveal loose volcanic ash and gravel filled with water between two solid walls of basalt. The contract was let on the basis of a tunnel to be cut through solid rock. When the gravel portion was undercut, the watery gravel collapsed, trapping and killing five workmen. It was then pointed out that the contractors, in constructing the approach, had destroyed certain stones which were considered sacred.

Such stories are part of the local repertoire for tourists. They become exaggerated, but even the exaggerations show the persistence of ancient beliefs in the kapu. The Hawaiian may be a devout Christian, but he does not harm the kapu place.

Another persistent belief has been associated with the

Hawaiian idea of power or mana—faith healing. The ancient rites of healing did not differentiate between psychological and medicinal treatment. *Lomilomi* massage, use of certain herbs, and preparation of objects considered to have healing power were included in the ritual. Dr. Nils Larsen, former Director of Queen's Hospital, made studies of Hawaiian medical practice and found it highly advanced both in medicinal value and psychological approach. For instance, since *nono* fruit has a large amount of citric acid, it is not surprising to find arthritic people who report themselves healed by nono fruit, massage, and prayer. Today some practitioners of Hawaiian healing are Christians, and verses of the Bible have become part of the psychological treatment. There have been cases of treatment in which a Bible or a crucifix was placed on the place of pain. Thus ancient Hawaiian practices persist while using aspects of the new faiths. There are also cases of the mixture of Oriental practices with the Hawaiian.[7]

To people of Hawaii, all this is natural. When dedicating a new building, a Chinese merchant (member of a Christian church) will follow the Chinese practice of using gongs and exploding firecrackers, but he will also have a Hawaiian ritual with salt water and maile leaves. No attempt is made to give intellectual explanation, but psychologically the mixture of religions is satisfying.

HEIAUS

After over a century of neglect, the ruins of Hawaii's past are now recognized as archeologically important. Most sites of historical significance have been set aside by the

State of Hawaii as historical sites. The City of Refuge at Honaunau, which has undergone restoration, is a National Historical Monument. It is one of the most impressive Polynesian archeological sites in the entire Pacific. In ancient days women and children were safe within its boundaries during wartime. Anyone who violated the sanctuary was sacrificed at the heiau.

At South Point, where there were ancient villages with canoe landing sites, the ancient heiau Kakekea was uncovered. Heiaus exist in Puna, Hilo, Ka'u, and along the Hamakua Coast, but the historically important ones are in west Hawaii. Hikiau Heiau at Napoopoo was probably the heiau that Captain Cook's body was taken to. At Kailua was Ahuena Heiau, next to the fort that Kamehameha built. Much of this heiau has been destroyed. Also near Kailua is Kealakowaa Heiau.

The Puu Kohala Heiau at Kawaihae is not only one of the most imposing archeological ruins of Hawaii but the last major heiau constructed in Hawaii. Kamehameha decided on the construction before his final conquest of the other islands. The heiau was built in 1792. Keoua, king of Ka'u, outranked Kamehameha and had been in almost constant war with the chiefs of Kona led by Kamehameha. Some of these chiefs persuaded Keoua to come to Kawaihae for the dedication of the heiau. Upon the landing of Keoua's canoe, Keeaumoku thrust his spear into him. Keoua and most of the chiefs in his canoe became the dedicatory sacrifice of the new heiau. Then Kamehameha launched his conquest of the islands.

On Maui there are a number of heiaus: Loaloa at

Kaupo, Kanekauila near Kipohu, and Kaiwaloa at
Olowalu. Two at Wailuku, Haleki'i and Pihana, are
state historical sites. These were the heiaus of the great
kings of Maui. The kahunas at Haleki'i regarded their
heiau as the most sacred heiau of all Hawaii and were
reluctant to join the general abolition of the ancient
religion. Kamehameha II ordered the heiau destroyed.

Molokai has a great heiau at Mapulehu named Iliilio-
pae. This is one of the largest heiaus in the Islands. Near-
by are a bell stone and a sacred spring. On the road to
Halawa Valley is a sacred *kukui* grove that was once kapu
to all except the priests, and is still shunned by most
Hawaiians.

Lanai has little of historical interest, only a heiau at
Kaenaki on the northwest point, and Kaheu Heiau, destroyed for the building of a plantation railroad.

Oahu has a number of historic heiaus. One was Leahi
on Diamond Head and another was on Puuwaina (Punchbowl Crater). The largest was Puu O Kahuku Heiau,
overlooking Waimea Bay. The dedication of this temple
had so many sacrifices and the fires were so large that the
glow was seen on Kauai, one hundred miles away. In
1792 three English sailors from Vancouver's ship *Daedalus*
were captured and sacrificed at this heiau. Vancouver
insisted upon the execution of those guilty. The chief
believed to be responsible was not executed, and the
Hawaiians who were killed were probably innocent. This
was the only authenticated sacrifice of Europeans, in spite
of the fact that Captain Cook's body was taken to a heiau.

The Ke Aiwa Heiau above Aiea is one of the finest restored sites. This was a school for training in Hawaiian healing. The use of medicines, massages, and chants was taught here. There was no human sacrifice, but other types of sacrifice, which were part of the healing ritual, were used. Near Wahiawa was a birth center with birth stones where alii women gave birth to their children. Other heiaus were at Kolekole Pass, Makua, and Waianae. The Ulu Po Heiau near Kailua is of very ancient construction, reportedly by the *menehune*s (dwarfs).

On Kauai there was an ancient religious center by the Waialua River. This included a temple of refuge, a birth center for the alii, and, above them, Holu Holuku with a bell stone. Other heiaus are Polihale, near the Barking Sands, Kekaha, and Haena.

Perhaps the most fascinating ruins on Kauai are those associated with the menehunes. About A.D. 1000 a major migration from Tahiti landed in Kauai and found evidence of human settlements. Legend was to tell of menehunes whose magical powers became part of Hawaiian folklore. The menehunes may have been Polynesians. They may have disappeared before the great migrations or may have been absorbed by the later arrivals, or they may have been related to the terrace builders of the Philippines. Dr. Katherine Luomala, after extensive research, decided the menehunes were simply "hard working, common Hawaiians whose work passed unnoticed to later Hawaiians."[8] Yet archeologists have discovered shaped and fitted stones, whereas all Hawaiian stonework is with rough stones, crudely arranged into walls. The Menehune Ditch beside the Waimea River and the Alakoko Fish Pond are constructed in a manner superior to later Hawaiian construction.

1. Kenneth Emory, "Religion in Ancient Hawaii," *75th Anniversary Lectures,* The Kamehameha Schools Press, Honolulu, 1965, p. 91.

2. Martha Beckwith, *Hawaiian Mythology,* Yale University Press, 1940, p. 60.

3. Sir Peter Buck, *Anthropology and Religion,* Yale University Press, 1939, p. 51.

4. Samuel Kamakau wrote articles for Hawaiian newspapers printed in Hawaiian. This is from *Nupepa Kuokoa,* No. 265. Kamakau wrote for over thirty years, and sometimes statements made in later articles are not in harmony with those of his earlier years. Translation by Westervelt.

5. Abraham K. Akaka, "The Statehood Sermon," *The Hawaiian Statehood Service,* LP record, Radio Station KAIM recording, 1959.

6. John Dominis Holt, *On Being a Hawaiian,* Star Bulletin Press, Honolulu, 1964, p. 15.

7. John H. Wise and Nils P. Larsen, "Hawaiian Medicine," *Ancient Hawaiian Civilization,* Charles E. Tuttle Company, Tokyo, 1965, p. 260–67.

8. Katherine Luomala, *Voices on the Wind,* Bishop Museum, Honolulu, 1955, p. 136.

2. Hawaiian Royalty and Religion

The Kingdom of Hawaii had eight monarchs, and they and the other chiefs of high rank influenced greatly the life of the land, including religion. Perhaps no country has had rulers with greater benevolent concern for their people. The legacy of that concern still exists in Hawaii in the benevolent trusts established by members of these royal families. Details of their religious influence will be presented in the appropriate sections describing individual faiths. However, a survey of the period of the monarchy will show the relationship of the religious life of Hawaii to the events of that century.

Ancient Hawaii was never a political unity. Each island had its own chiefs. For centuries these chiefs engaged in wars. Defeat might mean the annihilation of an entire family of chiefs, with victorious new chiefs assuming rule. The death of a chief might mean reshuffling of the ownership of an entire island.

The situation might have been chaotic except that the position of the chiefs was determined by their kapu status. The social structure and its fixed religious sanctions did

not change, and new chiefs and priests assumed the
duties and privileges of their position. When Captain
James Cook discovered Hawaii, Kahekili was ruler of
Maui and was later recognized as overlord of all the
islands except Hawaii. Kalaniopuu was ruler of Hawaii.
When he died in 1782, his son Kiwalao became king.

KAMEHAMEHA I

Kekuhaupi'o, an elderly chief, persuaded five chiefs of
Kona to band together to resist any reassignment of lands.
These five chiefs, Kamehameha, Keeaumoku, Kame-
eiamoku, Kamanawa, and Keaweaheula, found themselves engaged in a war in which they ultimately conquered
not only the island of Hawaii but also united all the islands
under the sovereignty of Kamehameha. Kamehameha and
the Kona chiefs had a somewhat dual attitude toward the
ancient religion. They built the great heiau of Puu Kohala
with scrupulous regard for the correct religious kapu, but
Keeaumoku killed Keoua when he came as honored guest.
Keopulani, the granddaughter of the great king of Maui,
Kahekili, was of such high rank that under kapu restrictions Kamehameha could not stand in her presence, but
he determined to marry her so that his sons would have
her high rank.

The success of Kamehameha in war was due to his
English gunners and sailors. These foreigners married
Hawaiian women but were exempt from the kapu system.
As increasing numbers of ships came to the Islands, no
effort was made to enforce the kapu on the foreigners.
Kamehameha held to the ancient faith, but before his

death he refused to permit human sacrifices on his behalf.

As the traditions of the past were being challenged, Kamehameha increasingly felt an obligation as ruler. In "Ke Kanawai Mamalahoa" (The Law of the Splintered Paddle) he established the principle of security for noncombatants in war.

A Russian visitor, seeing the well-ordered and disciplined social system under Kamehameha, showed his estimate of the Hawaiians in these words: "Were it possible to introduce the Christian faith and the art of writing among the Sandwich Islanders, they would in one century reach a state of civilization unparalleled in history.... If a few well educated, patient people, capable of observing things carefully, should settle ... they would soon become famous as enlighteners of this people."[1]

LIHOLIHO (KAMEHAMEHA II)

Before his death, Kamehameha designated his son, Liholiho, as king and Queen Kaahumanu as *kuhina nui*, a sort of prime minister. Some of the chiefs, including Kaahumanu, believed the authority of chiefs could be maintained without the ancient religion, so the old religious practices were abolished. Hawaii became a nation without religion.

When the first missionaries arrived a few months after this, Liholiho gave permission for them to teach. The missionaries, however, reported that he felt that having abolished one religion he did not wish to establish another.

When Queen Kamamalu showed interest in learning to read, Liholiho pointed out that accepting the new religion

would mean he could have but one wife, and since Kamamalu was his half sister she could not be his wife.

Liholiho and Kamamalu died in London. The journey
was made on impulse, and the motives for the journey are
vague. Desire to discuss the American missionaries with
British leaders probably was one motive.

In the Hawaiian preface to the Church of England Book
of Common Prayer that King Kamehameha IV translated, he wrote that Liholiho ". . . went to a distant and
powerful country to hasten the advent of that which your
eyes now see . . ." (i.e., the arrival of the Church of England clergy).[2]

This was probably not uppermost in Liholiho's mind,
but he undoubtedly would have preferred British to
American influences in all things, including religion.

KAUIKEAOULI (KAMEHAMEHA III)

The second son of Kamehameha and Keopuolani, Kauikeaouli, became Kamehameha III. Twelve years old when
he became king, Kamehameha III divided authority with
a series of strong-willed women. Queens Kaahumanu,
Kinau, and Kekulauohi were kuhina nui and made most
of the decisions in regard to the American missionaries and
the banning of the French Catholic missionaries.

Kamehameha III was a capable administrator. He
enlisted the support of men from other nations, and during
his thirty years of rule he managed to keep Hawaii
independent.

When still a young man, Kamehameha III was married
to his sister, Nahienaena, in a Hawaiian pagan ceremony.

This marriage, from the standpoint of the Christian leaders, was incestuous, polygamous, and pagan, but it was in the tradition of the chiefs of Maui. Nahienaena's early death removed the problem. Later in his long reign, Kamehameha III sometimes drank excessively.

These differences in moral codes raised questions in the missionary community about the king's Christian convictions. Yet missionaries William Richards and Gerrit P. Judd resigned from the Mission to work with the government.

Kamehameha III provided the land for Kawaiahao Church and participated in the planning. He approved a balcony in the church, although this placed the seats of commoners higher than the Royal Pew. The Royal Pew in which he sat is preserved in Kawaiahao.

During the time of the Roman Catholic troubles, Kamehameha III had his capital in Lahaina, while Kaahumanu, and later Kinau, had charge in Honolulu. Urged by the Reverend William Richards, Kamehameha III abolished the penalties which were enforced on Oahu by Kinau. The death of Kinau and the information that the French were sending a warship to return Catholic priests to Hawaii permitted Kamehameha III to act before the arrival of the warship in such a way as to insure freedom for Hawaii as well as to satisfy the French demands. The king then provided the means for building Our Lady of Peace Cathedral.

Kamehameha III tried to keep independence for Hawaii while satisfying foreign powers. In 1842, when France took over Tahiti and the Marquesan Islands,

Kamehameha sent a delegation to Europe. While this delegation was in Europe, Captain Lord George Paulet forced the cession of the Islands to Great Britain. Admiral Thomas of the British Navy restored the Kingdom of Hawaii to the king.

The service of restoration, held in a field now called Thomas Square, was followed by a service of Thanksgiving at Kawaiahao Church. At this service Kamehameha III voiced his guiding philosophy. Only this fragment was preserved:

> He aupuni palapala kou
>   Aia i ka lani ke Akua.
> O ke kanaka pono, oia kou kanaka.
> Ua mau ke ea o ka aina i ka pono.
>
> My kingdom is one of knowledge
>   Which is of God above.
> Men of righteousness are my men,
>   For the life of the land is perpetuated
>   by righteousness.

The last line—"Ua mau ke ea o ka aina i ka pono"—was placed on the Hawaiian Coat of Arms and has now become the state motto of Hawaii.

IOLANI (KAMEHAMEHA IV)

Alexander Liholiho, son of Kinau and nephew of Kamehameha III, became Kamehameha IV and took the name of Iolani.

Whereas Kamehameha III had favored American

advisers, Kamehameha IV made a Scotsman, Robert C. Wyllie, his chief aide. Gerrit Judd had taken the two Hawaiian princes Alexander Liholiho and his brother Lot Kamehameha on a tour to Europe. In the United States at least two incidents of racial prejudice took place. The memory of such slights coupled with Queen Emma's enthusiasm for all things British led Kamehameha IV to ask for missionaries of the Church of England, which led to the establishment of the Anglican, or Episcopal, Church.

The principal legacy of this royal couple was in the founding of Queen's Hospital. The Queen Emma Trust, owning the land on which the International Market Place in Waikiki is located, still aids in the support of Queen's Hospital. The great influence of this royal couple and their establishment of St. Andrew's Priory and Iolani School will be discussed in the section on the Episcopal Church. Kamehameha IV died a year after the English missionaries arrived. However, Queen Emma continued in the dedication which had brought the Church of England to Hawaii. The summer home of her last years is maintained as a public museum.

KAPUAIWA (KAMEHAMEHA V)

Lot Kamehameha succeeded his brother as Kamehameha V. His favorite residence had been his Kapuaiwa lands on Molokai. Although he continued to support the Church of England missionaries, he also seemed to favor the resurgence of ancient Hawaiian practices. His sister, Victoria Kamamalu, was still an infant when their mother, Kinau, died. This infant girl was designated kuhina nui, although Kekulauohi was acting kuhina nui until her death. William Lunalilo was the son of Kekulauohi. When Lunalilo wanted to marry the young princess Kamamalu, her brothers opposed the marriage. Victoria Kamamalu refused to join her brothers in support of the Anglican Church. She died in 1866, not yet thirty years old. Although she was a member of Kawaiahao, the mourning for her followed ancient Hawaiian practices. Mark Twain was in Honolulu and one night witnessed the wailing, dirges, and dancing, which he termed "pagan deviltry."[3]

Mark Twain's account is marred by his ridicule of the Hawaiian ceremonies, so we are unable from his account to know whether the ceremonies used were spontaneous reactions to grief or deliberate use of pre-Christian forms. When Kamehameha V proclaimed a month of mourning, he consulted Bishop Staley, who did not object to the Hawaiian plans. Mark Twain made the Bishop responsible for an entire resurgence of paganism.

After a month of mourning, the interment was held. The young minister of Kawaiahao, Henry Parker, had just begun a pastorate that was to continue for fifty-four years. Parker conducted a funeral service at the palace, but Bishop Staley refused to let him conduct the interment at the Royal Mausoleum, which had been consecrated according to the Church of England regulations. Moreover, because Princess Victoria Kamamalu was not a member of the Reformed Catholic Church of Hawaii, Bishop Staley would hold only a brief committal service.

All the incidents of the funeral indicate that a strong antimissionary feeling had developed. After 1866, though individuals of the royal and noble families supported religious work, there was never again strong support of religion as a part of government policy. Kamehameha V officiated at the laying of the cornerstone of St. Andrew's, but little work was done on the building.

Also in 1866, by orders of Kamehameha V, persons having leprosy were sent to Kalawao on Molokai. The spread of this disease created a mood of despair among the Hawaiians. On the Kalaupapa peninsula ninety per cent of these first exiles would have nothing to do with the churches.

Yet Honolulu was prosperous. The present Judiciary Building was built as the official capitol building. Kamehameha V, in his final illness, asked his cousin, Princess Bernice Pauahi, to be ruler. Pauahi, who was married to Charles Reed Bishop, a banker, declined. She was the last survivor of the Kamehameha dynasty and before her death inherited a great portion of the personal lands owned by the various members of that family. When she inherited this property she decided to set up schools for Hawaiian children. Her estate, the Bernice P. Bishop Estate, maintains the Kamehameha Schools as a distinctive educational institution for children of all or part aboriginal blood.

LUNALILO

Since Princess Pauahi, the logical successor, declined the throne, the legislature elected the king. William Lunalilo, grandson of a brother of Kamehameha I, was chosen. Sick with tuberculosis and having a reputation for exces-

sive drinking, he ruled a little more than a year. His
father, Kaiana, governor of Oahu, sought to reinstate the
strong leadership of the chiefs in matters of religion and
morals. Lunalilo was buried in a special mausoleum at
Kawaiahao Church. His father was also interred there,
and on Lunalilo's birthday, January 30, the mausoleum
is opened and a special service conducted. Lunalilo owned
a section of land, stretching from sea to mountain, that
included the Diamond Head, the Kaimuki, and the
Maunalani Rise sections of Honolulu. His will provided
for the establishment of a home for aged Hawaiians.
A home was built, and his land sold for $300,000, which
became an endowment fund which still has the same
worth. A decade later the Kamehameha lands of Bernice
Pauahi Bishop were evaluated at about the same amount,
but these lands were kept in trust and by 1966 had an
evaluation of about $200,000,000. The difference between
these two trusts is painfully apparent to Hawaiians who
fight for the preservation of the lands and estates endowed
by the royal families.

KALAKAUA

After the death of Lunalilo the legislature held another
election, and David Kalakaua became King Kalakaua.
This election revealed the great rift which had developed
between the Hawaiians and the business community.
Queen Emma, widow of Kamehameha IV, was the un-
successful candidate. Her supporters were mostly Hawaiians who were excluded from voting because of property
qualifications. They rioted after the election.

Iolani Palace was built, and the "Merry Monarch" fluctuated between reviving the ancient Hawaiian practices and instituting European monarchial practices. The entire period of Kalakaua's reign was one of religious cynicism and commercial opportunism. The Reciprocity Treaty with the United States brought prosperity. The new prosperity required more plantation workers. Workers were brought from every part of the world. The plantation system was to be the formative factor of a new Hawaii. Most of the alii families that owned land prospered. Many Hawaiians remained in little valleys untouched by the new prosperity; others flocked to the cities, where, if they were successful, they became police officers and minor administrators or, if they were not able to find employment, the landless poor. On the plantations a stratified society developed with a stratified religious system. The managerial group attended English-speaking churches established by missionaries' families of the second and third generations. The supervisors *(lunas)* were at first Hawaiians, then Portuguese, Germans, or other Europeans. The Germans were Lutheran, the Portuguese were Roman Catholic, and the field laborers, mostly Oriental, were Buddhists, Shintoists, and Taoists. At times those descendants of missionaries who had missionary consciences sought to enroll the new arrivals into Protestant churches, but they did this by establishing ethnic-language churches rather than by bringing the immigrants into their own English-speaking churches. This pattern of religious stratification was to continue in the 20th century, but the beginnings came in Kalakaua's reign.

Kalakaua's reign had so much political upheaval that at last the men of the new commercial plantation economy became the real rulers of Hawaii. Although the missionary descendants were a small minority of the commercial community, they provided the leadership for this new Hawaii.

Kalakaua's queen, Kapiolani, showed a great concern for the Hawaiians and established hospital care for Hawaiian mothers. This has now grown to the Kapiolani Maternity and Gynecological Hospital.

LILIUOKALANI

King Kalakaua designated a line of successors. They were to be his sister, Liliuokalani, wife of General John Dominis; another sister, Princess Likelike, wife of Governor Archibald Cleghorn; and their daughter Princess Kaiulani.

If these had no direct heirs, the succession would pass to nephews of Queen Kapiolani: Prince Kuhio Kalanianaole and Prince David Kawananakoa.

Queen Liliuokalani was unwilling to accept the dominance of the commercial group, which had forced King Kalakaua to accept a new constitution. She made plans to abrogate that constitution, and to obtain funds she made a promise of an opium concession to a group of Chinese. The opium plan alienated a number of Hawaii's leaders, and her decision to set up a new constitution divided the country.

The commercial group formed a Committee on Public Safety, which took over the government and forced the queen to surrender her powers. The landing of a company of American marines to protect Americans kept her supporters from rallying to her aid. The Committee of Public Safety asked the United States to annex the Islands. President Grover Cleveland rejected the idea and asked that Queen Liliuokalani be restored to her throne.

The provisional government now established the Republic of Hawaii, and again asked for annexation when McKinley was elected president. The Senate of the United States failed to ratify the treaty of annexation by the necessary two-thirds, so a concurrent resolution annexing Hawaii was pushed through both houses of Congress.

Queen Liliuokalani, deprived of her throne, became a tragic symbol to native Hawaiians. Almost her only support in the business community had been the British bishop, Alfred Willis, and his handful of staunch Englishmen. For thirty years she had been a firm friend of the Reverend Henry Parker of Kawaiahao Church, but he had turned against her over the opium grant.

Now she turned to Bishop Willis. When, after annexation, the Episcopal Church in America assumed charge, Queen Liliuokalani did not approve. She showed some interest in the Church of Latter-day Saints. Late in life she again showed an interest in St. Andrew's. She became the patron of many community activities, such as the Girl Scouts.

Her lands were left in an estate named the Liliuokalani Trust, a fund administered for orphans and other children in indigent circumstances. The Liliuokalani Trust has become a modern social service organization which emphasizes the psychological and social rehabilitation of Hawaiian children rather than the orphanage care of its earlier days.

Queen Liliuokalani wrote a hauntingly beautiful prayer during the months of her imprisonment in Iolani Palace.

> O! Lord Thy loving mercy,
> Is high as the heavens,
> It tells us of Thy truth
> And 'tis filled with holiness.
>
> Whilst humbly meditating,
> Within these walls imprisoned,
> Thou art my light, my haven,
> Thy glory my support.
>
> Oh! Look not on their failings,
> Nor on the sin of men,
> Forgive with loving kindness
> That we might be made pure.
>
> For Thy grace I beseech Thee,
> Bring us 'neath Thy protection,
> And peace will be our portion,
> Now and forever more.
>   Amen.

OTHER HAWAIIAN ROYALTY

Each person in the order of succession that King Kalakaua established is remembered by the Hawaiians.

Princess Kaiulani was a gentle, beautiful woman who

died at twenty-four. She founded the Kaiulani Trust, which maintained a home for Hawaiian girls working in Honolulu.

Prince Jonah Kuhio Kalanianaole considered refusing to accept American citizenship, but after seeing the Home Rule Party win the first election after the annexation, he decided to cooperate with the Americans. His example was the reconciling force which made Hawaii a loyal part of America. This man, who would have been king of Hawaii, was elected a delegate to Congress, and for twenty years he represented Hawaii in the Congress of the United States. He was foremost in the organizing of Hawaiian societies in which Hawaiian tradition was effectively combined with the American tradition of clubs and secret societies. His long service in Congress is remembered best for the Hawaiian Homes Act, which provided virtually free land for Hawaiian homes to persons at least fifty per cent Hawaiian.

Prince David Kawananakoa and his wife, Princess Abigail, became members of the St. Augustine Catholic Church and provided a baptismal font for the church. Princess Abigail was buried in the Kalakaua tomb. Because Bishop Sweeney would not permit ancient Hawaiian services in a Catholic Church, the service was held at Kawaiahao, where after a long lying in state, during which the Hawaiian societies chanted in the old Hawaiian manner, a Christian minister conducted a brief service. The same type of service was held for her son, David Kawananakoa, and her daughter, Kapiolani Field, wife of State Senator Harry M. Field.

Many churches boast some memento of a link to these members of Hawaiian royalty. Waialua Protestant Church is often called Liliuokalani Church and has a calendar clock which was a gift of the queen. St. Andrew's has stained-glass windows in its gallery, gifts of the alii. In services of dedication Dr. Abraham Akaka uses a calabash that was reputedly King Kamehameha's. The Temple Emanu-El has a pointer for reading the Torah that is known as the Kalakaua Pointer.

All this indicates the support the alii gave the religious life of the land.

THE HAWAIIAN MONARCHS

Regal Name	Reign	Other Names	Consort
Kamehameha I	*?–1819*		*Keopulani (queen of highest rank) Others included: Kaahumanu, Kalakua*
Kamehameha II	*1819–24*	*Liholiho*	*Kamamalu*
Kamehameha III	*1824–54*	*Kauikeaouli, Kaleiopapa*	*Queen Kalama, Nahienaena*
Kamehameha IV	*1854–63*	*Alexander Liholiho, Iolani*	*Queen Emma (Rooke)*
Kamehameha V	*1863–71*	*Lot Kamehameha, Kapuaiwa*	*(Not Married)*
Lunalilo	*1871–72*	*William Lunalilo*	*(Not Married)*
Kalakaua	*1872–91*	*David Kalakaua*	*Queen Kapiolani*
Liliuokalani	*1891–93 (died 1917)*	*Lydia Kamakaeha*	*General John Dominis*

1. Klaus Mehnert, *The Russians in Hawaii,* University of Hawaii Bulletin, Honolulu, April 1939, p. 67.

2. Meiric Dutton, *Preface to the Book of Common Prayer,* composed by Kamehameha IV, Advertiser Publishing Company, Honolulu, 1959, p. 14.

3. A. Grove Day, *Mark Twain's Letters from Hawaii,* Appleton-Century, New York, 1966, p. 161.

3. Henry Opukahaia. From an engraving, 1817.
Artist not named.

3. The Hawaii Conference of the United Church of Christ

A Hawaiian youth named Opukahaia inspired the first Christian missionaries in their decision to come to Hawaii.

A chief named Kaiana was the first of the alii to journey to a foreign land. The ship returned from China to Kona, and Kaiana had with him many Chinese supplies, including gunpowder. Kamehameha appointed him chief over Ka'u. In 1795, when Kamehameha invaded Oahu, Kaiana deserted him. With his soldiers from Ka'u, Kaiana landed at Waimanalo and joined the forces of Oahu. Kaiana was killed in the battle of Nuuanu Valley. (A *kahili* staff, a feather standard symbolic of royalty, was made for Kamehameha from the leg bones of the chiefs slain on Oahu. This is on exhibit in the Bishop Museum, and Kaiana's shin bone has been identified.)

In Ka'u, Namakeha, brother of Kaiana, led the people in revolt. Kamehameha ordered the Kona chiefs to invade Ka'u. One family hid in a cave. The Kona warriors found the hiding place and killed the entire family except for one young boy whose name was Opukahaia. Tradition says that Opukahaia ran away, carrying his baby brother on his back. A Kona chief threw a spear which pierced the body of the baby and knocked Opukahaia to the ground. After hesitating whether or not to kill the boy, the chief decided to take him to Kona.

In Kona, Opukahaia located his grandmother and an aunt through his name chant, that is, through the recital of his genealogy. The aunt's husband was Pahua, the chief kahuna in the Hikiau Heiau at Napoopoo. Opukahaia learned the chants and rituals of the heiau. Pahua began the construction of a subsidiary heiau where Opukahaia would officiate.

Then Opukahaia decided to leave Hawaii. The *Triumph,* a vessel from New Haven with Captain Caleb Brintnall in command, anchored off Napoopoo. A Hawaiian, Thomas Hopu of Kohala, was on board as cabin boy. Opukahaia swam out to the ship and joined the crew. The *Triumph*'s voyage was to the North Pacific for seal skins, to China to sell them, and then around Africa to New York, arriving in October 1809. Captain Brintnall took the two Hawaiians with him to New Haven. Opukahaia lived at the Brintnall home and Hopu with a Dr. Hotchkiss. The Yale students treated them as curiosities, but began to teach them. Edwin Dwight, son of the president of Yale, Dr. Timothy Dwight, showed special concern for Opukahaia, and after a few months Opukahaia went to live in the Dwight home.

SAMUEL MILLS

The American Foreign Missions' endeavor originated

when some Williams College students took refuge in the lee of a haystack during a rain and made a prayerful dedication of themselves to go out as foreign missionaries.

Samuel Mills was the leader. In the next few years he inspired the founding of the American Board of Commissioners for Foreign Missions. To provide scripture in other languages, he led in the forming of the American Bible Society. He started the first work in New York for immigrants. To return freed Negro slaves to Africa he helped found the American Colonization Society. On a return trip from Africa, where he surveyed the work which led to the formation of Liberia, he died at the age of thirty-one.

In Liberia, in the American University of Beirut, and in countless other places, Samuel Mills' vision preceded the work. He inspired Adoniram Judson to go to Burma, even though Judson's Baptist views led to the organization of a Baptist Foreign Missionary Society. The warmth, charm, and intelligence of this thoroughly dedicated youth showed its fineness in his treatment of Opukahaia. On a visit to Yale, Edwin Dwight introduced Mills to Opukahaia. Mills, then a student at Andover Seminary, saw Opukahaia as the instrument for the conversion of Hawaii. During the summer of 1810 Opukahaia lived and worked on the Mills' farm. As they worked Samuel Mills taught Hebrew and Greek to his fellow worker.

When Mills returned to the seminary, Opukahaia went with him. Opukahaia had a part-time job, and the students all helped him with his studies. A few months later Mills arranged for Opukahaia to study at Bradford Academy. When Mills graduated and was ordained, one of his first acts as a minister was to baptize Opukahaia, the first known Hawaiian to be baptized. Although Samuel Mills was the pastor of a church, his main interest was foreign missions. He raised money for a school for students from other lands at Cornwall, Connecticut. Opukahaia was the outstanding student in this school and soon became a favorite speaker in New England churches.

Just as Samuel Mills' dream of returning Opukahaia to Hawaii as a Christian leader was taking shape, Opukahaia became ill and died of typhus fever on February 19, 1818. Samuel Mills rode on horseback for two days and arrived the day before Opukahaia's death. After Opukahaia's death, his diary, letters, and a narrative of his early life were collected. Edwin Dwight compiled them into a book entitled *Memoirs of Obookiah*. This book, written by the first Hawaiian author, enlisted the interest of thousands, and a year later the first missionaries were on their way from Boston to Hawaii.

In 1920, in celebration of the centennial of the mission, a tablet was placed near the heiau at Napoopoo in honor of Opukahaia, and in 1957 a memorial shrine was dedicated at the old cemetery in Punaluu, Ka'u, the birthplace of Opukahaia.

In 1968 the Sesquicentennial of Opukahaia's death was observed in many ways, including a pilgrimage from Hawaii to the grave of Opukahaia in Cornwall. The *Memoirs of Obookiah* was reissued at the same time.[1]

THE FIRST COMPANY OF MISSIONARIES

The American Board of Commissioners for Foreign Missions authorized a mission to Hawaii. The missionaries who volunteered were mostly unmarried young men, and the Board insisted upon sending only married couples. But by mid-October 1819 the first missionaries were ready, and at the Park Street Church in Boston they were commissioned and formed a church.

They sailed from Boston on October 23, 1819, on the ship *Thaddeus*. There were two ministers, both recently married, the Reverend Hiram Bingham and the Reverend Asa Thurston; a physician, Thomas Holman, M.D., who married the sister of Samuel Ruggles a week before sailing; a printer and his wife, Mr. and Mrs. Elisha Loomis; two teachers and their wives, Mr. and Mrs. Samuel Ruggles and Mr. and Mrs. Samuel Whitney. The only ones past thirty were Mr. and Mrs. Daniel Chamberlain, who had five children.

Their purpose, as stated in their commission, was:

> You are to aim at nothing short of covering these islands with fruitful fields and pleasant dwellings, and schools and churches; . . . to obtain an adequate knowledge of the language of the people; to make them aquainted with letters, to give them the Bible, with skill to read it, to introduce and get into extended operation among them, the arts and institutions of civilized life and society.[2]

With these missionaries and the others to follow came a number of Hawaiian youths who in one way or another had sailed to New England. In the first company were four who had been in the school at Cornwall with Opukahaia.

Thomas Hopu had been Opukahaia's companion on their trip to America. Hopu had sailed and fought on an American ship during the war of 1812, perhaps the first Hawaiian to serve in the armed forces of the United States. Two others were William Kanui and John Honolii. Also with the group was George Kaumualii, the son of Kaumualii, king of Kauai. Kaumualii had entrusted his son to a captain to be taken to America to be educated; the captain, appropriating the gifts, had abandoned the young man. George Kaumualii enlisted on the U.S. frigate *Enterprise,* and was wounded in her historic battle with the *Boxer*. He returned to Kauai, where King Kaumualii gave the ship's captain a thousand dollars' worth of sandalwood and showed great interest in the work of the missionaries.

Among the first missionaries, there was no doubt of the commanding leadership of the Reverend Hiram Bingham. He was the leader of the work of translation, the organizer and planner of the first missionary education, and the first pastor of Kawaiahao. His forceful personality commanded the respect and enlisted the support of the chiefs, while enlisting the cooperation or arousing the hostility of the Europeans and Americans who came to the Islands.

As shown by stories by the descendants of other missionaries, Hiram Bingham's uncompromising sense of duty could antagonize even his fellow workers, but there is no doubt of his influence upon Hawaii. He was in Hawaii for twenty years. He left in 1840, never to return. When he arrived, there was not a single Hawaiian who

could read or write. When he left, there were thousands
who could read and write their own language, and
Hawaii was in process of becoming a literate nation.
When he arrived, Hawaii was still a land where the chiefs
had the power of life and death. Before he left, Kamehameha III had promulgated the first constitutional
guarantees. When Bingham arrived, there were no books,
in fact no written language. When he left, numerous books
were being printed and the first Hawaiian newspaper had
appeared. When he arrived, there were no Christian
services. When he left, three thousand people crowded
the usual Sunday services at Kawaiahao Church. When
he arrived, there were no places of Christian worship;
when he left, Kawaiahao Church as it stands today was
being erected according to his plans. The Sunday bulletin
of Kawaiahao Church states, "The work that began here
has been assessed by historians as the most significant in
Hawaii's whole development."

THE MISSIONARY INFLUENCE

Since the Hawaiian chiefs were all-powerful, the achievements and failures of the missionaries were closely related
to the decisions of the chiefs. The Hawaiians saw the work
of the missionaries as being twofold: *pule* (worship) and
palapala (learning). The chiefs saw the immediate value
of literacy. King Liholiho designated young men to learn,
one of whom, John Ii, became a judge of the Supreme
Court in later life. The missionaries believed that in the
Bible was the message of God for the saving of men, and
therefore men had to read the Bible. Thus they had to

translate the Bible into Hawaiian and teach the people
to read. But first they had to make a written language.

How great this influence was can be shown in a symbolic
way. Before the mission press could start the printing of
books, Hawaiians had to be taught to read and an alpha-
bet had to be devised. Opukahaia could not pronounce
"r" and used "k" sounds in speaking. When the missionaries arrived in "Honoruru" (Honolulu), they found a confusion of sounds. Guided by Opukahaia's attempts to
write Hawaiian, they voted to use "l" in place of "r" and
"k" instead of "t." They probably made a wrong decision, but not even the people who disparage their work
insist on calling a certain famous beach, Waititi. The
influence of the missionaries set the pattern of *Hawaii nei*.

At first Liholiho and Kaahumanu, who was kuhina
nui, did not support the missionaries to the extent most
other chiefs did. Even Hewahewa, kahuna nui, high
priest of the old faith, welcomed the new teachers. In
Kona, Kuakini aided the work of the missionaries. King
Kaumualii on Kauai aided the missionary teacher Samuel
Whitney. Queen Keopuolani, mother of Liholiho, had
married Hoapili, and together they made Lahaina the
center of Christian learning. Kalanimoku, who had been
Liholiho's commander-in-chief, was to become a leader
at Kawaiahao. The first missionaries received tremendous
aid from the Reverend William Ellis, an English missionary from Tahiti. He had with him some Tahitians, one of
whom, Taua, became a personal teacher to Queen Keopuolani. In a short time Mr. Ellis and the Tahitians were
preaching in Hawaiian.

The initial indifference of Kaahumanu changed to whole-hearted support. Liholiho died, and during the boyhood of Kamehameha III Kaahumanu was virtual ruler. Kalanimoku served as her chief of state. Together they exercised strong leadership, seeking to re-establish the social control that had disappeared with the overthrow of the old kapu system. Kaahumanu traveled about the Islands establishing schools, enlisting the support of chiefs, seeking to ban alcoholic liquors, and, by her example, supporting the entire Christian enterprise. At times she showed a dictatorial spirit, but when she died in 1832, the people mourned. Kamehameha III, now a man, hesitated in appointing another kuhina nui, but Hoapili and Kuakini persuaded him to appoint his sister, Kinau, who was as strong a supporter of the mission as Kaahumanu had been.

With such support every enterprise of the mission flourished. The printing presses printed primers, portions of the Bible, and books of every type. Schools were everywhere. At first these provided no more than simple instruction in reading the Hawaiian language, but soon boarding schools appeared on the major islands. Lahainaluna was the first. Here the Reverend William Richards and the Reverend Sheldon Dibble saw that Hawaiian youths learned not only the Bible but the secular learning as well, which varied from navigation and the making of copper plates for book illustrations to advanced geometry. Sheldon Dibble organized a historical society, and two of his scholars, David Malo and Samuel Kamakau, wrote historical accounts of ancient Hawaii. Other schools were

Hilo Boarding, Waioli, Kawaiahao Seminary, and a school for chiefs' children conducted by Mr. and Mrs. Amos Starr Cooke.

Hundreds wanted to learn to study, to attend the churches. Chiefs like Kuakini and Laanui were imitated in almost every locality, the former in the building of Mokuaikaua in Kona and the latter in the building of a church at Waialua, Oahu. The king himself donated the land and led in the building of Kawaiahao Church.

At first there was antagonism between the missionaries and the commercial shipping interests. A movie version of the burning of Lahaina makes it seem virtually a war. Yet almost from the start, concern was shown for the sailors. One Seamen's Bethel was established in Honolulu and another in Lahaina. The Reverend Samuel C. Damon started Hawaii's oldest publication, the *Friend* (full title, *Seamen's Friend and Temperance Advocate*).

From 1820 to 1848 twelve companies of missionaries came to Hawaii, fifty-two ordained ministers, eight physicians, fourteen teachers, five printers, and three business agents. Two others came to work with sailors. These eighty-four left a deep imprint upon the Islands.

GREAT HAWAIIAN CHRISTIANS

Many Hawaiians became Christian leaders who gave remarkable testimony to their faith. Kapiolani Nui is the most famous. Kapiolani Nui had had two husbands. She was the first of the alii to decide this was wrong. She chose Naihe, the orator or talking chief of Kona, as the

4. Mokuaikaua Church, Kailua-Kona (1837). The
oldest church in Hawaii still used for worship.

one to keep. Together they governed the Napoopoo-Honaunau portion of Kona. They would go by canoe to Kailua to attend services or send a canoe for someone to preach. They built a church at Kaawaloa and a home for a pastor. In 1824 the Reverend and Mrs. James Ely came in response to Kapiolani's request.

Kapiolani discovered that a priestess of Pele was again active and that there was a resurgence of fear of the goddess Pele. Kapiolani was determined to challenge this fear of Pele. With a large following, she walked from Kona to Kilauea. Missionary Joseph Goodrich in Hilo heard of her decision and went to Kilauea to meet her. Meeting her near the volcano was the priestess of Pele, who warned her that Pele would destroy her. For over a century Halemaumau in Kilauea Crater was a lake of fire, rising and falling as molten lava flowed and ebbed in its underground sources.

Kapiolani asked Mr. Goodrich to have a service of prayer and worship. About fifty Hawaiians went with Goodrich and Kapiolani to the brink of Halemaumau. There Kapiolani told her faith. "Jehovah is my God. He kindled this fire. I fear not Pele." She ate *ohelo* berries, sacred to Pele and kapu to women. Then there was praise and prayer. This was on December 22, 1824.

This heroic act made Kapiolani's name famous. Alfred Lord Tennyson and, more recently, John Oxenham have written poems about this event. The artist Peter Hurd painted the scene as one of the great events in Hawaiian history. The Church College of Hawaii has a painting of this event as marking the triumph of Christianity. Since

Tennyson's *Kapiolani* is seldom printed in his collected poems, it is given here.[3]

KAPIOLANI

When from the terrors of Nature a people
  have fashioned and worship a Spirit
  of Evil
Blest be the Voice of the Teacher who
  calls to them,
    "Set yourselves free!"

Noble the Saxon who hurled at his Idol a
  valorous weapon in olden England!
Great, and greater, and greatest of women,
  island heroine
  Kapiolani
Clomb the mountain, and flung the berries
  and dared the Goddess, and freed the people
    Of Hawaii.

A people believing that Pele the Goddess
  would wallow in fiery riot and revel
    On Kilauea,
Dance in a fountain of flame with her devils
  or shake with her thunders and shatter
  her island,
    Rolling her anger
Thro' blasted valley and flowing forest
  in blood-red cataracts down to the sea!

Long as the lava-light
    Glares from the lava-lake,
    Dazing the starlight;
Long as the silvery vapor in daylight,
    Over the mountain
Floats, will the glory of Kapiolani be
    mingled with either on Hawaii.

What said her Priesthood?
"Woe to this island if ever a woman should
    handle or gather the berries of Pele!
Accursed were she!
And woe to this island if ever a woman
    should climb to the dwelling of
    Pele the Goddess!
Accursed were she!"

One from the Sunrise
Dawned on His people and slowly before him
None but the terrible Pele remaining as Gods
    and Goddesses,
Vanished shadow-like
        Kapiolani
    Ascended her mountain,
Baffled her priesthood,
    Broke the Taboo,
    Dipt to the crater,
Called on the Power adored by the Christian
    and crying, "I dare her, let Pele
    avenge herself!"
Into the flame-billows dashed the berries,
    and drove the demon from Hawaii.

Popular among mission stories was that of Blind Bartimea, or Puaaiki. Born deformed, he was buried alive by his mother, but a protesting uncle rescued him. Neglected by everyone, he was taught the craft of a kahuna, including the rites for praying a person to death and methods of committing undetectable murder if the prayers did not avail. When the kapu system was abolished, dances ceased to have religious significance and Puaaiki attained the status of a court jester through his burlesques of the hula. Drinking excessively, he became blind and would have died except for the compassion of John Honolii, one of the youths who had returned with the missionaries. Puaaiki became a Christian. He listened intently to sermons and years later could repeat from memory a sermon that he had heard only once. His work aided the establishment of Haili Church in Hilo and Kaahumanu Church in Wailuku, Maui.

David Malo was the greatest of the early Hawaiian Christian leaders. Brilliant as a student at Lahainaluna, he assisted the Reverend William Richards in the translation of seventeen books of the Bible. He became the supervisor of schools on Maui. His book *Hawaiian Antiquities* is the best source of knowledge of Hawaii before the arrival of Captain Cook. David Malo saw clearly the destiny of Hawaii to be engulfed by men from many nations and believed the only hope of Hawaii was in Christian education. He asked to be buried high above Lahaina so that his grave would not be lost in the waves of foreigners who would sweep over Hawaii's shores.

THE MISSIONARIES AND THE GOVERNMENT

Many of the chiefs wanted to establish schools, control alcohol, and save their people from exploitation. They sought the advice of the missionaries. To what extent the missionaries determined the policy of the government is still a matter of debate, but in 1838 the king asked the Reverend William Richards to enter the service of the monarchy. Richards resigned from the Mission to do this. Richards drafted important documents, including the edict of religious tolerance and the constitution of 1840. In 1842 Kamehameha III sent Sir George Simpson of the Hudson's Bay Company, Richards, and alii Timothy Haalilio as envoys to the United States, France, and Great Britain. Haalilio was the official head of the group, but the king gave to Richards blank sheets signed by him so that Richards, in the king's name, could make any agreements he felt necessary.

Richards was completely successful, gaining recognition from all three governments for the independence of Hawaii. When Richards left on this mission, his place was taken in the government by Dr. Gerrit Judd. Dr. Judd also resigned from the Mission and became a citizen of Hawaii.

Richards returned from his successful journey in 1845 and became Minister of Education. A Scotsman, Robert Crichton Wyllie, became Foreign Minister, and Dr. Judd became Minister of the Interior. Richards died in 1847, having succeeded in keeping Hawaii independent in the troublous 1840's. Since Richards had resigned from the

Mission, his wife was destitute until she received a pension from the king.

The pastor of Kawaiahao Church, the Reverend Richard Armstrong, became the Minister of Education. Like Richards and Judd, he resigned as a missionary and became a Hawaiian citizen. As long as Kamehameha III ruled, Judd was the dominant figure, so much so that Samuel Harrison entitled his book about Judd *The White King*.[4] Such things as the Great Mahele, which provided for fee simple ownership of land, were in great part Judd's work. Judd made a trip to Europe with the two princes who were later to be kings of Hawaii, and with Chief Justice William L. Lee and Judge John Ii drew up the constitution of 1852.

Although Hawaii had remained independent through the difficulties with France and Britain, Judd was not certain independence would continue. A petition to the government asked for annexation to the United States, and Judd started negotiations. The United States government never acted upon this request.

The smallpox epidemic of 1853 disrupted every aspect of life in Hawaii. Large flourishing churches declined to dispirited handfuls, and the missionary influence ebbed. When Kamehameha IV became king, R. C. Wyllie became the dominant figure in government and Dr. Judd retired. After Dr. Judd no missionary ever again held a dominant position, although Armstrong remained as Minister of Education. On Maui the Reverend Lorrin Andrews and the Reverend Jonathan Green resigned as missionaries of the American Board in protest against the

Board's receiving missionary money from slave owners. Green, who supported himself by farming, founded an independent school. Andrews was appointed a judge on Maui and later an Associate Justice of the Supreme Court. His great work was a dictionary of the Hawaiian language. The mission printer, E. O. Hall, resigned to become printer and publisher for the government.

THE MISSIONARIES AND THE CHURCHES

Eighty-four missionaries were appointed by the American Board, yet only thirty-three remained under the Board until their death or until the Board closed its work in Hawaii. Most faithful were the ordained ministers.

Twenty-three ministers served until death or retirement. Asa Thurston of the first company lived for forty-eight years in the Islands. One minister, Ephraim Clark, left the Islands to supervise the printing of Bibles in Hawaiian for the American Board. Only one minister, the Reverend Samuel G. Dwight, was dropped by the Board. Dwight, of the Yale Dwight family, was one of the few unmarried missionaries to come to Hawaii. When almost forty years old, he married a young Hawaiian girl. Since every Foreign Mission Board at that time had a policy forbidding such marriages of missionaries, Dwight was released.

Most of the ordained missionaries who came to Hawaii were men with a dedication which lasted to their lives' end. The one who received the greatest aloha from the Hawaiians was the Reverend Lorenzo Lyons. He was twenty-four years old when he sailed to Hawaii with his eighteen-year-old bride Betsy. They went to the chill uplands of

Waimea, Hawaii, where Lyons was to labor for fifty-four years. The winters were too much for Betsy and she died. Lyons continued his work, later remarrying.

His dedication was complete. When the Reverend J. S. Green resigned from the mission because the American Board had taken gifts from slave owners, Lorenzo Lyons felt deep concern but remained at his work. He saw missionary teachers such as Amos Starr Cooke and William H. Rice and business agents such as S. N. Castle and E. O. Hall resign from the mission to start businesses that made them or their descendants wealthy, but Lorenzo Lyons never wavered. He saw the sons of missionaries enter into the business world, but when his own son, Curtis, was given land for surveying the Hamakua coastlands, he persuaded him to sell the land so a new Imiola Church could be built. For years he translated the Sunday school lessons into Hawaiian. For this he received no pay, and when the printer found a substantial profit after seven years and gave Lyons $1,200, Lyons used the money to bring out a new edition of the hymn book *Hoku Ao Nani*.

The hymns Lorenzo Lyons translated are his great gift to Hawaiian music. The missionaries had taught the Hawaiians to sing. To the rather stilted translations of Hiram Bingham and the adaptations of Tahitian hymns by the Reverend William Ellis, Lorenzo Lyons added hundreds of hymns in a lyrical Hawaiian. Not least of these is "Hawaii Aloha," a patriotic hymn which has been termed the "My Country 'Tis of Thee" of Hawaii. When Lorenzo Lyons died, King Kalakaua provided a Hawaiian flag to be placed over the casket.

Besides these hymns of the missionaries, the Sunday schools provided much musical training. A feature of the Sunday school was the *Hoike,* a quarterly or annual rally. These rallies provided competition, and many rallies had songs with original words and music. Some of the Hoike songs that tell Bible stories are religious classics which ought to be preserved as genuine folk music. The great Hawaiian choirs and the translation of some of the world's great choral music into Hawaiian were later developments.

THE MISSIONARIES AND THE SCHOOLS

Although the missionaries made a tremendous impact upon Hawaii, the churches they established never enrolled a large percentage of the population because of the regulations enforced on church members. The greatest influence was felt by way of schools, such as the Chiefs' Children's School, Kawaiahao Seminary, Maunaolu Seminary, Lahainaluna, Kohala Boarding School, and Hilo Boarding School. These schools provided a pattern for education which still influences Hawaii. They taught the dignity of work with a daily work period, and to this day few are the schools in Hawaii, either public or private, which do not have a janitorial or cafeteria work-squad. So important was education to King Kamehameha III that he persuaded the principal of Lahainaluna, the Reverend William Richards, to take over the setting up of public schools. Two years later Mr. Richards died, and the Reverend Richard Armstrong became the superintendent of schools.

Armstrong's son, Samuel Chapman Armstrong, while a student at Yale, organized an army company. Later he became the commanding officer of Negro troops. At the close of the Civil War he was twenty-six years old and a Brigadier-General. After the war he established Hampton Institute for Negro students. The principles which his father followed at Lahainaluna became his guide at Hampton.

Numerous other schools came from the missionary influence. To educate their own children in English, they founded Punahou in 1841. When the Chinese arrived, they started Mills Institute and Mid-Pacific School of Theology. Later these schools, along with Kawaiahao Seminary, combined into Mid-Pacific Institute. So great was the desire for education that when the last of the Kamehameha dynasty, Mrs. Bernice Pauahi Bishop, died, she bequeathed her wealth to the establishment of the Kamehameha Schools.

THE HAWAIIAN BOARD

The first missionaries were stationed at Kailua, Honolulu, and in Kauai. Two years later they held an annual meeting, and these annual conferences *(Aha Paeaina)* are still an outstanding event in the church. As early as 1850, there were some who suggested that Hawaii was now a Christian nation and that the American Board should use its resources in other fields. In 1863 what had been the General Meetings of the Mission became the Hawaiian Evangelical Association, organized "to consist of all native and foreign Congregational and Presbyterian clergymen on the Sandwich, Micronesian and Marquesan Islands."

As the American Board slowly withdrew, the Board of the Hawaiian Evangelical Association, to consist of not less than eighteen members, was formed. Like the American Board, the Hawaiian Board was a separately incorporated legal entity, handling the business of the Association and investing funds, and in final analysis not subject to denominational control.

Most ordained missionaries who had been appointed by the American Board remained at their posts after 1863. Titus Coan was at Haili Church, Hilo; Lorenzo Lyons in Waimea; John D. Paris in Ka'u and Kona; and Elias Bond in Kohala. On Maui, William P. Alexander and Dr. Dwight Baldwin at Lahaina were to remain as supervising rather then active ministers. Kaumakapili Church had Dr. Lowell Smith, its founder, as pastor, and Benjamin Parker still served in Kaneohe. In Waialua, John S. Emerson served until his death in 1867. On Kauai Daniel Dole had left the mission and had an independent school and a foreign church (i.e. English speaking, not Hawaiian speaking). At Waimea, Kauai, George B. Rowell also had a foreign church, and after 1865 he worked independently of the Board.

A few sons of missionaries followed in their fathers' footsteps. Two, Luther H. Gulick and Hiram Bingham II, became missionaries to Micronesia. (Luther Gulick later became Secretary of the Hawaiian Board.) Anderson O. Forbes became the minister at Kaluaaha Church in

Molokai, and later at Kaumakapili. Oramel H. Gulick, after a short time in Hawaii, became a missionary to Japan in 1870. He returned to Hawaii in 1894 to take charge of the Japanese work for the Hawaiian Board. William DeWitt Alexander, after some years of teaching, became the president of Punahou. Sereno E. Bishop became principal at Lahainaluna. Henry H. Parker became pastor of Kawaiahao Church, June 28, 1863, the last missionary appointed under the American Board. He served as pastor of Kawaiahao for fifty-four years.

HAWAIIAN MINISTERS

Most of the replacements for the missionaries were Hawaiian ministers. Stephen L. Desha, Sr., served Haili Church in Hilo for forty-five years. A supporter of Queen Liliuokalani, Desha also worked to preserve ties with the Hawaiian Board. As a long-time Territorial Senator, he was to wield political as well as religious influence. His son, Stephen L. Desha, Jr., trained for the law and was a Circuit Court Judge for years. At the death of his father, Stephen Jr. took charge of Haili Church and decided to become a minister. He entered San Francisco theological Seminary and later became the chaplain of the Kamehameha Schools.

The Reverend J. Kauhane of Waiohinu was also elected Territorial Senator. Men like C. M. Kamakawiwoole on Hawaii, Isaac Iaea on Molokai, Isaiah Kaauwai on Kauai, L. B. Kaumeheiua on Maui, and the Reverend Henry Poepoe on Oahu gave many years of service. The North Pacific Missionary Institute provided training for many of these ministers, as well as students from Samoa, Micronesia, and in later years the Philippines and the Oriental countries.

The Hawaiian churches with their Hawaiian-speaking ministers developed a very successful pattern with Christian Endeavor, Sunday school, and church services, all in Hawaiian. However, after the public schools made English the medium of instruction, the church had the same problems that German and Scandinavian language churches in the Mid-West had. Young people slipped away from churches to those that had English services. Some ministers, like the Reverend Edward Kahale and the Reverend Samuel Keala, both of whom taught Hawaiian at the University of Hawaii, were bilingual. Outstanding in these years of eloquent Hawaiian leadership was the Reverend Henry P. Judd, grandson of the missionary physician Dr. Gerrit Judd. For a number of years his activities were numerous. He served in various capacities on the Hawaiian Board, working with the Hawaiian churches. He served many of the Hawaiian churches and was much in demand. For years he taught Hawaiian at the University of Hawaii, and collaborated on the publication of a Hawaiian-English dictionary.

The Reverend Akaiko Akana was the first Hawaiian to attend a mainland seminary. A number attended, but Abraham Akaka was the only Hawaiian before 1950 to receive a completely accredited ministerial training. Since then, Gilbert and Abraham Williams, Leopold Waiau, William Kaina, John and Thomas Kalili, James Merseberg, David Kaupu, Henry Boshard, David Kaapu, and Tyrone Reinhardt have graduated from accredited seminaries.

SILOAMA

Siloama, the Church of the Healing Spring at Kalawao, is the story of dedicated Hawaiian ministers and laymen at Kalaupapa Settlement. Four hundred sufferers of leprosy arrived in the first year after the establishment of the settlement. A general lawlessness arising from despair prevailed in that first year. There had been a church at Kalaupapa before the settlement started, and one deacon of the church, D. G. Kawaluna, lived at Kalawao. The *lanai* (Hawaiian veranda) of his home became the place for religious services. A plaque in Siloama Church commemorates the organization of the church with these words: "Thrust out by mankind, these 12 women and 23 men, crying aloud to God, their only refuge, formed a church, the first in the desolation that was Kalawao."

Later a Mrs. Kawaluna was a patient, and she might well have been the wife of this dedicated deacon. One of the early pastors, the Reverend John Hanaloa (1878–89), did come when his wife was sent to Kalaupapa and he would not forsake her.

The Maui Association appointed pastors in charge if there was no ordained minister at the settlement. These were usually the pastors at Kaluaaha. The first, the Reverend Anderson O. Forbes, made the trip down the great cliff to organize the church. A later pastor at Kaluaaha, the Reverend David Kaai, who served three years as a missionary in the Gilbert Islands, became pastor at

Kaluaaha in 1896 and until 1918 was interim pastor at
Kalaupapa. The Reverend Daniel Mahihila, also a missionary in the Gilberts, was pastor at Kalaupapa from
1918 to 1930. The Reverend Alice Kahokuoluna went to
Kalaupapa as pastor in 1938 and served until her death
in 1957. This first woman in Hawaii to be an ordained
minister had the aura of sainthood.

The story of Siloama Church with its dedicated Hawaiians was unknown until Mother Alice found the old record
book in a storage place beneath Siloama Church. This led
to the rebuilding of the church as a memorial shrine. At
the centennial celebration of the church in 1966, over four
hundred people attended.

THE HAWAIIANS BECOME MISSIONARIES

The American Board saw Hawaii as only one of its ob-
jectives among the many islands of the Pacific. In 1852 the
first missionaries to Micronesia started their work. They
were the Reverend and Mrs. Albert Sturges, the Reverend
and Mrs. Benjamin Snow, and the Reverend and Mrs.
Luther Gulick. En route they stopped at Honolulu where
Gulick had been born. The Hawaiian Mission Children's
Society, now a social organization of missionary descendants, was organized to help "Cousin" Luther in his mission
work. To aid the American Board's Micronesian Mission,
the Hawaiian Missionary Society was formed. Two
Hawaiians, both deacons, volunteered, and the missionary
community rallied to their support. Mr. and Mrs. Daniel
Opunui went to Kusaie, and Mr. and Mrs. Berita Kaai-
kaula to Ponape. Both men died at their place of service.

The following year Hawaiians went to the Marquesas Islands. A Hawaiian youth from Maui married the daughter of Chief Matanui of the island of Fatuluva in the Marquesas. Chief Matanui, with his Hawaiian son-in-law, came to Lahaina in March 1853 and asked for missionaries to go to his island. When told that no missionaries were available, he appealed to the Hawaiians to be the missionaries. Eight Hawaiians volunteered—the Reverend and Mrs. James Kekela, the Reverend and Mrs. Samuel Kauwealoha, Mr. and Mrs. Lot Kauaihelani, and Mr. and Mrs. Isaia Kaiwi. The Reverend Benjamin Parker had visited the Marquesas in 1834 and offered to go to the Marquesas to make suitable arrangements for the mission before returning to Hawaii.

Thus thirty years after the first missionaries arrived in Hawaii, the Hawaiians were sending missionaries to the other islands of the Pacific.

The Reverend James Kekela wrote a journal of his life as a missionary, and the chief facts of his life are stated on a monument in the Kawaiahao churchyard.

Reverend James Kekela, Kekela o ka lani
Born in 1824 Mokuleia, Oahu
Educated by James Hunnewell at Lahainaluna
Ordained at Kahuku, December 21, 1849

In 1853 he went as a pioneer missionary to the Marquesas Islands where for 46 years he exercised a remarkable influence against cannibalism and tribal influence, a true spiritual guide.

In 1864 he was signally awarded by Abraham
Lincoln for rescuing an American seaman from
cannibals.

Died in Honolulu, November 1904.

O ke aloha, oia ka mole o mea pono ame na mea ioaio a
pau. Love is the root of all that is good and true. Kekela.

The Reverend James Kekela remained in the Marquesas until 1899, when the churches were turned over to the
French Protestants.

The work in Micronesia has continued to the present
day. Many Hawaiian ministers worked on the various
islands, and their stories are myriad.

Men with names still familiar in Hawaii, such as
Paaluhi, Kanoho, Mahoe, and Nawaa, were ministers in
the Marshalls, at Kusaie, and in the Gilberts.

In 1856, the American Board decided a small sailing
vessel was needed so that the missionaries could travel
among the scattered islands. They named the ship the
Morning Star and appointed Hiram Bingham, Jr., as missionary. Hiram Bingham, Jr., became the missionary to
the Gilberts. He translated the Bible into Gilbertese. While
he was in Honolulu to supervise the printing of the Gilbertese Bible, his son, Hiram Bingham III, was born.
Hiram Bingham III is renowned for his discovery of the
ancient Inca city Macchu Bicchu. He later became a
United States Senator from Connecticut, and his son,
Jonathan Bingham was elected to Congress from New
York. In 1866 Hiram Bingham, Jr., had obtained a larger
ship, the *Morning Star II*. Other ships named the *Morning*

Star came in later years. Mission work in Micronesia almost ceased during the years of Japanese occupation, but in 1947 the *Morning Star VI* sailed to Micronesia. One of the crew was Mr. Daniel Akaka, now Minister of Music at Kawaiahao Church. Soon after this, the Reverend Eleanor Wilson was left in charge of the Micronesian Mission, including the *Morning Star VI*. A delightful book of her missionary activities and experiences with *Morning Star VI* was published under the title *The Lady Was a Skipper*.[5]

In 1958 the Reverend and Mrs. Tuck Wah Lee of Hilo were appointed as missionaries by the American Board. They have worked at Ponape, in the Truk Islands, and in the Marshall Islands.

POLITICS

The Reverend John P. Erdman, at the 1920 centennial of the arrival of the first missionaries, wrote *A Brief Historical Sketch of the Hawaiian Board of Missions*.

> During the last thirty years of the 19th century the general work of the Hawaiian Board did not sustain the strong record made in the early years of the Mission. Briefly stated, the retarding factors were these: First, the unprecedented and rapid commercial growth in the Hawaiian Islands, which introduced a materialistic tendency having a decided influence toward reducing the number of church adherents and the stability of the native Christians; Second, the influx of thousands of contract laborers from the Orient, bringing an entirely new element into the social organism and perforce in-

troducing new evils to the community; and Third, heated political disturbances. This third factor was perhaps the most serious.[6]

The Hawaiians had great aloha for their missionary pastors, such as Samuel Whitney at Waimea, Kauai; Lorenzo Lyons at Imiola; Titus Coan at Haili; and John Emerson at Waialua. These men lived with their congregations, suffered privation with them, died in service to their people and were buried in the cemeteries beside their churches. However, only seven or eight unordained missionaries remained until death or retirement. Samuel N. Castle was the business manager for the American Board and then entered into partnership with Amos Starr Cooke to form Castle and Cooke.

Moreover the Hawaiians saw the sons and sons-in-law of the missionaries assuming more and more leadership in economics and politics. Henry P. Baldwin wanted to become a physician like his father. When he lost an arm, he went into sugar raising and began to develop what is now the largest sugar plantation in Hawaii. And his building of the East Maui irrigation project is a success story in the American tradition. The children of Elias Bond in Kohala, of the Rices and Wilcoxes on Kauai, of the Castles and Cookes on Oahu, and of the Alexanders and Baldwins on Maui were to dominate economically the areas in which they lived. No less important were the sons-in-law. When Benjamin Dillingham came ashore from an Oregon-bound ship to do some sightseeing, he was thrown from his horse and had to remain in Hawaii with a broken leg. He subsequently married the daughter of the Reverend Lowell Smith. Joseph Ballard Atherton married the daughter of Amos Starr Cooke. Such men were not missionaries, but the Hawaiians saw them as part of the missionary families. As these men prospered in business, while many of the Hawaiians did not, resentments grew which had an adverse effect on the churches.

Mr. Erdman's third point was the political upheaval. Since the constitution of Kamehameha V had a property qualification for voting, many Hawaiians could not vote and the legislature had a high proportion of American and British descendants.

In the later years of King Kalakaua's reign, friction developed between the commercial interests and the king. This was not lessened when Queen Liliuokalani became the ruler. The tragic years that followed culminated in the annexation of the Islands by the United States. Although Queen Liliuokalani was a member of Kawaiahao Church, the Reverend Henry Parker supported those who opposed her. Many of the churches of the Hawaiian Evangelical Association opposed Queen Liliuokalani's attempt to license opium, but the congregations divided in sentiment when she was forced to abdicate. The Royalist element was credited with the burning of Wainee Church in Lahaina. The Reverend Stephen L. Desha, Sr., of Haili Church in Hilo, managed to support Queen Liliuokalani while maintaining his position as a leader in the Hawaiian Evangelical Association. But for many of the churches, as Dr. Erdman noted, the heated political disturbances reduced the number of church members.

THE CHINESE

Mr. Erdman's second point was the influx of contract laborers from the Orient. The sandalwood trade established early contact with China, and numerous Hawaiians went on voyages to China. Some Chinese came to Hawaii on the return voyages, and one of these brought the grinding stones for a sugar mill that he established on Lanai in 1802.

The Chinese were few before 1850; then immigration brought hundreds to Hawaii. Many settled in the area of downtown Honolulu still called Chinatown. As this was near the Seamen's Bethel (on Bethel Street), the Reverend Samuel Damon began religious work among the Chinese in 1868.

A Chinese church was developed by working from the Seamen's Bethel, and designated the Fort Street Chinese Church. This later became the First Chinese Christian Church and, as one of the strongest churches in Hawaii, can look back on a century of work. United States Senator Hiram Fong is a member of this church, who, incidentally, as a youth selected the name of Hiram when he learned of the Christian leadership of Hiram Bingham.

Probably because of his father's work with the Chinese, Francis Damon studied Chinese in China. In 1884 he started a school for Chinese boys and assumed charge of the work with the Chinese in Hawaii. Within every community where there was a significant number of Chinese, a Chinese minister worked. In Kohala the old Chinese Church has united with Kalahikiola Church, and in

Wailuku the Chinese Church merged with Wailuku Union. In Hilo the Chinese Church has taken the name United Community Church, and has employed pastors of other racial groups to promote an interracial church.

In Honolulu a second Chinese Church developed after the Chinatown fire of 1900. Kaumakapili Church was destroyed in that fire, and the congregation rebuilt it at its present site. The Beretania Street Chinese Church was built on the old Kaumakapili site. Some years later tension developed between the older and more conservative Chinese-speaking element and the younger group, particularly those having a college education, typified by Hung Wai Ching, who attended the University of Hawaii and Chicago Theological Seminary and was a Y.M.C.A. worker before becoming a very successful businessman. These men organized the Community Church of Honolulu, and now have a strikingly beautiful church at the Pali Highway and Wyllie Street.

The Beretania Street Church continued until, as the United Church of Christ, it was rebuilt at Liliha and Judd streets in 1951. The Reverend Charles Kwock of First Chinese and the Reverend Richard Wong of the Community Church were Island youths, while the Reverend Harold Jow of the United Church came from San Francisco Theological Seminary in 1947. Reverend Kim On Chong has been chaplain of Mid-Pacific Institute for twenty-five years. Dr. Kwai Sing Chang, who received his doctorate at the University of Edinburgh, was pastor in Hawaii for some years and is now a professor at Colby College.

THE JAPANESE

The first Japanese laborers arrived in Hawaii in 1868. There were few married men among them. Some of the unmarried men married Hawaiian women, and their families merged with the Hawaiians. The great influx of Japanese came almost twenty years later.

Christian missionary work among them started with the Methodist Church. When the Methodists withdrew temporarily, the work was assumed by the Hawaiian Board, and in 1894 the Reverend Oramel Gulick, born in Hawaii, resigned from his missionary work in Japan to take charge of the Japanese work in Hawaii. The former Methodist Church became Nuuanu Congregational Church.

Mr. Gulick persuaded a young Japanese minister to come to Hawaii. The Reverend Takei Okumura, ordained in 1909, became the inspired leader of the Makiki Christian Church. The Makiki and Nuuanu churches established dormitories for students from other islands and in many ways exerted leadership among the Japanese Christians.

In many plantation communities, church work was established with a Japanese-language school. As Japanese workers left the plantations, churches like Lihue Christian, Holy Cross in Hilo, and Iao Congregational became strong. The Reverend Kwon Higuchi was one of the early pastors. The Reverend Paul Waterhouse, a missionary's grandson with years of service as a missionary in Japan, returned to be pastor at Kalihi Union Church.

As the Japanese young people came to the University

to study, they often abandoned their Japanese past. A special service for such young people was started at the Mission Memorial Building. When the Reverend Galen Weaver came as minister, the Church of the Crossroads resulted. This church has given community leadership in many ways.

Partly through the Church of the Crossroads, a number of outstanding young men of Japanese ancestry entered the ministry. The Reverend Paul Osumi, now pastor of Nuuanu Congregational, was pastor at Lihue, Kauai, in 1941 and acted as agent for the Japanese Consulate. When the Consular officers were interned, Mr. Osumi was among them. In the relocation camp in Arizona, he began to write little devotional messages, and now he publishes a thought each day in the *Honolulu Advertiser*. The Reverend Mineo Katagiri, after holding pastorates in Hawaii, has become a secretary for the National Council of the United Church dealing with racial problems. The Reverend Seido Ogawa is executive secretary of the Hawaii Council of Churches. The Reverend Hiro Higuchi and the Reverend Masao Yamada became chaplains with the 442nd Infantry Regiment. Mr. Higuchi has become known for building churches, having built Waipahu Community Church, Pearl City Community Church, and Manoa Valley Church. Mr. Yamada is now chaplain of the State Hospital. Dr. Thomas Okuma, after years as a missionary in Angola, Africa, returned to Hawaii as a Professor of Religion at Hawaii Loa College. Dr. Mitsuo Aoki is head of the Department of Religion at the University of Hawaii, and was chairman of the University Faculty Senate in 1967–68. The Reverend Paul Miho was in charge of the University Y.M.C.A. for many years. These men of Japanese ancestry are vital influences in the religious and community life of Hawaii.

THE PORTUGUESE

The majority of the Portuguese have remained Roman Catholics, but a significant number of Portuguese names are also found in other churches. Among the Portuguese Negroes of the Cape Verde Islands who came to Hawaii in 1867, one Mr. Jose Manuel became a worker for the Hawaiian Evangelical Association. He became a pastor of the Hawaiian Church of Kaneohe, and although the Association went on record as releasing him from that church to engage in evangelistic work among the Portuguese, he was content to remain with the Hawaiian Church. Mr. Manuel was the first Negro minister to work in Hawaii.

As the Portuguese community grew, Miss Knight, sister of Mrs. Charles M. Hyde, began a little Sunday school. In 1890 a Portuguese minister from Springfield, Illinois, was recruited by the Hawaiian Board. The Reverend Antonio V. Soares soon had a sizable congregation, and in June 1892 he dedicated the Pilgrim Church at Miller and Vineyard streets. This church remained in the Portuguese community until 1940, when it united with Central Union Church.

In Hilo the Reverend Ernest da Silva established and ministered for years a Portuguese church which later took the name Central Christian. This is now the only Portuguese Protestant church in the state. Mr. G. Santos worked on Maui and established a small church, which has since dissolved, the members joining other churches.

THE CAUCASIANS

Since Americans came as foreigners to Hawaii, a number of churches they established were termed foreign churches. The chapel of the Seamen's Bethel was sometimes designated First Foreign Church. English-speaking residents of Honolulu attended, but the major emphasis of the chapel was on work with sailors. In 1852 the second foreign church, with the name of Fort Street Church, was established. The Reverend Daniel Dole came to Hawaii to establish Punahou School, but later moved to Koloa, Kauai, where he established a school of his own and later an English-speaking church. The Reverend J. S. Green established an independent congregation in 1844 that developed into Makawao Union Church. The Foreign Church of Waimea, Kauai, in 1865, and also the First Foreign Church of Hilo, in 1868, were formed as the Hawaiian Evangelical Association became entirely a Hawaiian-speaking organization.

As the plantation communities grew, provision was made for English services. Ewa, Lihue, Kohala, and Kahului were plantation communities where English services led to the formation of churches.

Kohala is a good example of the development of churches in a plantation community. Kalahikiola Church was the Hawaiian church where Father Elias Bond was pastor. When the plantation was started, a Chinese church soon came. Later Kohala Union Church came into being for English-speaking residents, followed by a Japanese church in 1894 and a Filipino church in 1933. By 1942 all churches except the Filipino church were having services in English. The Japanese and Chinese churches merged, and a few years later all except the Filipino church merged with Kalahikiola.

After a fire destroyed the Bethel church, the Bethel congregation merged with Fort Street Church to form Central Union and built its edifice at Richards and Beretania. Central Union built its present building in what had been the Dillingham gardens in 1922. Central Union was an independent church with ministers from the Presbyterian as well as the Congregational churches. Dr. Albert W. Palmer, pastor when the present church was built, later became president of Chicago Theological Seminary. Dr. Allen Hackett, after a mainland pastorate, became General Secretary of the Metropolitan Boston area of the United Church of Christ. Dr. Thomas L. Crosby, pastor from 1951 to 1970, led Central Union until it was one of the largest churches of the United Church of Christ in America, both in membership and total financial giving.

THE FILIPINOS

Although a number of Filipinos came to Hawaii earlier, the largest migrations came when the Oriental Exclusion Act of 1924 closed all Asian countries except the Philippines as a source of plantation labor. Cooperative planning and work began with the Methodist Mission. Some pastors were brought from the Philippines, and young men came to study at the Theological School. The Reverend C. C. Cortezon on Kauai, the Reverend Simeon Ibera on Hawaii, the Reverend Romualdo Barientos on Maui, and the Reverend F. M. Santa Ana on Oahu were pastors. Some, like the Reverend George Garcia, returned to the Philippines.

During the 1950's the Hawaiian Board and the Methodist Mission ended their united work. Some churches became Methodist, and the majority of the Filipino Congregational churches merged with other churches. Waipahu Evangelical merged with Waipahu Community to form the Waipahu United Church of Christ. Waialua Evangelical merged with Waialua Pilgrim Church, and the Koloa Church became part of the Koloa Union Church. Only Puunene Congregational Church and Kohala Pilgrim Church remain.

THE SAMOANS

Just as the American Board of Commissioners for Foreign Missions was an independent organization but working mainly with Congregationalists, the London Missionary Society represented Independent or Congregational Churches of Great Britian. The London Missionary Society evangelized Samoa. There was fraternal good will but little contact between the Samoan and the Hawaiian Congregational fellowships. This is still true even in American Samoa.

A few Samoans came to Hawaii to study, and the

Reverend John Samoa Likelesa was pastor of Imiola Church from 1902 to 1910. Most Samoans who did come to Hawaii were Mormons and lived at Laie. However, the abolition of the Pago Pago Naval Base brought a large number of naval civilian employees and their dependents to Pearl Harbor. Almost all were Congregationalists. Some preferred to call themselves Congregational while others insisted upon the designation of L.M.S. (London Missionary Society), but both groups became part of the Oahu Association. No Samoan minister came to Hawaii. Deacon P. Malae was licensed to minister to the Samoan Church L.M.S., and N. L. Malepeai was licensed for the First Samoan United Church of Christ. These churches are across the street from each other, near the Moanalua Shopping Center. Other Samoan churches are the First Samoan United Church of Christ at Maile and the Samoan Church of Hawaii L.M.S. at Nanakuli.

TOWARD THE HAWAII CONFERENCE

When the Hawaiian Evangelical Association was formed, it became in fact an independent denomination existing only in Hawaii. The ties which kept the churches in touch with the American Board and with Congregational churches were fraternal. The only official relationship of the churches in Hawaii to those in the United States was through their joint effort in Micronesia. Organizations such as the Women's Board for the Pacific kept contacts with other churches.

The Hawaiian Board elected secretaries who acted at least in part as administrative officers. The Reverend

Anderson Forbes, the Reverend Oliver P. Emerson, and the Reverend Oramel Gulick, all the sons of missionaries, served as secretaries. Mr. Francis Damon, another missionary son, became superintendent of Chinese work.

In 1894 Mr. Theodore Richards, principal at the Kamehameha Schools, became a Field Secretary of the Board, and later its treasurer.

By 1900 the position of General Secretary had become established. Dr. Doremus Scudder served from 1904 to 1908, and then became pastor of Central Union Church. The Reverend William B. Oleson, first principal of the Kamehameha Schools, after many years in mainland churches, returned to Hawaii to head the Board. In 1907 the Reverend John P. Erdman began a service of thirty-two years with the Hawaiian Board. In 1932 he became the General Secretary. Associated with him for years were the Reverend Henry P. Judd, Field Secretary of Hawaiian Churches, and the Reverend Norman Schenck, who started to work as Chinese Superintendent in 1915. Later he also assumed charge of the Filipino work and the youth work. The Reverend Norman Schenck became the General Secretary in 1939. Associated with Mr. Schenck was Dr. J. Leslie Dunstan, who had been in charge of the School of Religion associated with the University of Hawaii.

Mr. Schenck, who worked with the Hawaiian Board for almost thirty years, was General Secretary for only a few years. Next Dr. Dunstan served as General Secretary until 1954, when he became Professor of Missions at Andover Newton Seminary. Dr. Nelson Dreier, who had been superintendent of the Washington Council, came to Hawaii as General Secretary, followed by Dr. Joseph Bevilacqua, who served from 1961 to 1968. In 1969 Dr. Chester Terpstra was elected general secretary.

The Hawaiian Evangelical Association was an independent denomination until 1923. The Reverend Henry P. Judd was instrumental in negotiations with the National Council of Congregational Churches, which drew up a plan of organic union with the Hawaiian Evangelical Association in 1921. The Plan of Organic Union was adopted on June 21, 1923.

The union of the Congregational and Christian Churches in 1931 aroused little notice in Hawaii, and it was not until 1951 that the Association voted to be called the Hawaiian Evangelical Association of Congregational Christian Churches.

The negotiations for the forming of the United Church of Christ were protracted. The issue was to what extent would the churches have to give up Congregational prerogatives to form the United Church of Christ. Eighty of the churches voted to join the United Church; thirty-two did not vote or voted to abstain. So in 1961 the Hawaiian Evangelical Association voted to become the Hawaii Conference of the United Church of Christ, but with the provision that churches not belonging to the United Church could still be members of the island associations and the state conference.

New England Congregationalism in town meetings had concern for the community. The Hawaii Conference inherited that New England concern. The Metropolitan

Mission of the Hawaii Conference is involved with urban renewal, slum clearance, and the social effects of tourism. The Campus Ministry at the University of Hawaii with its "Off-Center Coffeehouse" not only has discussions in the town meeting tradition, but has become an action group in regard to University and community policies.

This community involvement led a visiting professor at the University of Hawaii to comment, "After having been in Hawaii for a year, the United Church in Hawaii seemed to be the most vital and lively and dynamic group."[7]

THE CONTINUING CONGREGATIONAL CHURCHES

When the Hawaiian Evangelical Association voted to become the Hawaii Conference of the United Church of Christ, a provision was adopted that churches could be members of the Hawaii Conference without being members of the national body. A number of churches, like Haili Church in Hilo and Mokuaikaua Church in Kailua-Kona, have done this. Others, like the Bernice Pauahi Bishop Memorial Church (the chapel church of the Kamehameha Schools) which is nondenominational, retained an affiliation with the Hawaii Conference. However, a few churches no longer have that affiliation. Nanaikapono Church in Nanakuli, with a Missionary Church pastor, withdrew and became independent. Lihue Congregational Church is also independent.

Four churches, under the leadership of the Reverend John Kalili, have termed themselves the Hawaii Congregational Christian Churches Association and have made contacts with the Continuing Congregational Church on the mainland, which did not enter the United Church of Christ. These churches and some other churches which had not joined the United Church held an Ecclesiastical Council and ordained the Reverend David Kaapu. Such proceedings were according to the old Congregational practice but not according to the regulations of the United Church of Christ. Since the churches and ministers involved had not accepted the constitution of the United Church, a dilemma has developed. Are the churches and ministers that remained Congregational to be governed by old Congregational practice or by regulations of the United Church?

The answer will require Christian charity and aloha.

1. Edwin Dwight, *Memoirs of Obookiah,* 150th anniversary edition, The Women's Board of Missions for the Pacific Islands, Honolulu, 1968.

2. Oscar Maurer, *How the Gospel Came to Hawaii,* pamphlet privately printed, 1945, pp. 9–10.

3. Quoted from *The Friend,* vol. 77, no. 4, p. 90, April 1920.

4. Samuel B. Harrison, *The White King,* Doubleday, New York, 1950.

5. Moribelle Cormack, *The Lady Was a Skipper,* Hill and Wang, New York, 1956.

6. *The Centennial Book,* Hawaiian Board of Missions, Honolulu, 1920, pp. 77–78.

7. *Delegates Handbook,* 146th Aha Paeaina (Annual Conference), Honolulu, 1968, p. 11.

5. *The Compassionate Christ*—an altar fresco by Jean
Charlot. St. Catherine's Church, Kapaa, Kauai.

4. The Roman Catholic Diocese of Honolulu

There is a remote possibility that a Spanish priest came to Hawaii four centuries ago. When the English missionary the Reverend William Ellis heard the story of Paao, he conjectured that Paao was a Spanish priest who was ship-wrecked on the island of Hawaii. The Catholic historian Father Reginald Yzendoorn presented a long argument to support this view.[1] Most archeologists do not accept this theory, but it is faintly credible. More credible is that a Spanish ship did visit the islands and that the white sail-like banner that served as a symbol of the god Lono during the Makahiki festival became a symbol after this visit.

One of the advisers to Kamehameha the Great was Don Francisco de Paulu Marin, a Spaniard. Marin (after whom Marin County in California was named) received land on Oahu, planted vineyards (Vineyard Street takes its name from these), and raised cattle. He had two Hawaiian wives and lived much in the fashion of a Hawaiian chief. Nominally a Roman Catholic, he was careful not to have his religion bring him in conflict with the chiefs either before or after the abolition of the kapu. In fact, he had, as a

chief, assisted in the pagan ceremonies of the old days.
After the arrival of Protestant missionaries, Marin apparently became more open in his religious faith, teaching
his children prayers and reading the Mass on Sundays.
He claimed to have baptized over three hundred children,
yet the first thirteen baptisms recorded in the Catholic
mission in Honolulu were performed by a Mexican merchant, Don Thomas Milandrez. Two of those baptized
were Marin's wives. Seven were children of the two wives.
Another child was his granddaughter. Moreover, when
the Catholic missionaries arrived, Marin refused to give
them any substantial aid for fear of offending the chiefs.

The first known Roman Catholic priests came on French
ships. Just after the death of Kamehameha I, the French
warship *Uranie* arrived in Kona. Abbe De Quelan baptized Kalanimoku in the first baptismal service in Hawaii.
Kalanimoku had a fair understanding of the Christian
faith, and when the Protestant missionaries arrived, he
was a strong supporter and one of the first members of
Kawaiahao Church. On this same voyage Abbe De
Quelan also baptized Boki, the governor of Oahu.

The Catholic Mission came to Hawaii through the influence of Jean Rives, one of those ingratiating rascals who
have made Pacific history so colorful. A teen-age boy when
he arrived in Hawaii, Rives became the close friend of
Liholiho. King Kamehameha made Rives a chief of rank
so that he could eat with Liholiho. Queen Kaahumanu
treated him like a favorite son, so much so the Hawaiians
called him Luahine (Old Woman). When Liholiho became
king, Rives acted as his secretary. Rives started to teach

Liholiho to read, but they found card playing more divert-
ing. Rives had a Hawaiian wife and twin daughters. He
was given extensive land, and built a home where the
Honolulu Gas Company now stands on Bishop Street.
Rives' descendants still live in Hawaii.

In 1823 Liholiho decided to go to England. In the royal
party, besides a number of Hawaiians, were Rives and
James Kanehoa Young, the *hapa haole* (half white) son of
John Young. James Young was left in Rio de Janeiro,
either by accident or by some trickery on the part of Rives.
Young managed to get another English captain to take
him to London. Meantime, the visit of the royal party had
had a tragic ending. Both King Liholiho and Queen
Kamamalu had died in London.

While Liholiho was living, Jean Rives had sought to
make some commercial contacts in England. When the
king died, Rives left very abruptly. He went to Paris with
a Hawaiian youth, Marie Joseph Kanui, who was baptized
and educated by the Order of the Sacred Hearts. The
Congregation of the Sacred Hearts of Jesus and Mary had
worked to reclaim France from the teachings of the French
Revolution. From 1800 to the present, it has been a strong
influence in France. At the request of Jean Rives and with
the approval of the Pope, the Sacred Hearts decided to
send a mission to Hawaii.

Meantime, Rives received the backing of the French
merchants and the French government to found a colony
in Hawaii. Rives sailed from France in April 1826, promising to be in Hawaii when the mission arrived. The
ship stopped in Mexico. There Rives learned from a

Captain Sommers that the Hawaiian party, including James Young, had returned from England with many accusations against Rives. Angry, Kaahumanu had confiscated all lands which had been given to Rives subject to revocation by the king, and adopted his twin daughters. Rives and the French merchants, in uncertainty, sold or traded all their merchandise. The French merchants returned to France with their ship, and Rives remained with Captain Sommers.

On November 20, 1826, the second ship, *La Comete*, sailed from Bordeaux. Three priests, Fathers Alexis Bachelot, Abraham Armand, and Patrick Short, and three lay brothers, Theodore Bossier, Melchior Bondo, and Leonore Portal, comprised the mission. Rives had assured the captain of *La Comete* that the passage of the mission would be paid upon arrival in Honolulu. When *La Comete* arrived in Honolulu, not only was there no Rives but an angry Kaahumanu had made his name taboo in her presence.

However, Boki, the Governor of Oahu, permitted the priests to land. Boki disliked Kaahumanu and had once sought to enlist other chiefs in open war against her. So Boki provided Kaahumanu a second reason for disliking the new arrivals. The third reason was religious. Kaahumanu, after some years of indifference, had become a most zealous supporter of the American missionaries. When the French missionaries arrived, the Americans made social calls and showed some personal friendliness, but, on the other hand, they preached against Catholic doctrine.

All these factors led Kaahumanu to order the priests to

leave. The Captain of *La Comete* refused to take them since the priests' passage was unpaid. Boki supported the Catholic mission. For a time his support kept Kaahumanu from taking action. Then Boki embarked on an adventure to gather sandalwood in the South Seas, and his ship was lost at sea. In 1831 Kaahumanu forced the priests to leave. The lay brother Melchior Bondo was left in charge of the mission. They returned after the death of Kaahumanu, but found Kinau also in determined opposition. When another French ship arrived in port with Father Louis Maigret aboard, Kinau forced all the priests to leave. However, a year later her opposition did not prevent two Irish priests who were British citizens from remaining. One, Father Arsene Walsh, was to become the founder of many Catholic churches. There was less opposition to the Irish priests than there had been to the French ones.

Kinau proceeded to act against Hawaiians who had become Catholics. At least twenty-eight persons were imprisoned and many were harassed by various chiefs. Kinau died on April 4, 1839, and on June 18 Kekauluohi forbade the use of force against Catholics. Previously, Kamehameha III had given the same order on Maui. However, some Catholics were still imprisoned in Honolulu when the French warship *L'Artemise* arrived on July 9. Captain La Place demanded that Catholics receive the same rights as Protestants, a site for a church and other provisions which included rights of French merchants to trade.

Captain La Place insisted that the insult to France owing to the expulsion of French priests had originated with Protestant missionaries. But, actually, before the arrival of the French ship, the Reverend William Richards of Lahaina had persuaded Kamehameha III to end the persecution on Maui, and was to explain the persecutions as an unfortunate event due to the political rivalries of the chiefs.[2] Mr. David Gregg, American Commissioner in 1853 and a Roman Catholic, decided that the American missionaries were indirectly to blame because they attacked Catholicism in their sermons, but he was satisfied that the missionaries did not recommend persecution and that many of them had urged the chiefs to stop the punishment of the Catholics. That even in such a conflict the aloha of Hawaii was working is shown by Mrs. Laura Judd. She was exchanging seeds with the lay brother, who was an enthusiastic horticulturist.

Yet Kinau and the other chiefs saw a real danger in the coming of the French. Within a few years Tahiti and the Marquesans were taken over by the French, and Captain Paulet raised the British flag over Hawaii. Admiral Thomas restored the government to Kamehameha III, and France and England agreed to respect the independence of Hawaii. For years some French priests acted as French Consuls, and there was confusion between the acts of the church and the acts of the French government. Father Yzendoorn says, "The priests even fostered perhaps a secret hope that France might annex the islands."[3] The chiefs had the fear of French annexation, and the persecutions might be understood as coming in part from this fear. Many of the priests of the Sacred Hearts came from Belgium, and their devotion to their work was to make the Catholic Church in Hawaii the least involved of the churches in the political turmoil that brought about annexation.

Besides the school at the Cathedral, the mission founded a college, Ahuimanu, on Windward Oahu. Ten sisters arrived in 1859 and started a school for girls, Sacred Hearts Academy. St. Louis was established for boys in 1881, and in 1883 the Marianists arrived to take over the teaching at St. Louis.

BISHOP LOUIS MAIGRET

The history of the Diocese of Honolulu can follow the bishops who served. All the first bishops in Honolulu were missionary Vicars Apostolic, being titular bishops of some other locality. Bishop Stephen Rouchouze, Bishop of Nilopolis, was consecrated as bishop in 1833. His diocese extended from Easter Island to Hawaii, and his headquarters was at Mangareva, west of Tahiti. Bishop Rouchouze directed the mission to Hawaii but did not come to Hawaii himself until May 15, 1840. He settled all questions relating to Catholics in Hawaii. Part of the understanding was the building of a church, and on July 9, 1840, which was the Feast of Our Lady of Peace, Bishop Rouchouze broke ground for the building of the Cathedral of Our Lady of Peace. He sailed from Hawaii on January 3, 1841, for France. Almost two years later he sailed on his return trip, and the ship with all on board was lost at sea. Left in charge of the mission in Honolulu was Father Louis Maigret, who must be regarded as the real founder of Catholic work in Hawaii. His immediate concern in 1840 was the building and dedication of the Cathedral.

The clock in the tower is from Valparaiso, Chile, where it had been in a church of the Sacred Hearts. Memorial plaques honor Father Bachelot and Father Damien, who was ordained and said his first mass in 1864. Behind the episcopal throne is the tomb of Bishop Maigret. The altar is of Italian marble, dedicated in honor of the centennial of the mission. The bells in the tower, installed in 1853, are from France. The smaller one is dedicated to Louis Maigret and the larger to Father Aubert. In the courtyard is a statue to Our Lady of Peace to commemorate the centennial of the mission.

Father Louis Maigret had sailed to Honolulu in 1836 but was not allowed to leave the ship. After a long delay following the disappearance of Bishop Rouchouze, Rome named Father Louis Maigret as Titular Bishop of Arathia. Bishop Maigret went to Rome and was consecrated October 30, 1847. During his return trip to Hawaii he translated *Imitation of Christ* into Hawaiian. Earlier he had brought a printing press, and a great number of Catholic publications appeared. Bishop Maigret sent priests to California during the Gold Rush days. One concession made for Catholics in the Pacific area was permission to eat meat on Fridays. For over a century before Vatican Council II, Catholics in Hawaii ate meat on Friday, except for Lent and on days of obligation.

In 1866 Mark Twain wrote this judgment of Bishop Maigret:

The French Roman Catholic Mission here, under the

Right Reverend Lord Bishop Maigret, goes along quietly and unostentatiously; and its affairs are conducted with a wisdom which betrays the presence of a leader of distinguished ability. The Catholic clergy are honest, straightforward, frank, and open; they are industrious and devoted to their religion and their work; they never meddle; whatever they do can be relied on as being prompted by a good and worthy motive. These things disarm resentment—prejudice cannot exist in their presence. Consequently, Americans are never heard to speak ill or slightingly of the French Catholic Mission. Their religion is not nondescript—it is plain, out-and-out, undisguised, and unmistakable Catholicism. You know right where to find them when you want them. The American missionaries have no quarrel with these men; they honor and respect and esteem them—and bid them Godspeed. There is an anomaly for you—Puritan and Roman Catholic striding along, hand in hand, under the banner of the Cross![4]

FATHER DAMIEN

To millions of Catholics around the world Father Damien represents the Roman Catholic Church in Hawaii. Joseph De Veuster was born in Belgium, educated at Louvain, ordained at Honolulu, and worked in Puna and Kohala. In 1873 he volunteered to go to Molokai. At first he worked not only at Kalawao but on the top side of Molokai as well. In east Molokai he built two churches. However, in increasing measure he had to work for the lepers. The settlement at Kalaupapa was established in 1866, and the first group managed to establish some sort of community. However, in 1873 the government ordered an intensive drive and literally dumped hundreds of sick and afflicted on a most desolate shore. Father Damien became carpenter, and aided many. He was nurse to many and not only conducted committal services for the dead but often constructed the coffins for their burial.

Disregarding many precautions in dealing with the sick, he became the unofficial nurse for those who refused to enter the hospital. When Father Damien became aware that he was a leper, he announced it in a sermon in which he spoke of "we lepers." Father Damien died on April 15, 1889, and was buried beside the Church of St. Philomena, which he had built. His body remained there until 1935, when it was exhumed, returned to Belgium, and reburied in the Monastery of the Sacred Hearts, where he had studied for the priesthood. But the empty grave and the Church of St. Philomena remain a shrine of this apostle of Christian charity.

In every account of Father Damien some mention must be made of the controversy which followed his death. Dr. Charles M. Hyde wrote a most ungracious letter to a friend, who sent it to a person in Australia who published the letter. Robert Louis Stevenson wrote "An Open Letter" savagely attacking Dr. Hyde. The conscience of the world today would say Dr. Hyde was wrong, and Robert Louis Stevenson unjust.

Dr. Hyde, as Protestant head of the North Pacific Theological Seminary, had visited Kalaupapa, written in praise of Father Damien's work, and helped persuade Charles Reed Bishop to build Bishop Home for Mother

Marianne and the Franciscan Sisters. If, then, Dr. Hyde was not the bigot depicted by Stevenson, why did he write a letter implying that Father Damien was immoral in his life?

Dr. Hyde wrote a reply which, after publication in a religious periodical, was reprinted in pamphlet form. Quickly some of his argument was shown to be based on false information and mistaken identity. Dr. Hyde was one of the founders of the Social Science Club of Honolulu, which dealt with all aspects of social problems in Hawaii. He had studied the problem of leprosy and viewed it in the following way: "By all that I saw and heard and read, I was soon convinced of this one fact, that leprosy is one of the results of licentiousness."[5]

Dr. Hyde visited Kalaupapa confident that he was in no danger of leprosy. He regarded Father Damien's leprosy as proof of licentiousness. Dr. Hyde should be regarded not as a religious bigot, but as a man with very faulty medical knowledge. What he called fact was erroneous belief.

Father Damien reported that once when he was hearing a confession in an open area, a patient had a hemorrhage from his lungs and coughed violently, covering Father Damien with blood. The judgment today would be that Father Damien, seeking to convince the patients that his dedication to them was complete, did not practice the precautions which all workers with leprosy usually do. Mother Marianne insisted upon such precautions, and the many years of dedicated service by the Franciscan Sisters indicates that while there was danger, much of the danger disappeared with due regard to sanitary procedures.

The 1965 Hawaii State Legislature passed a resolution naming King Kamehameha and Father Damien as the two persons from Hawaii to be honored by statues in the national capitol, the ceremony of presentation being held on April 15, 1969. There was general community support of this decision, and most people in Hawaii of every religious faith would rejoice if Father Damien received canonization, and was known as Saint Damien, Apostle of Christian charity.

The sculptor of the Damien statue, Marisol Escobar, was present for the presentation. She also came to Honolulu when a duplicate was placed in the new capitol of the state of Hawaii.

BROTHER JOSEPH DUTTON

In 1886 an American, Joseph Dutton, came to Kalawao to help Father Damien. A Civil War veteran, Joseph Dutton had an unfortunate marriage followed by years of drunkenness. Later he wrote: "In 1882, I had decided upon a life of penance for the rest of my years. I decided that the penitential system of the Catholic Church was best suited for my condition."[6]

After trying to be a Trappist Monk, he came to Kalaupapa. He lived and worked at the settlement until 1930. His forty-four years of work at Kalaupapa were a witness not only to his own dedication but to the spirit of Father Damien.

THE PORTUGUESE

Dr. Jaoa de Castro was a physician with the Kotzebue Russian expedition. He treated King Kamehameha, who was ill. Kamehameha became friendly with this Russian expedition and sat for his portrait by Louis Choris. Dr. de Castro is the first identified Portuguese to visit Hawaii.

The Portuguese came as whalers and sailors, and by 1860 about two hundred were living in Honolulu. In 1860 Bishop Maigret mentioned that a little chapel named St. Patrick had been built in Halawa, Oahu, and most of the funds had been contributed by a Portuguese man. In 1867 a group of Cape Verde Island Portuguese Negroes were working at Ewa Plantation.

The big Portuguese migration began in 1878. Since the Azores and Madeira Islands in the Atlantic are similar in many ways to the Hawaiian Islands, the Hawaiian government decided to contract laborers from the Azores. The Portuguese did not like field labor on the plantations, and as soon as their contract obligations ended they moved to Honolulu. Another group found the climate and soil of the Kula slope on Maui similar to the Azores and started farms. As the plantations turned to Japan for laborers, other Portuguese became the field bosses. The Portuguese speedily developed into skilled laborers and small private businessmen. In Honolulu they found land they could purchase on the slopes of Punchbowl. A Portuguese community of privately owned homes became a distinctive part of Honolulu by the beginning of the 20th century.

A Portuguese priest, Padre M. F. Fernandes, came to

Honolulu in 1889. He had a letter from the Archbishop of San Francisco and was willing to work in Hawaii. Bishop Koeckeman would not accept him because Father Fernandes was not a member of the Sacred Hearts, which had been assigned Hawaii as a mission field. Within a few days the Bishop received a petition with a hundred signatures, asking that Father Fernandes be assigned to work with the Portuguese. When the petition was denied, Father Fernandes went to Macao.

Some resentment in the Portuguese community may have led some Portuguese to leave the Catholic Church. However, they were few in number.

The Portuguese strengthened the Roman Catholic Church in Hawaii greatly, not only because of the loyalty of most Portuguese to their faith but also because of considerable intermarrying by them with the Hawaiians. The ukulele, regarded as the most Hawaiian of instruments, was introduced by the Portuguese. The Festival of the Holy Ghost, a Portuguese festival extending from Ascension Day to Pentecost, was for years a time of special observance. The Society of the Holy Ghost maintains a chapel of its own. The Church of the Holy Ghost at Kula, Maui, still maintains portions of the old festival.

LATER BISHOPS

In 1881 Bishop Maigret asked for help, and he received a co-adjutor, Father Herman Koeckeman, Titular Bishop of Olba. Instead of going to Rome, Bishop Koeckeman was consecrated in San Francisco, August 21, 1881, and served until 1892.

The bishops had all been members of the order of Sacred Hearts, and Bishop Koeckeman had appointed Father Gulstan Ropert as vice provincial of the order for the Islands. So Father Ropert became bishop. He was consecrated in San Francisco as Titular Bishop of Pana-polis on September 25, 1892. Bishop Ropert was involved in controversy concerning Catholics being members of secret societies and, with the Board of Health, concerning regulations at Kalaupapa. The last found the Protestant groups acting with the Catholics against Board policies.

Bishop Ropert died of cancer, and before his death Father Libert Boeynaems was acting as his successor. Bishop Boeynaems was consecrated at San Francisco on July 25, 1903, as Titular Bishop of Zengma. Bishop Boeynaems established three orphanages and aided in the building of churches, such as St. Joseph's in Hilo, St. Anthony in Wailuku, and Sacred Hearts on Wilder Avenue. He had a chronic heart condition and, almost four years before dying, asked for appointment of Father Stephen Alencastre as his successor. Bishop Boeynaems died on May 13, 1926.

BISHOP STEPHEN ALENCASTRE

Bishop Stephen Alencastre was born in the Madeira Islands, and his family came to Hawaii when he was five years old. His name then was Peter, and he became an altar boy, helping the priests at Hana, Maui. He attended St. Louis High School, and then he went to Belgium, where he studied, taking the name of Stephen when taking his vows as a member of the Sacred Hearts. He was ordained as a priest in the Cathedral of Our Lady of Peace.

He was the first priest raised and ordained in Hawaii to become a bishop. He was consecrated at Los Angeles on August 24, 1924, as Titular Bishop of Arabissus. One of his first acts was to arrange for the Maryknoll Fathers to come to the Islands, realizing that the Order of Sacred Hearts, with its headquarters in Belgium, did not reflect the change in Hawaii following the annexation to the United States. Bishop Alencastre also strengthened parish status, erecting more and more schools of parochial type. On May 9, 1927, the Sisters of St. Francis opened St. Francis Hospital with fifty beds. The St. Francis School of Nursing began in 1929. Since then the hospital has grown with additions over the years, culminating with the Mother Marianne Wing built in 1959. The state's new requirements for nurses' education led the sisters to close the School of Nursing and to cooperate with the University of Hawaii School for Nursing. Sister Jolenta and Sister Maureen have been capable administrators of the hospital. Bishop Alencastre also built rectories at the churches for the priests. Bishop Alencastre died aboard the ship *Matsonia* on November 9, 1940.

DIOCESE OF HONOLULU

The German occupation of Belgium limited the work of the Order of Sacred Hearts. Archbishop John J. Mitty of San Francisco wanted Hawaii under his jurisdiction. The Catholic Church in Hawaii had grown too large and its ties with America too many for the Church to remain under the supervision of a missionary order based in Europe. Consequently, the time was ripe for Hawaii to become a diocese. On May 20, 1941, it was announced that the Right Reverend James J. Sweeney of San Francisco was to be the first Bishop of Honolulu. The consecration took place on July 25, 1941, in San Francisco. Bishop Sweeney arrived in Honolulu in September, and on September 10 the formal erection of the Diocese of Honolulu was made. The Diocese contained forty-two parishes and fifty-three missions. There were nineteen schools and eighty-two priests.

During World War II Bishop Sweeney had responsibility for Catholic chaplains and troops in the Pacific. Many of the plans for the Diocese had to be postponed until the end of the war. But he did establish the Catholic Social Service in 1943, in order to bring the Catholic charities into more modern lines. In 1948 the Catholic Social Service was chartered. It directs all aspects of social service. The orphanages have been closed and children placed in foster homes. The Service now has its own center, with a large staff of competent, trained social workers. Sister Mary Grace, long-time worker and director of the Catholic Social Service, became Coordinator of the Social Work Program at the Training Center at Maryknoll, New York. Sister Helen Mary Bauman is the first nun to be executive director. In the past a priest has been the diocesan director and one of the sisters the executive secretary.

Few priests in the Church were Island born or raised.

Bishop Sweeney set out to change this. In 1946 St. Stephen's Seminary opened with three Sulpician Fathers to staff the Seminary. After a discouraging beginning (twelve of the first fourteen students left in the first year), the Seminary grew until the 1965–66 academic year had fifty-eight students studying for the priesthood. Father Louis H. Yim, who finished his course at St. Stephen's in 1949, was ordained in 1957. In 1954 the Marianist Sisters arrived to care for the domestic life of the Seminary.

Bishop Sweeney suffered a long period of illness in 1953 and 1954. On July 14, 1954, Pope Pius XII appointed Father John J. Scanlan as Bishop of Canae to serve as Auxiliary Bishop in the Diocese of Honolulu. Bishop Scanlan served as pastor of the Cathedral parish.

Bishop Sweeney and Bishop Scanlan attended the first sessions of the Vatican Council. Later Bishop Sweeney was excused from the third and fourth sessions. The first effect of the Council's decision upon Hawaii was the use of English in some portions of the Mass. The regulations regarding fasting and eating of meat on Friday adopted by the bishops of the United States now became the regulations of the Diocese of Honolulu. In line with the Vatican Council's decision that the Pope should have a Senate of Bishops to aid in the government of the Holy See, Bishop Sweeney, in 1967, organized a Senate of nine priests to aid in the decision-making of the Diocese.

The tremendous growth of the Roman Catholic Diocese can be attributed in part to the arrival of the Portuguese and Filipino immigrants, but in much greater part it is due to the educational program.

CATHOLIC SCHOOLS

The Catholic school system had thirty elementary schools and ten high schools in 1966. In 1946 Bishop Sweeney voiced his hope to have a school named in honor of Father Damien, and in 1962 the Christian Brothers from Ireland arrived to staff Damien Memorial High School. Brother Regan was principal from 1962 until 1968. Monsignor Daniel Dever has been superintendent of the Catholic schools since 1954 and is faced with all the problems of a modern school system.

The Marianist Brothers opened Chaminade College in 1955. Very quickly Chaminade became a four-year, fully accredited liberal arts college. Father Robert MacKay served as president for ten years. The college is coeducational and has a special program for training young men who desire to become Marianist Brothers.

There have been two seminaries, St. Stephen's and Sacred Hearts. In 1968 the two seminaries were combined.

The Confraternity of Christian Doctrine has been a supplementary educational program. One purpose was to train lay catechists who would give religious instruction to children who attend the non-Catholic schools. Sister Clotilde has spent twenty-five years in this work, and has prepared manuals and courses for lay teachers. In 1965 there were 22,613 students and 1,103 teachers in these released-time classes.

TWENTY-FIFTH ANNIVERSARY

In May 1966 the community joined the Catholic churches

in celebrating the twenty-fifth anniversary of the Diocese of Honolulu and of Bishop Sweeney's appointment.

The anniversary of the Diocese showed that the Roman Catholics had become the most numerous religious faith in Hawaii. Besides the two bishops, there were 173 priests, 27 diocesan priests, and 146 members of religious orders. Lay brothers, mostly in teaching positions, numbered 486. Sixty-two parishes had resident priests, and these parish priests also served forty-eight missions. There were also forty-one chapels in schools, hospitals, and other institutions.

When Bishop Sweeney came to Hawaii, one Hawaiian youth was studying for the priesthood, Charles A. Kekumano. He became an inspiration for Island youth. Father Kekumano became the chancellor of the Diocese and pastor of Saint Pius X Church. He became a Monsignor in 1961 and in 1968 was appointed pastor of the Cathedral Parish, Our Lady of Peace. Father Vincent Meyer is a member of the Order of Sacred Hearts and has acted as Provincial Director. Father Thomas Miyashiro was the first Japanese priest. However, a number of Portuguese born in the Islands became priests over the years, Monsignor Benedict Vierra being one of the most outstanding.

Yet graduates of St. Stephen's Seminary include Island-born priests such as Francis Chun, Michael Chong, Russell Ho, Edward Morikawa, Louis Yim, Alan Nagai, and Henry Sabago. These priests testify to the vision of Bishop Sweeney in seeking to provide Island-born priests for the Diocese.

In 1968, Bishop Sweeney's health led to his resignation.

The Most Reverend John Joseph Scanlan, who had been Auxiliary Bishop, succeeded him. On April 25, 1968, the Most Reverend Archbishop Luigi Raimondi, the apostolic delegate to the United States, consecrated Bishop Scanlan. Bishop Scanlan was born and educated in Ireland, but ordained in San Francisco and assigned to parishes on the West Coast. After serving as Bishop Co-Adjutor of Seattle, he came to Honolulu and served as pastor of Our Lady of Peace parish as well as Auxiliary Bishop.

Bishop Sweeney died on his seventieth birthday, June 19, 1968, and the sorrowful tributes to his memory showed how tremendous had been his influence.

THE RELIGIOUS ORDERS

Sixteen religious orders are now working in Hawaii.

1. *The Congregation of the Sacred Hearts of Jesus and Mary* was assigned Eastern Oceania as their province in 1826. For almost a century all parish priests in Hawaii were members of the Sacred Hearts. They maintained their own seminary at Hauula until 1968. All bishops who acted as Apostolic Vicars were of this order. The Order of Sacred Hearts, which had been directing the work from Belgium, relinquished control only in 1940.

2. *The Sisters of the Sacred Hearts and of Perpetual Adoration* founded Sacred Hearts Academy in 1859. Later they conducted Sacred Hearts Convent School and Our Lady of Peace School. The Sacred Hearts Sisters also opened Immaculate Conception School at Lihue, Kauai. They also founded St. Theresa's School on School Street.

3. *The Society of Mary* (Marianist) assumed charge of St. Louis School in 1883. The Marianist lay brothers and priests have taught the school since then. In 1954 they established Chaminade College, and in 1968 St. Louis and Chaminade became an administrative unit under the direction of Father Robert MacKay. They also direct St. Patrick's School.

4. *The Sisters of the Third Order of St. Francis,* inspired by Father Damien's story, came to Hawaii to help Father Damien at Kalaupapa. They still live and work at Kalaupapa. They established St. Francis Hospital on Liliha Street, St. Francis Convent School, and St. Francis School of Nursing. St. Francis Convent School is now in

Manoa Valley, and St. Francis School of Nursing closed in favor of a cooperative plan with the University of Hawaii.

5. In 1924 Bishop Alencastre invited *The Maryknoll Fathers* to Hawaii. The Maryknoll Fathers, an American Missionary Order, assumed charge of many parishes, beginning with Sacred Hearts Church on Wilder Street near Punahou.

6. *The Congregation of the Maryknoll Sisters of St. Dominic* joined the Maryknoll Fathers by working in the Sacred Hearts School. Soon after, they established Maryknoll High School, the first coeducational Catholic high school in Hawaii. They also serve in the Catholic Social Service.

7. *The Sisters of St. Joseph of Carondelet* provided the staff for St. Theresa's School after 1941, and at the close of World War II they established St. Joseph's School in Waipahu. They opened St. Anthony's School in Kailua, Oahu in 1952.

8. *The Franciscan Sisters of Christian Charity* opened St. Theresa's School at Kekaha, Kauai, in 1946.

9. *The Sisters of Charity of the Blessed Virgin Mary* started Holy Cross School in Kalaheo, Kauai, and St. Catherine's at Kealia, Kauai, in 1946.

10. *The Marist Fathers* provided parish priests, mostly serving on the island of Kauai.

11. *The Sulpician Fathers* came to staff, and teach at, St. Stephen's Seminary.

12. *The Missionary Sisters of the Society of St. Mary* now provide the housekeeping staff at St. Stephen's Seminary.

13. *The Sisters of Notre Dame de Namur* came to staff Star

of the Sea School, beginning an elementary school and a high school for girls. They also staff Holy Family School.

14. *The Dominican Sisters of the Holy Rosary* took charge of St. Elizabeth's School in Aiea in 1964.

15. *The Sisters of St. Joseph of Orange* came to Hawaii in 1945 to staff St. Joseph's at Makawao, Maui.

16. *The Christian Brothers of Ireland* came to establish Damien Memorial High School. Bishop Sweeney had hoped to build a diocesan high school after World War II, but it was 1962 before the Christian Brothers arrived. Some of the teachers were born in Ireland, but the majority are from the American mainland.

1. Reginald Yzendoorn, *History of the Catholic Mission in the Hawaiian Islands,* Honolulu Star Bulletin, Honolulu, 1927, pp. 8–16.

2. Ralph S. Kuykendall, *The Hawaiian Kingdom,* University of Hawaii Press, Honolulu, 1957.

3. Reginald Yzendoorn, *History of the Catholic Misson in the Hawaiian Islands,* Honolulu Star Bulletin, Honolulu, 1927, p. 165.

4. A. Grove Day, *Mark Twain's Letters from Hawaii,* Appleton-Century, New York, 1966, pp. 175–76.

5. *Dr. Hyde's Reply,* privately printed pamphlet, p. 8.

6. Sister Adele Marie Lemon, *Hawaii, Lei of Islands,* Tongg, Honolulu, 1956, p. 97.

5. The Church of Jesus Christ of Latter-day Saints

THE MORMON BACKGROUND

The most important social fact of American life in the 19th century was the American frontier. Life on the frontier was fluid, providing new opportunities for individuals and also for social groups. Consequently, churches developed which utilized the fluid concepts of the frontier. Some churches, such as the Methodist and Baptist, used evangelistic techniques, such as revivals and camp meetings.

Lawlessness was one phase of frontier life, and churches insisted on a personal morality in opposition to that lawlessness, so such prohibitions as those against drinking and gambling were common in these churches. Since ordained ministers in the scholarly tradition of European churches were almost nonexistent on the frontier, emphasis was placed on leadership by the laity, often with a disregard of everything European, and a discounting of the scholarly tradition of Greek and Hebrew exegesis in favor of a literalistic interpretation of the Bible. At times these literalistic interpretations led to new interpretations amounting to new revelations.

The Church of Jesus Christ of Latter-day Saints came into being during this sociological ferment of the frontier. Its prophet, Joseph Smith, presented a new book of revelation: The Book of Mormon. The church used the King James Version of the Bible with literal interpretations. As an American church it disregarded the European past of Christianity in favor of a revelation that placed the past emphasis and also the future hope of the church in America. Lay participation, common to all churches on the frontier, was raised to the point of making every member a priest and a working evangelist who had to spend two years as a missionary. In personal morality, use of alcohol and tobacco were prohibited.

Two ideas made the Church of Jesus Christ of Latter-day Saints different from other frontier churches. One was the hierarchial structure. Lay participation made Martin Luther's priesthood of all believers a reality, but this participation was channeled through priests, bishops, and counselors to culminate in the Apostles, with a presidency. Lay participation and hierarchial control made for strong denominational control.

Secondly, the doctrine of revelation counted as authentic sources not only the Old and New Testaments and the Book of Mormon, but revelations given in the church through its leadership. Some of these revelations are printed, such as the Pearl of Great Price. Others are declarations of policy. The decision to allow multiple marriages and also the decision to abolish multiple marriage came as ongoing revelations to the church leaders.

The Mormons, with their tight organization, aroused

conflict. The governor of Missouri objected to their semi-military organization, and they moved to Illinois. Here a mob killed Joseph Smith. Faced with the fact that law enforcement officials objected to Mormons arming to defend themselves but did not provide protection if Mormons remained unarmed, they moved to Utah. Mormon President Brigham Young was one of the outstanding personalities in the American settlement of the West. His leadership was determinative for the founding of Utah.

THE MISSION TO HAWAII

The Latter-day Saints moved to Utah in 1846. Three years later the gold rush to California ended Utah's isolation. A group of young men left Utah for the gold fields to do missionary work, but the church leaders decided that the gold fields were not a favorable site for missionary work. Elder Charles C. Rich, one of the twelve Apostles, ordered them to go to Hawaii. The men obeyed and sailed from San Francisco on November 22, 1850. On December 12, 1850, they arrived in Honolulu. The young men were Presiding Elder Hiram Clark, Thomas Whittle, John Dixon, Henry W. Bigler, Thomas Morris, William Farrer, James Hawkins, James Keeler, Hiram H. Blackwell, and George Q. Cannon.

They rented a house and on the second day climbed up Pacific Heights overlooking the city; here they held a service of prayer. This is commemorated in a mural in the lobby of Church College of Hawaii. These young men had come to persuade English-speaking people. The English-

speaking people of Honolulu were either stalwart supporters of Protestant or Catholic missionaries, or were
persons opposed to every type of missionary effort. Dis-
couraged, four of the young men returned to Utah. The
Presiding Elder, Hiram Clark, decided to go to the South
Pacific, where he is honored as the founder of work there.
"The spirit of the work took possession of the five Elders
who remained: George Q. Cannon, James Keeler, H. W.
Bigler, James Hawkins and William Farrer, and they
studied hard to acquire the language."[1] The leader was
George Q. Cannon.

GEORGE Q. CANNON

George Q. Cannon was born in Liverpool, England, in
1827. His uncle, John Taylor, was a forceful leader whose
missionary zeal led at last to the presidency of the church.
The family were some of the first converts to the church in
England, but the father died en route to join the church.
George Q. Cannon was only twenty-three when he arrived
in Hawaii. He was unwilling to abandon Hawaii as a
missionary field before visiting the other islands.

The trial was very successful. In less than a month
Cannon reported, "The progress I had made in learning
the language surprised the Elders at Honolulu. I was able
to converse tolerably well with the natives and understand
what they said."[2]

The Mormon missionaries established the first branch
of the Church on August 8, 1851, at Kealakou, Maui, and
four other branches soon after.

Among these first converts was Mr. Jonathan H.

Napela, who had attended Lahainaluna School. He understood English and was fluent in Hawaiian. Later in life his wife was sent to Kalaupapa. Napela went with her and, faithful to his church, established a branch at Kalaupapa.

In January 1852 Cannon began translating the Book of Mormon into Hawaiian. He would translate a few pages and then discuss the meaning of the pages with Napela. Then Cannon would read his translation and ask Napela to explain the meaning. The corrected text was later revised by using the same method with Elder Kauwahi on Kauai.

Two years passed in translating. Elder Cannon was transferred to California, and there he supervised the printing of the Hawaiian translation of the Book of Mormon. In January 1856 the books were sent to Hawaii.

George Q. Cannon was the real founder of his church in Hawaii. Later he was a delegate from the Territory of Utah to Congress. He returned to Hawaii for the fiftieth anniversary of the first mission.

LANAI

Nine other missionaries came in 1853, and five Hawaiian elders from Maui, including J. H. Napela, went on mission tours. Within four years after the first arrival, there were 4,000 baptized members in branches on all the islands. Just as converts in America went to Utah, so it was decided to establish a gathering place for the Hawaiian church. The "City of Joseph" was established in Palawai Valley on the island of Lanai. Livestock, seed, tools, and building

material were transported to Lanai. Joseph F. Smith,
later to be sixth president of the denomination, was in
charge of the work on Lanai from 1854 to 1858. In 1858
all missionaries were recalled to Utah. The Hawaiian
elders took charge.

Then Walter Murray Gibson arrived. Gibson is an
incredible figure in the history of Hawaii. He had been
an adventurer in the East Indies. The Netherlands
was in control, but there were still semi-independent
rulers. Gibson entered an alliance with a Sultan on
Sumatra and may have tried to set himself up as ruler of
a neighboring sultanate. The Dutch officials seized his
ship, accusing him of piracy. Gibson escaped with his ship
and soon after enlisted support in the United States Congress for action against the Netherlands. When the government of the Netherlands provided evidence against him,
he lost the support of the congressmen. Then he drifted
west. In 1860 he sought to convince Mormon leaders in
Utah that New Guinea would be an admirable place for
the Mormons. Brigham Young was not convinced but
did give Gibson a vague commission for work in the South
Pacific. Gibson became a member of the church.

Gibson had been able to persuade congressmen and
Mormon leaders, so when he came to Hawaii with a commission signed by Brigham Young, the Hawaiian leaders
accepted him.

Gibson duplicated the Utah organization with himself
as president, and ordained apostles, priests, and bishops.
He either was ignorant of or ignored many of the church's
teachings, and some older members complained to Presi-

dent Brigham Young. Brigham Young sent two Apostles, Ezra T. Benson and Lorenzo Snow, to investigate. Three elders, including Joseph F. Smith, were also with them. (When they landed at Lahaina, their small boat was capsized in the heavy surf. They brought Lorenzo Snow to shore seemingly dead, but revived him by mouth to mouth resuscitation. Lorenzo Snow lived to become the fifth president of the Church.) They found conditions were as described by the Hawaiians. The Apostles excommunicated Gibson. Gibson had recorded all property in his own name and was able to retain the lands on Lanai. Some of the Hawaiians decided to remain with him. Gibson, during the reign of King Kalakaua, became trusted adviser to the king. His grandiose ideas had not lessened, and Kalakaua sought to establish an Empire of the Pacific. The Bayonet Constitution of 1887 forced Kalakaua to dismiss Gibson, but many Hawaiians were to regard him as the Shepherd Saint of Lanai, who worked always to advance the Hawaiians. Others remembered his grandiose dream of the Empire of the Pacific as a venture which helped shatter Hawaii's independence and prepare the way for annexation.

LAIE

At Laie on Oahu, in ancient Hawaii, there was a city of refuge. It was to Laie that the Mormons turned. Elders George Nebeker and Francis A. Hammond, both former missionaries, returned to Hawaii in 1865 and decided to purchase Laie from the mountains to the sea. About 6,000 acres in size, the plantation had about 1,500 acres suitable

for farming. Elder Hammond made the purchase for
$14,000 while Nebeker was in Utah to obtain approval;
President Young provided $11,515, with the remainder
coming from the sale of livestock that was part of the
purchase. Elder Nebeker returned to become president of
the Hawaiian Mission and manager of the plantation.

Laie was to be the gathering place of church members,
but it was also to be a plantation. Church members came
in the dual capacity of plantation worker and church
member. At times, owing to drought, there was no work,
and hardship was the lot. As the plantation raised more
sugar, the reports reflect not so much the growth of the
church, but the ups and downs of plantation management.
The establishment of a power mill to replace the mule-
powered one and the drilling of an artesian well were
heralded as achievements of the church. Nebeker had to
ask for subsidies, and by 1879 $40,000 had come from the
church in Utah.

Criticism arose outside the church, and a law was
passed to stop what outsiders considered exploitation of
Hawaiian laborers. The law covered only the specific
problem of the plantation at Laie, and King Kalakaua
refused to sign it unless it covered all employees of
churches. The church at Laie felt this act was due to
religious opposition, but historians today, familiar with
union contracts, see that a plantation that paid daily
wages, the size of which depended on ability and availabili-
ty of cash, deserves some criticism. Often wages were
partly paid in scrip redeemable at the village store.

The dedication of church members did sustain them in

every difficulty. The presidents of the mission came mostly for short terms, eight serving in less than twenty years. Then the church appointed Samuel E. Wooley as president of the Mission and plantation manager. In 1898 he borrowed $50,000 to install an adequate pumping system. He remained in the dual capacity for twenty-four years and increased the sugar production by ten times. Nor was he less concerned about church affairs. He made plans for a temple. President Joseph F. Smith dedicated the site on his fourth visit to Hawaii.

Ralph Wooley, son of the Mission president, built the temple. Architects and artists from Salt Lake City planned the temple, which, in Renaissance tradition, was placed in a formal garden setting. Samuel Wooley had accomplished both his goals—a prosperous plantation and a temple that was a symbol of faith to all Latter-day Saints. The dedication of the temple, held on Thanksgiving Day, November 27, 1919, brought President Heber J. Grant to Laie.

President Grant praised the work of Samuel Wooley, but the next year he sent E. Wesley Smith to take the office of president of the Mission. The headquarters was moved to Honolulu, and Wooley remained as plantation manager. Laie was the site of the temple, but Honolulu was the area for Latter-day Saint work and growth.

The high sugar prices of World War I dropped. Samuel Wooley retired. Laie became a debt-ridden plantation. Beach property was sold to pay off debts. Then in 1931 the sugar acreage was leased to Kahuku Plantation, and after years of effort the Mormons reluctantly abandoned

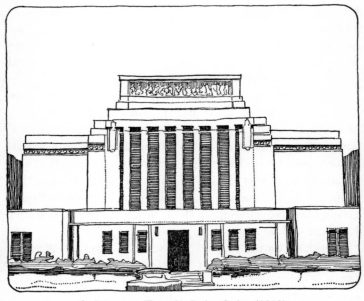

6. Mormon Temple, Laie, Oahu (1919).
ARCHITECTS: POPE & BURTON

the plantation as a way to provide jobs for their members.

ISRAEL IN THE PACIFIC

The Church of Jesus Christ of Latter-day Saints accepts the events related in the Book of Mormon as historical fact. These relate that in the era of the destruction of the kingdoms of Israel and of Judah, a group of Israelites came to America and there set up a kingdom which lasted from about 600 B.C. to A.D. 420. After the Resurrection, Christ visited and instructed these people. After two centuries of harmony, war broke out between two groups—the Nephites and the Lamanites. In a battle fought near the hill of Cumorah, not far from Palmyra, New York, almost all the Nephites were killed, including Mormon. Moroni, son of Mormon, had the Golden Plates with the story of Mormon, and he hid these plates before his death. Fourteen hundred years later Moroni was the angelic revealer of the Golden Plates to Joseph Smith.

This revelation, which is accepted by the Mormons, has had a slight change for the Pacific peoples. The book *Israel in the Pacific* presents the argument at great length with genealogical statements, but the basic argument is in these two paragraphs:

> THE SEED OF LEHI TODAY. The Book of Mormon states that the Nephites were entirely destroyed from off the face of the earth, and only the Lamanites were left. Then how do we explain the blessing which Lehi gave to his son, Joseph, whose seed was numbered with the Nephites, "for thy seed shall not utterly be destroyed?"

As explained in chapter ten [of *Israel in the Pacific*] there were descendants of this Joseph among the Lamanites. In further fulfillment of this blessing a branch of the Nephites was preserved in the Pacific, to become the people now called Polynesians . . .

THE MENEHUNE PEOPLE. In the Hawaiian legend of "Kumuhonua" and his descendants, the Polynesians are distinguished by the appellation of *ka poe Menehune*, "the Menehune people", said to be descended from Menehune (Isaac), son of Luanuu (Abraham), and grandfather of the twelve sons of Kinilau-a Mano.[4]

The use of Polynesian legends combined with Mormon interpretations created the belief that the Polynesian people are descendants of the Israelites, who were driven into exile. Although such an interpretation might find little support among scientific archeologists and philologists who have studied the Polynesian migrations, it did receive strong collateral support from Thor Heyerdahl and his voyage of the *Kontiki*. Thor Heyerdahl believed that the Polynesians came from South America, and his voyage on the raft *Kontiki* supported his theory. The scientists of the Bishop Museum in Honolulu have opposed Heyerdahl's theories, but in some areas these theories had considerable acceptance.

Using the example of the *Kontiki*, Mr. DeVere Baker built a raft to float to Hawaii from California. The first three attempts failed, but on the fourth he landed at Maui in the raft *Lehi IV*. Mr. Edwin Kekaula, a Hawaiian, was one of the crew who felt they had proved that the Polynesians had come from America.[5]

This theory of Israel in the Pacific provided strong emotional support to the Polynesians who accepted it. A Maori who could recite his name chant back through the generations until he named the canoe on which his ancestors arrived in New Zealand felt this genealogical listing could be continued through the Biblical genealogies until it came to Abraham and then back to Adam. The Hawaiian who found that an incident, the arrival of Captain Cook, was considered as the beginning of Hawaiian history found a new dignity in believing that his racial ancestry had roots in the plan of God for the preservation of a people driven from Jerusalem centuries before Christ.

THE MORMON STAKES

Few Hawaiians cared for the life of plantation worker. Even before the temple was built, more Mormons lived elsewhere than at Laie. The church had 6,000 members in 1900, with branches in many communities. From 1920 to 1935 church membership more than doubled in number. In the Church of Latter-day Saints, when a congregation is formed, it becomes a branch of the mission; when the branch grows to have sufficient members and is self-sustaining, it becomes a ward. A number of wards form a self-governing organization—the stake. After additional wards were created in Honolulu, the wards on Oahu organized the Oahu Stake in 1935. A large house at Beretania and Punahou became the mission headquarters, and during World War II it was a center for work with servicemen.

On this property the Oahu Stake erected its tabernacle,

facing Kalakaua Street, which was dedicated in 1941. The tabernacle was used by a number of wards. Workmen were putting the great mosaic in place when the attack on Pearl Harbor changed every aspect of work in Hawaii.

After World War II the Latter-day Saints were ready for vigorous expansion. Honolulu resident Edward L. Clissold led in the establishment of the Mission to Japan in 1948, and returned to Honolulu a few years later as president of the Hawaiian Mission. Elders Hilton Robertson and Henry Aki started the Hong Kong Mission, followed some years later by the South East Asian work.

The Centennial of the Mission in 1950 pledged the church to new activity. In 1954 there were sixteen wards totaling over 9,000 members in the Oahu Stake. The island of Oahu was then divided into the Honolulu and Oahu Stakes. The Oahu Stake Tabernacle became the headquarters of the Honolulu Stake. The Oahu Stake headquarters was placed in Laie, with Edward L. Clissold as president.

The division placed some wards in Honolulu in the Oahu Stake, with its headquarters at distant Laie. After some years these wards with the wards in Leeward Oahu formed the Pearl Harbor Stake, with George Q. Cannon III, grandson of the founder, as president.

In 1956 the Mission headquarters was transferred from the site next to the tabernacle to 3019 Pali Drive. Although the Hawaiian Mission has no direct authority in dealing with the stakes, it aids in many ways, primarily in directing the work of the missionaries. However, all the Latter-day Saint branches on the other islands are directed by the Mission headquarters. There have been about forty presidents of the Hawaiian Mission of Latter-day Saints since 1850. Most have returned to Utah, but a number have remained in Hawaii to become active in the business community.

THE SAMOANS

The temple at Laie was a temple for all the Pacific. The Latter-day Saints sent their first missionaries to the South Pacific and Australia in 1843. When the United States assumed control of part of Samoa, it assigned the government to the United States Navy. The Navy left most of the civilian government to the chiefs and Samoans, even those who worked at the naval base lived much as their ancestors had. A few Samoans who became Mormons moved to Laie. Thirty-three came in 1925, and by 1929 a Samoan village existed at Laie.

The Navy closed the base at Pago Pago in 1952 and transferred the personnel to other bases. Samoans who were in the Navy were given the privilege of taking their dependents with them. The Navy sent the U.S.S. *President Jackson* to Samoa for the dependents, who numbered about five hundred. The steamship company announced a special bargain rate of $30 to Hawaii for other Samoans. Five hundred other Samoans decided to go, including about two hundred Mormons who decided to move to Laie.

The arrival of the one thousand Samoans in July 1952 created social problems for Hawaii, and the greatest impact was in the Samoan village at Laie. Not only did the Mormon Samoans go to Laie, but almost as many non-Mormons. The Samoans at Laie would not turn away anyone, and family homes had as many as forty people living in a home. Whereas the first Samoans who had settled at Laie had come solely for religious reasons, these later arrivals had come for economic reasons. Many of them left within a few years for San Diego. Yet the Samoan problem remained—basically the problem of a people whose culture deteriorated in an environment in which there was inadequate economic opportunity to move into the new culture.

At times friction developed between the church authorities at Laie and the Samoans, and was given newspaper notice. The newspapers gave such reports on the conflict as the Samoan complaint that the Mormon restrictions on smoking and drinking should not be enforced on non-Mormon friends.

The Church authorities at Laie saw the economic problems of the Samoan village and the culture conflicts, and to a remarkable extent were able to make the Samoans a vital part of the development of Laie, both as a religious community and as a tourist center. The Samoans at Laie have their own ward building and are part of the Mormon program of welfare assistance.[6]

CHURCH COLLEGE

David O. McKay visited Hawaii long before he became president of the Church of Jesus Christ of Latter-day Saints. He visited the public school in Laie in 1921. The flag-raising ceremony of the school is shown as the mural front to the entrance lobby to the Church College. At that time David McKay voiced the hope that some day a college would make Laie an intellectual as well as a spiritual center of the Pacific. Oahu Stake President Ralph Wooley appointed four members of the Oahu Stake Council in June 1947. They were Clinton Kanahele, J. Franklin Wooley, Lawrence Peterson, and George Zabricke, who made recommendations in regard to a college. They recommended the establishment of a high school to be developed into a junior college. Edward L. Clissold, who was Hawaiian Mission president at the time, advised the use of the old Waialae Training School. Dr. Wesley Lloyd of Brigham Young University made a study of possibilities, and in 1954 the presidency in Utah approved plans for a college in Laie and appointed Dr. Rueben D. Law of Brigham Young University as president.

David O. McKay, now president of the church, returned to Hawaii, and on February 12, 1955, he broke ground for the building of the college. The building was to take a number of years, but using many temporary structures, the college opened on September 26, 1955. The trustees of the new school were Edward L. Clissold, Ralph E. Wooley, George Q. Cannon III, Lawrence Haneberg, and Dr. Arthur Haycock, president of the Hawaiian Mission of the church.

With full support of the labor mission and President McKay, the trustees decided to build the college as a unit. The first three years of the college were carried on with the building program in full operation. Many students spent their Saturdays working with the labor mission.

The college has an enrollment of over one thousand. It is fully accredited with a full college program.

THE LABOR MISSION

Perhaps the most extraordinary missionary ever to come to Hawaii was Elder Joseph E. Wilson. A successful contractor in Englewood, California, Wilson came to Hawaii to build The Church College of Hawaii. The First Presidency in Utah called him as a missionary without salary. At the dedication of the Church College, Elder Wendell B. Mendenhall, chairman of the church building committee, paid this tribute to the labor missionaries:

> . . . The first eleven rows of this center section are people who are here as labor missionaries. They include men who have been called from their private businesses, men who have turned their business over to their young sons, men who have retired many years ago and were living a comfortable and peaceful life and have returned to activity. . . . People who have left their homes and their families and what they have to devote themselves to this great cause. . . .
>
> . . . Brother Joseph Wilson was called here along with Brother Lake, his assistant, and Milton Maynard, treasurer of construction, to get under way. These buildings cost a total of $3,580,000. There were 294,798 donated hours by the labor missionary group and the membership of the Church contributed to this great cause. There has been well over $1,300,000 saved. Where would you find a greater Christian spirit than to have the people be willing to give of time and of service and of

> sinew to build . . . for the good of the people and save
> $1,300,000.
>
> By this saving alone, we can build in other parts of the
> world fifteen or sixteen new chapels.[7]

Elder Joseph Wilson brought construction equipment
and helped recruit qualified construction supervisors.
Young men, given the option of being labor missionaries
for their two years of missionary duty, volunteered. Elder
Arthur Parker, patriarch of the Oahu Stake, had charge
of the labor missionaries from Hawaii.

The college was finished, but the labor missionaries still
came. Joseph Wilson's three and a half years as supervisor
of construction of the Church College were to extend to
ten and a half years of service, and the initial expenditure
of $3,580,000 for the college was to grow until Wilson had
supervised construction valued over $17,000,000. Addi-
tional expenditures were made at the Church College
over the years for other buildings. Landscape designer
Mr. Harry Hing of Honolulu directed the work of making
the college campus a show place of Island beauty.

No less spectacular was the building of the chapels for
the Mormon wards. Architect Harold Burton's designs
were adapted by Wilson. Zion Missionaries (that is,
appointed by the church in Utah) came for two years,
working with the volunteers from the churches in Hawaii.
Eight chapels on Oahu were built as part of a single project, and Wilson directed the flow of materials and men to
the eight chapels. Laie, Hauula, Waialua, Lanakila,
Halawa, Pearl Harbor, and Waianae chapels were com-

pleted within two years. The Kalihi Ward Chapel was rebuilt, incorporating in its building the headquarters for the Pearl Harbor Stake.

The branches on the other islands joined the surge of construction until every community in Hawaii having a strong branch of Latter-day Saints has now a fine modern structure.

THE POLYNESIAN CULTURAL CENTER

Since Mormons hold as a religious tenet that Polynesians are a branch of the House of Israel, their missionary work has been extensive in all of Polynesia.

A former president of the Pacific Island missions, Matthew Cowley, had this vision: "I hope to live to see the day when my Maori people down here in New Zealand will have a little village there at Laie, with a beautiful carved house. The Tongans will have a village, too, and the Tahitians and Samoans—all these islanders of the sea."[8]

Since one purpose for the Church College was the education of the Polynesians, students came from many Pacific islands. Almost at once these students began to entertain at church meetings and in various places on Oahu.

Labor Missionary Joseph Wilson constructed the Polynesian Cultural Center in line with the earlier vision. Polynesian Mormons who knew their culture came as labor missionaries for two years. Others came as students. Six villages were constructed—Fijian, Maori, Tahitian, Tongan, Samoan, and Hawaiian—with the detail work by craftsmen shaping authentic architecture for each island group. Others came to demonstrate and explain the techniques and mode of living for the various racial groups.

Along with the villages, an entertainment center was developed. Beginning with the students at the college, an entertainment group was developed which, with some modern stage technical aid, has become an outstanding entertainment feature for tourists. This has created some problems. The Musicians' Union blocked the Polynesian Cultural Center entertainers from appearing at the dedication of the Honolulu International Center. Since all profits of the shows go to the scholarship program, the church regards the student participation as a form of scholarship aid.

The Mormons, when criticism comes that the entertainers are exploited, simply ask people to look at it from a Mormon point of view. Since the church expects every member to spend two years as a missionary at his own expense if possible, a program where the missionary obligation is discharged at the same time a person receives his college education is highly worthy.

1. Compiled by Kate B. Carter, "The Mormons in Hawaii," *Daughters of Utah Pioneers,* November 1955, p. 136.
2. George Q. Cannon, *My First Mission,* 1933, reprinted in *Three Mormon Classics,* compiled by Preston Nibley, Publishers Press, Utah, 1944, p. 141.
3. David W. Cummings, *Centennial History of Laie,* Laie Centennial Committee, Honolulu, 1965.

4. William A. Cole and Elwin W. Jensen, *Israel in the Pacific,* Publishers Press, Utah, 1961, p. 90.

5. DeVere Baker, *The Raft Lehi IV, 69 Days Adrift on the Pacific Ocean,* Whitehorn, Long Beach, California, 1959.

6. Material for this section was taken from newspaper accounts and a Master of Arts thesis for the University of Hawaii in June 1956 on "Acculturation of Samoans in the Mormon Village of Laie," by Bernard Francis Pierce.

7. David W. Cummings, *Mighty Missionary of the Pacific,* Publishers Press, Utah, 1961, pp. 276–77.

8. *Building Missionaries in Hawaii, 1960–1963,* A Labor Mission Publication, n.d., p. 132.

6. The Reorganized Church of Jesus Christ of Latter-day Saints

When the Mormon Prophet Joseph Smith was killed in 1844, the Apostles became the leaders of the church. The ones who were in Illinois decided to take no action until all the Apostles were present. They especially waited for the return of Apostle Brigham Young. They chose him to become president of the Church of Jesus Christ of Latter-day Saints. However, in the church there was a minority group which favored the son of the prophet. The younger Joseph Smith, who was about twenty years old, did not obtain a strong following, and Brigham Young led the Saints to Utah. Some remained in the Mid-West, and young Smith became their leader. As controversy arose over the Mormons, their advocacy of polygamy and their militant organization in Utah, the group led by Joseph Smith III withdrew from association with the Utah Mormons. They were able to re-establish their headquarters in Independence, Missouri, and became a separate denomination— the Reorganized Church of Jesus Christ of Latter-day Saints. One of the statements of Latter-day Saints' teaching is the acceptance of the King James version of the Bible insofar as it is correctly translated. The Prophet Joseph Smith worked on an interpretative version of the Bible from 1830 to 1833. His wife had the manuscript at the time of his death. The Bible, together with these interpretations, was published by the Reorganized Church in 1866. The Utah Mormons do not accept this version of the Bible as an authentic revelation of the prophet. Such religious differences are accentuated by the sociological differences that developed. The Mormons in Utah were completely in control of a society in which the church was active in state and business. The Reorganized Church coexisted with churches of all types in which there was separation of church and state, and church and economic life. After a century the Reorganized Church was, sociologically, more like the Protestant denominations of the Mid-West than like the Mormons of Utah.

The Reorganized Church began work in Hawaii in 1890. Elder Gilbert J. Waller was a Honolulu businessman of English birth who had been converted and baptized in Oakland, California. Promptly Mr. Waller asked for a teacher, and Elder and Mrs. Albert Haws were sent. En route they met Mr. and Mrs. C. H. Luther, members of the Utah Church. Elder Haws convinced them that the Reorganized Church was faithful to Joseph Smith, and Mr. and Mrs. Luther joined the Reorganized Church.

Gilbert Waller welcomed them to Honolulu and arranged for the group to meet in the law office of Judge Kaulukou. Mr. Waller and the missionaries were the entire congregation. Like the Mormons from Utah, they

found little response among the Caucasians. They rented
the Odd Fellows Hall, and soon a number of Hawaiians
began attending, with Mr. Joseph M. Poepoe acting as
interpreter. During the troubled years ending in the
American annexation of Hawaii, all American church
groups found a lessened response among the Hawaiians,
so little growth took place until the 1900's. The first church
was dedicated on October 13, 1907.

Mr. Waller was the leader of the Reorganized Church
in Hawaii until his death. Later the church at Lewalani
and Mott-Smith Drive was built along with a chapel dedicated to the memory of Mr. Waller. Branches and missions
were developed in other localities on Oahu and the other
islands. Elder Isaac Harbottle was the leader of the
Kaneohe Branch. Elder Stephen A. Black served as president and pastor of the Headquarters Church, and Elder
Delbert D. Smith, member of the Council of Seventy, was
missionary pastor of the Hilo area.

At the present time the president of the Hawaiian District is Elder V. Newton Ward, with Elder Donald Mahi,
Elder Ray Kekoa and Elder Akira Sakima some of the
branch leaders. Elder Akira Sakima of the Kalihi Branch
is a member of the Hawaii State Legislature.

7. St. Andrew's Cathedral, Honolulu. Completed in 1958.

7. The Protestant Episcopal Church of the United States of America

BEGINNING WITH CAPTAIN COOK

The Church of England provided the first contacts the Hawaiians had with Christianity. When a sailor died on one of Captain Cook's ships, he was buried beside the heiau at Napoopoo in January 1779. A monument there commemorated this first Christian service on Hawaiian soil. Regrettably the second service on Hawaiian soil was for the burial of Captain Cook.

Englishmen were the first Caucasians to live in Hawaii. "Padre" Howell, reputedly a clergyman of the Church of England, lived in Kona for some months. He was a clerk in an American ship and remained in Kona to secure a cargo of sandalwood. There is a tradition that he urged King Kamehameha to change his religious practices.

More important were the English seamen John Young and Isaac Davis. Kamehameha gave them the rank of chiefs, but specifically exempted them from the kapu regulations. They were the king's aides in the conquest of the islands and in all his dealings with foreign ships. John Young had a Church of England prayer book. A chaplain of a visiting English ship officiated at the wedding of James Kanehoa Young to the daughter of Isaac Davis. One of John Young's daughters married Dr. T.C.B. Rooke, an English physician who had the first private medical practice in Honolulu. The Rookes adopted Emma, the daughter of Fanny Kekela, sister of Mrs. Rooke. Dr. and Mrs. Rooke attended Kawaiahao Church and sent Emma to the Chiefs Children's School. In their own home the Rookes maintained a fine religious atmosphere, and prayers were read from the English prayer book each morning and communion was received whenever a visiting British ship had a clergyman aboard.

KAMEHAMEHA IV AND QUEEN EMMA

Emma Rooke grew up with the home life of an English girl. When Kamehameha IV asked her to marry, she asked that the service used be that of the Church of England. They were married in Kawaiahao Church, but according to Queen Emma's wishes.

Kamehameha IV and his brother, Lot Kamehameha, had journeyed to England. Impressed by the Church of England, with the king as the head of the church, they shared Queen Emma's hope that the Church of England would come to Hawaii. Political events favored this hope. The American missionaries William Richards and Dr. Gerrit Judd had been instrumental in preserving Hawaii's independence during the many years that both Great Britain and France were threatening that independence. During this time some Americans felt that ultimately a foreign nation would take possession of

Hawaii. After California became a state, a committee of thirteen Americans (none of whom were connected with the missionaries) drew up a petition asking for annexation. King Kamehameha III approved negotiations. No formal treaty was ever submitted, but the issue was debated in the United States Senate. The Hawaiian chiefs opposed the project, and Dr. Judd, who as foreign minister had taken part in negotiations, resigned. Robert C. Wyllie, a Scotsman, took Judd's place.

Wyllie wished to strengthen ties with England to counteract the American influence. Since the religious hopes of Queen Emma coincided with the political desires of King Kamehameha IV and his chief adviser, they asked for an Anglican Church in Hawaii. Contact was made with missionary societies in England and in America. Bishop Ingraham Kip of California was interested, and when he was in England in July 1860, the possibility of a joint mission to Hawaii was discussed. The outbreak of the Civil War in America prevented the joint effort. Missionary societies in England raised funds. Kamehameha IV promised land for church buildings and a personal gift of 200 pounds annually. The Reverend Doctor Thomas Nettleship Staley was consecrated bishop.

Finally, after long delays, the missionary party sailed for Hawaii. The members of the party were Bishop and Mrs. Staley and their seven children, the Reverend and Mrs. George Mason, and the Reverend Edmund Ibbetson.

Meantime, in Hawaii the king and queen were preparing for this new church. King Kamehameha IV translated portions of the Book of Common Prayer. The

queen planned for the baptism of her little son by the
bishop. The child, designated "The Prince of Hawaii,"
was sickly. The little prince died, but shortly before his
death he was baptized in Kawaiahao Church.

BISHOP THOMAS NETTLESHIP STALEY

Bishop Staley arrived in Honolulu on October 11, 1862.
Prime Minister Wyllie purchased on that same date the
Methodist Church, which was being sold at public auction,
so a church building was available. Services in English
may have been held on the following Sundays. On November 9, 1862, the service of Morning Prayer in Hawaiian
was held for the first time. As soon as the royal couple
returned from Maui, the king held a royal audience to
welcome Bishop Staley. At this audience the king assured
Bishop Staley that the services for Morning and Evening
Prayer would be ready in a few days. The king wrote an
explanation of the prayer book. It was printed at the end
of the first edition but became the preface of succeeding
printings. In it Kamehameha IV wrote: "The Church is
established here in Hawaii through the breathings of the
Holy Spirit and by the agency of the chiefs. Vancouver,
years ago, was requested to send us the True God. . . . Your
king [Kamehameha II] went to a distant and a powerful
country to hasten the advent of that which our eyes now
see . . . the very Church here planted in Hawaii, but how
long we have waited."[1]

Queen Emma was baptized, and her name is the first
in the Register of Baptisms of St. Andrew's Cathedral.
The enthusiasm for the church was strong. Land for the

Cathedral of St. Peter's was provided. St. Alban's School for Boys was to be started. The Reverend George Mason went to Lahaina to found the Holy Cross School and make preparations for a church.

There were also problems. Bishop Staley held Anglo-Catholic religious views. In Hawaii the name of the church was to be The Reformed Catholic Church of Hawaii. Some English businessmen in Honolulu wanted an English service but did not share Bishop Staley's views. Bishop Staley organized a separate English service and congregation.

The legislature granted land but did not make the church the official church of Hawaii like the Church of England was in England. Most of the alii supported the royal couple. A few, such as Liliuokalani, Lunalilo, and Bernice Pauahi Bishop, remained at Kawaiahao.

ST. ANDREW'S CATHEDRAL

Then tragedy interrupted the promising beginning: Kamehameha IV died on St. Andrew's Day in 1863. In his honor the projected Cathedral was renamed St. Andrew's, and St. Alban's School became Iolani. Although Kamehameha V was a member of the church, he did not have his brother's enthusiasm, so Queen Emma became its chief supporter. A wooden Procathedral was built on the Cathedral grounds for temporary use.

Queen Emma went to England on behalf of the Cathedral project. She secured architectural plans for an elaborate Gothic cathedral. The plans were detailed sufficiently so stones for the arches were carved. Queen Emma

received contributions amounting to $30,000. One enthu-
siastic helper was Miss Lydia Sellon, whose Anglo-
Catholic views had led to the founding of the Society of
the Holy Trinity, the first order of nuns to be organized in
the Church of England since the Reformation. In 1865
Miss Sellon, as mother superior, sent three members of the
order to Hawaii. These sisters taught at Lahaina. The
mother superior also promised Queen Emma she would
visit Hawaii.

Queen Emma returned to Hawaii with the stones which
would make the skeleton of the Cathedral and the plans
which provided for local material to be used for the walls.
On March 5, 1867, King Kamehameha laid the cornerstone for the Cathedral. Some work was done on the
foundation and choir section.

THE PRIORY

Three weeks after the laying of the cornerstone, Miss Sellon
arrived from England. With her were three sisters of the
Holy Trinity. The founding and building of St. Andrew's
Priory was an immediate need and received priority over
the Cathedral plans. Miss Sellon personally donated
$7,000 for the building. Sisters Bertha, Beatrice, and
Albertina were the first Priory teachers. In 1870 Sister
Bertha returned to England to become mother superior
following Miss Sellon's death. Within a few months St.
Andrew's Priory began its work as a school for girls. The
centennial of St. Andrew's Priory in 1967 demonstrated
the tremendous impact of the school on the life of Hawaii.

When Miss Sellon returned to England, four Hawaiian

girls went with her to enroll at Ascot Priory, where the Sisters of the Holy Trinity taught. Three of the girls died. Their graves at Ascot Priory are in a beautiful cemetery. The fourth girl, Keomailani, was a granddaughter of a brother of Kamehameha I. After she returned to the Islands, she married Mr. Wray Taylor, who was organist at St. Andrew's Cathedral. Their children, William Bishop Taylor and Mrs. Emma Strauss, were leaders in Hawaiian societies. Mr. Taylor served as trustee of Lunalilo Home and was in charge of the Royal Mausoleum. Mrs. Strauss, a godchild of Queen Emma, was in charge of the Queen Emma Museum.

Bishop Staley realized that the congregation of St. Andrew's was not large enough for the ambitious plans for the Cathedral. He journeyed to America and to England. In 1870 he decided not to return to Hawaii and resigned. Bishop Staley's daughter, Dr. Mildred Staley, served as a missionary physician in India. Upon retirement, she lived in Hawaii until her death.

On his journey to America, Bishop Staley saw Bishop Henry B. Whipple of Minnesota. George Whipple, a brother of the bishop, had been tutor for the children of Captain James Makee at Ulupalakua, Maui. George Whipple had later studied for the ministry and served in Minnesota. Bishop Whipple pledged support of his brother, and Bishop Staley assigned him to Maui, where he established the Church of the Good Shepherd at Wailuku. When the Reverend and Mrs. George Whipple came to Maui, they brought a twelve-year-old part-Indian girl from Minnesota. This girl, Clara Rohrer, served as organist and later married William F. Mossman. Their many descendants are prominent in Hawaii.

BISHOP ALFRED WILLIS

Following Bishop Staley's resignation, the Archbishop of Canterbury sought American cooperation and asked Bishop Whipple to accept the Bishopric in Honolulu, but he declined. The bishop selected was the Reverend Alfred Willis, a bachelor with private means. Some years later, in September 1883, Bishop Willis married.

In 1872 Bishop Willis arrived. He used the designation "The Anglican Church in Hawaii." Realistically, he revised the plans for the Cathedral, eliminating the transepts and adopting a plan by which the Cathedral would be built in sections. Finally on Christmas Day, 1886, Bishop Willis conducted services in the completed portion, the present choir and first bay. Two more bays of the nave were completed by 1902.

There were a number of Englishmen who did not like the High Church ritual used at St. Andrew's and asked that a second English congregation be organized. The Honorable A. S. Cleghorn, husband of Princess Likelike, and businessman Theophilus H. Davies, son of a Welsh Congregational minister, were British first and churchmen last. Bishop Willis resented the church view of Davies in particular. The bishop finally gave permission. The Englishmen of wealth and leadership preferred the second congregation. Theophilus Davies had never been confirmed but was allowed to take communion. Bishop Willis and Davies came to an open break on many matters.

The Anglican Church in Hawaii grew slowly. English families in Kona founded Christ Church at Kealakekua. Hawaii was changing. The prosperity of sugar plantations brought first Chinese and then numerous other races to the Islands.

Chinese boys and girls enrolled at Iolani and the Priory. Among these was Sun Yat Sen, the future founder of the Republic of China. Bishop Willis took a personal interest in the Chinese work and established St. Peter's Church. He gave Episcopal Ordination to the Lutheran Pastor Shim Yin Chin, who founded St. John's Church in Kula, Maui.

Strongly British in his sympathies, Bishop Willis was a royalist by conviction. He supported Queen Liliuokalani even when most ministers, including her own pastor at Kawaiahao, criticized her. The issue of licensing opium dealers, which led to most of the criticism, was to Bishop Willis secondary to the question of the queen's royal prerogative. The bishop never lessened his opposition to annexation or his support of the queen. Some members of the second congregation did not share the bishop's views.

When Bishop Willis was attending the Lambeth Conference in 1897, a Canadian priest, Canon John Usborne, was in charge. Some of the St. Andrew's members who were opposed to Bishop Willis started the Parish of St. Clement. Canon Usborne approved the new parish, including the provision that the title to the church property be in the name of certain trustees instead of the Anglican Church in Hawaii. When Bishop Willis returned he refused to recognize the new parish.

Annexation did not diminish Bishop Willis' royalist views. The Church of England and the Protestant Episcopal Church in the United States agreed that the work in Hawaii should be transferred to the Americans. Bishop Willis went to Tonga as Missionary Bishop. With him was a young Chinese man, Wai Sang Mark. Mark was ordained in Tonga but later returned to Hawaii as pastor of St. Peter's. In the last year of his service, Bishop Willis completed two more bays of the nave and arranged for the consecration of St. Andrew's as the Cathedral.

BISHOP HENRY BOND RESTARICK

The Right Reverend Henry Bond Restarick was consecrated as Bishop of Honolulu in 1902. Bishop William F. Nicholas of California received the transfer of the Anglican Church in Hawaii and established the authority of the Protestant Episcopal Church of the United States of America. Bishop Nicholas took no notice of the two English congregations but appointed the clergymen concerned as canons, and selected laymen from both congregations on the Cathedral Committee. When Bishop Restarick arrived in August, he assumed the position of Dean of the Cathedral. Soon afterward he reinstated Canon Usborne, who became pastor of St. Clement's. Soon after Bishop Restarick's election, a Miss Drant of Cincinnati volunteered to serve in Hawaii. He suggested that businessman W. C. Proctor provide her salary. Deaconess Drant's work in Palama led to St. Elizabeth Church. The Proctor family provided the funds for the building of the church and the mission house.

Bishop Restarick was a reconciler. Whereas Bishop Willis had assailed the sons of the American missionaries for their part in annexation, Bishop Restarick recognized that in many communities the missionary descendants attended Episcopal churches since the Congregational Church services were in Hawaiian. In 1908 two more bays were added to the nave of St. Andrew's. After the death of Theophilus H. Davies, the Davies family built the Davies Memorial Hall.

A Korean congregation developed, and John Park was ordained in 1911 and took charge of St. Luke's Mission. A third Chinese mission led to St. Mary's on King Street, and in Kaimuki work among the Japanese brought about the organization of Epiphany Church. A member of the Cathedral's Hawaiian congregation, Mrs. Alexander Karratti, appealed for help to start a Sunday school in Kapahulu. St. Mark's was largely a work for Hawaiians, and the first services were in Hawaiian. Philip T. Fukao, baptized and confirmed as an Episcopalian in Japan but ordained a Presbyterian clergyman, had come to Hawaii to work for the Hawaiian Board but later became an Episcopalian. Licensed as a lay reader, Fukao started Holy Trinity Mission. Through Holy Trinity, work was started among a group of Russians, and a priest of the Russian Orthodox Church worked with them for a time.

Bishop Restarick resigned in 1920 but remained in charge until his successor, the Right Reverend John D. La Mothe, arrived in August 1921.

BISHOPS LA MOTHE AND LITTELL

The Right Reverend John D. La Mothe served seven years as Bishop of Honolulu. In the early years of his work in Honolulu, he officiated at the funeral of Prince Kuhio Kalanianaole, the last member of the Kawananakoa dynasty to have been designated heir apparent to the throne of Hawaii.

Bishop La Mothe established St. Luke's Parish on Judd Street, and moved Iolani to the former Theo. H. Davies estate at Judd and Nuuanu streets. On his way to the General Convention in 1928, he became ill and died. His daughter, married to an army officer, Colonel Thomas Aaron, returned to Honolulu after his retirement. Colonel and Mrs. Thomas Aaron lived at the Diocesan House for years and served as hosts for military personnel.

A missionary who had served thirty years in China, the Right Reverend Harrington Littell was the next Bishop of Honolulu, and his consecration service was at St. Andrew's. He expanded work on the other islands. He established the Shingle Memorial Hospital on Molokai. This church hospital was transferred to the territory twenty years later.

Bishop Littell also purchased a twenty-five-acre site for Iolani School between Date Street and the Ala Wai. When Bishop Littell resigned, Bishop Stephen Keeler of Minnesota arrived to supervise the work of the Diocese as well as the war-time work of the Episcopal Church.

BISHOP HARRY KENNEDY

The Right Reverend Harry S. Kennedy was elected Bishop in October 1943. He was an Army chaplain on duty. Even after he arrived in Honolulu Bishop Kennedy was asked to spend much time in ministering to the military in the forward area of the Pacific. Under Bishop Kennedy's leadership, the number of churches has increased. Perhaps the most successful in a new suburban area was Holy Nativity Church in Aina Haina, where the Reverend John Morrett was pastor for years until becoming Dean of St. Andrew's. Other suburban churches were established as missions and grew to self-support.

Iolani School moved to its present location, and Hawaii Preparatory Academy at Kamuela was established in 1949. In 1964 Seabury Hall (a school for girls) was established on Maui.

The Diocese of Honolulu has charge of the Pacific Area Jurisdiction. As early as 1904 American Samoa came under the Diocese of Honolulu, but the bishop of the Church of England in charge of Western Samoa sends the clergyman who serves in Samoa. Wake, Midway, and Guam became part of the Diocese in 1948 and Okinawa in 1951. The work in Okinawa has a number of missions, including one in a leprosarium. Bishop Kennedy accepted the responsibility of serving Episcopal chaplains during the Korean War. Bishop Kennedy sent the Reverend Theodore T. Y. Yeh to Taiwan in 1954.

In 1955 the Diocese of Honolulu was host to the General Convention of the Episcopal Church, the first time a major denominational convention of a national organization has been held in Honolulu. Virtually all the bishops of the church attended this convention.

The Diocese of Honolulu has established a conference center at Mokuleia and also Canterbury Hall for university work.

The growing churches and their close ties with the denomination has brought many fine young men to the Islands who later moved to places of leadership, such as Anson Phelps Stokes III, who is now Bishop of Massachusetts.

Island youths, also, from the time of Bishop Willis, have studied for the Episcopal priesthood and become ordained priests. The Very Reverend Lani Hanchett, who is of Hawaiian ancestry, was designated Suffragan Bishop of Honolulu. The Service of Consecration was held on December 30, 1967. The Reverend Charles Crane, of Caucasian ancestry, is a member of a Maui family and pastor of the Church of the Holy Nativity. The Reverend James Nakamura, of Japanese ancestry, is at St. James Church in Kamuela, and the Reverend John Liu, who is Chinese, is at St. Augustine's Church in Kohala. The Reverend Norio Sasaki at St. Clement's is of Japanese ancestry, and the Reverend Guy Piltz at St. Mary's is part Hawaiian.

At present, a recent emphasis on urban programs in Honolulu in which the churches cooperate has brought the Reverend George Lee and the Reverend Don Guynes to work in this area, the latter as Waikiki Minister in a program sponsored by the Hawaii Council of Churches for the great number of people in Waikiki who need aid of all types.

The Missionary Diocese of Honolulu set the goal of becoming a self-sustaining diocese by the centennial year of 1962, then reset the goal for 1970. The Diocese has about 11,000 communicants in forty-five parishes and missions, with forty-eight active clergymen. There are eight self-sustaining parishes: St. Andrew's, St. Clement's, St. Peter's, St. Christopher's, Good Shepherd (Wailuku, Manu), Holy Nativity, Epiphany, and St. George's. The thirty-two missions include the missions on Wake, Guam, Midway, and Okinawa.

After service at St. Andrew's, Samuel Van Culin, a part-Hawaiian, was at the National Cathedral in Washington and then became one of the denominational secretaries. Significantly, Bishop Kennedy's leadership and influence with the younger clergy is shown by his own sons, three of whom are ordained and a fourth who is studying for the ministry.

St. Andrew's was completed in 1958. The West Window is the most striking work of stained glass in Honolulu. The dedicated Cathedral served as a center of the centennial services in 1962.

Bishop Harry S. Kennedy retired at the beginning of 1969 and Suffragan Bishop Lani Hanchett took over his duties.

1. Kamehameha IV, *Preface to the Book of Common Prayer,* Meiric Dutton, Honolulu, 1959, p. 14.

8. Eastern Orthodox Church

In 1799 Tsar Paul of Russia charted the Russian-American Company with headquarters at Sitka. Russian ships began to visit the Islands, and in 1815 a Russian ship was beached at Waimea, Kauai. A German physician, Dr. Gregor Scheffer, was sent to recover the cargo and to see about making some sort of settlement as a base for the Russians from Alaska. Dr. Scheffer visited King Kamehameha and bought land for a plantation on Oahu. He established a trading post at Honolulu Harbor and began to build a fort. John Young, acting as governor of Oahu, became alarmed and forced Scheffer to leave. Kaumualii, king of Kauai, welcomed Scheffer, and Scheffer promised support to Kaumualii in retaking Oahu and Maui from the conquerer Kamehameha. Scheffer received land at three locations and built a fort at Waimea. The agreement with Kaumualii took the following form:

> His Highness Kaumualii, son of Kaeo, King of the north Pacific Sandwich Islands, Kaui and Niihau, born

prince of the islands Oahu and Maui, asks His Highness
the Lord Emperor Alexander Pavlovitch, the all-Russian
autocrat, to accept the above islands under his protection.
He wishes with his successors to be loyal forever to the
Russian sceptre and has accepted as sign of his loyalty
and submission the Russian flag off the ship *Discovery,*
belonging to the Russian-American Company. Signed by
the king with a cross. Translated in the Sandwich language and proclaimed to the inhabitants of Kauai and
Niihau by the king himself.[1]

Scheffer stated that this pledge of the king was made on
the Gospel and the Cross (Russian Icon?). Kaumualii
apparently did not understand the import of the vow of
allegiance, and a year later he forced the withdrawal of
the Russians after a little battle in which some Hawaiians
and three Russians were killed. The advisers to the tsar
as well as the officials of the Russian-American Company
disavowed Scheffer's actions, and the Russian influence
in Hawaii ended.

No definite evidence survives of the building of a church
at the Russian fort at Waimea. However, regular weekly
Russian Orthodox services were held by the Russian-
American Company at such places as Fort Ross in Cali-
fornia, and it must be assumed that they were held at the
Russian fort at Waimea.

Probably, then, the first regular Christian services ever
held in Hawaii were those of the Russian Orthodox
Church.

UKRAINIANS

The sugar plantations sought for labor in many areas. In

1897 Hackfeld and Company contacted a group of Ukrainians from the Austro-Hungarian province of Galicia. Over five hundred men, women, and children came to Hawaii. The first ship arrived on July 27, 1897, and a second on October 6, 1898, with a few arrivals at other times. They were assigned to plantations on all islands. They probably held some religious services, but no churches were organized. Mention of an observance of Russian Christmas indicates at least some were Eastern Orthodox. The names are German: Bodnar and Meyer; Polish: Rutkowski and Turezyuski; Slovak: Kaczka and Klaczek; as well as Ukrainian.

Within a few years, as soon as they had worked off their passage contract, many moved to the United States mainland. Most of those who remained in Hawaii intermarried with the island groups, and their descendants lost their identity as Galicians or Ukrainians.

GREEKS

George Lycurgus, born in Sparta, Greece, came to Hawaii in the closing years of the monarchy. The "Volcano House" at Kilauea Crater made "Uncle George" world famous. At special occasions, some observance in the Greek Orthodox tradition would be held.

The Greek families which came to Honolulu did establish a community which from time to time held religious services, often with an Episcopal priest officiating. Mr. George Michopulos has been the Honolulu leader of the Greek community.

RUSSIAN IMMIGRANTS

Quite a number of Russian immigrants came to Hawaii from 1910 through 1912. Like other immigrant groups, many moved to Honolulu as soon as they finished their plantation contract. In 1916 Bishop Restarick arranged for a priest of the Russian Orthodox faith to come to Hawaii. The Reverend John T. Dorsh, a married priest, conducted the Orthodox Russian service. The Russians held their services in Holy Trinity Church on School Street. On one Christmas at least, they held a midnight processional service in the Cathedral. This was on January 6, Christmas Day on the Eastern Orthodox calendar.

The Russian Revolution in 1917 divided the Russians in Hawaii. A number went to Siberia when the Soviet government promised them land. Most of the others went to the American mainland. Father Dorsh returned to the mainland, and the few Russians who remained either affiliated with Episcopal churches or dropped their membership as Russian Orthodox members.

EASTERN ORTHODOX CHURCH

Eastern Orthodox communicants in the armed forces are sufficiently numerous for the appointment of Eastern Orthodox chaplains. Navy Chaplain (Lt. Commander) Nicolas Karros conducted services for Greek and Eastern Orthodox civilians as well as those in the military services.

After his term of service ended, Archbishop Athenagoras of the Greek Orthodox Church arranged for an Air Force chaplain to be assigned to Hawaii. Chaplain William

Basil Stroyen was assigned. The Eastern Orthodox Church was organized and a rectory obtained at 1080 Wanaka Street in the Moanalua Shopping Center area. Services in Greek and Russian are held in the chapel at the Hawaii Conference of the United Church of Christ. Chaplain Stroyen, author of the book *Religion Under Communism,* developed a strong permanent congregation.

The Eastern Orthodox Cathedral of Saint Sophia in Los Angeles sent a priest to Honolulu for Easter services even before the local church was organized. The permanent civilian priest, the Reverend Dean Gigico, arrived in October 1968. Arrangements were made to hold services at the Epiphany Episcopal Church.

The Greek Orthodox bishops and priests organized the Eastern Orthodox work in Honolulu. However, in May 1969 the announcement was made that Pravoslavna Cerkov became a co-founder of the Orthodox Church of Hawaii. This meant that the Eastern Orthodox churches that use the old Slavic ritual have also come to Hawaii, with Priest John Bolifka as organizer.

1. Klaus Mehnert, *The Russians in Hawaii,* University of Hawaii Bulletin, Honolulu, April 1939, p. 27.

8. An altar cross by Erica Karawina, displayed at New York World's Fair. Palolo United Methodist Church, Honolulu.

9. The United Methodist Church

The Methodist Church had two beginnings in Hawaii. The first was in 1855 when the San Francisco District Conference sent the Reverend W. S. Turner to start a church. A number of former Methodist Church members had heard Turner speak at a Fort Street Church service the previous year and had made the request. A Honolulu businessman, John T. Waterhouse, gave a lot, and a church able to seat two hundred was built. After two years of successful work, a number of problems and conflicts in which the pastor was involved led to his resignation. Two other ministers served, the Reverend John McClay and the Reverend C. V. Anthony, but the past problems could not be overcome; the church was mortgaged to pay its indebtedness and then sold to pay the mortgage. Prime Minister R. C. Wyllie purchased the building on October 11, 1862, the day that Bishop Staley arrived from England.

The second beginning came with the Japanese immigration. A young samurai, Kanichi Miyama, became a Christian in San Francisco and then became a pastor working with Japanese in California. These new converts in California decided to help their countrymen in Hawaii.

In October 1887 the Reverend Kanichi Miyama arrived, and after two months returned to California. A request was sent to the Bishop of California asking for Miyama's return to Hawaii. This request was seconded by the Hawaiian Evangelical Association, and the bishop agreed on the condition that this would be definitely a Methodist Church work, although the Hawaiian Evangelical Association would also have Japanese work.

With this understanding, the Reverend Kanichi Miyama, his wife, and two other workers, Mr. Takeshi Ugai and Mr. Gannosuke Mitani, arrived in Hawaii. They made great progress, not least among the converts being the Japanese Ambassador Taro Ando and his family. Ambassador Ando also acted as interpreter for services conducted by Dr. C. M. Hyde and other ministers of the Hawaiian Evangelical Association.

A former missionary to Japan, the Reverend M. C. Harris, was in charge of Japanese work for the Methodists of the Pacific Coast. Just a few months after the Japanese missionaries started work, Mr. Harris came to Honolulu and organized the church. The new congregation obtained use of the old church built by the first Methodists, at Kukui and Nuuanu.

In 1892 the Reverend F. N. Fisher, in charge of the Methodist Mission in Hawaii, decided that the Hawaiian Evangelical Association was better organized and could do the work of evangelism among the Japanese. The former Methodist Church then became the Nuuanu Congregational Church. However, the Reverend Kanichi Miyama persisted in maintaining the Methodist fellowship, and Dr. Harris sent other ministers. A church was organized on River Street, which later was named Harris Memorial Church.

The Reverend Harcourt Peck had come to Hawaii as educational secretary of the Honolulu Y.M.C.A. Mr. Fisher held some services for Methodist Caucasians in 1892, and in 1894 these Methodists organized the First Methodist Church of Honolulu, with Mr. Peck as their minister. This church has grown into one of the outstanding churches of Honolulu.

Mr. Peck reorganized the work among the Japanese. In November 1895 a Reverend Kihara started work in Lahaina. One convert, named Akazawa, was the proprietor of a Japanese saké shop. Akazawa studied for the ministry and returned to Japan, where he became a bishop of the Methodist Church in Japan.

Dr. George L. Pearson, in 1897, came to First Methodist Church as pastor, and he also served as adviser to Japanese pastors. He founded the church in Aiea where the Reverend Tahei Takahashi served as pastor. Other Japanese ministers were the Reverend Gennousuke Motokawa, founder of the church now called Wesley Memorial; the Reverend Tokuji Momuro, who served for a time at Lahaina; and Mr. Jutsuzo Morimoto, who organized a plantation church at Kaanapali.

In 1903 Miss L. Blois established the Susannah Wesley Home, where Christian concern and care was given to orphans and neglected children. Also in 1903, the first Koreans arrived. Mr. Sung Ha Hon was their first unordained pastor. In 1905 the Reverend M. C. Harris was elected a missionary to Japan, so the Hawaii Mission of the Methodist Church was established with Dr. John W. Wadham, former missionary in Japan, as the first superintendent. The second superintendent, Dr. William H. Fry, who served for thirty-three years, shaped the Methodist Mission into its present form.

The Hawaii Mission adapted itself to the pattern of plantation life. Newspapers in Japanese and Korean were printed, and a Korean Benevolent Society formed. In these churches there was usually a day school, an ethnic-language school (Japanese or Korean), an English-language school, and a day nursery. The Kahuku Church conducted the nursery and school six days a week from 4:30 A.M. to 4:30 P.M., while both men and women worked in the fields. When the Hawaii Mission was organized in 1905, there were 19 mission charges with 419 members and 23 Sunday schools with 1,279 students. Of the 6,000 Koreans who came to Hawaii, about a third had had contact with Christianity in Korea, usually through the Methodist Church.

The superintendents of the Methodist Mission have been outstanding leaders in community activities as well as in their own denomination. The Reverend J. W. Wadham was leader of the Antisaloon League while he was superintendent of the Mission from 1906 to 1914. The Reverend William Fry, superintendent from 1914 to 1946, saw his persistent support of workers rewarded with increasingly strong churches. Two former missionaries followed, the Reverend Roy L. Ruth of Korea and Dr. Leonard Oelschli of Singapore and Malaya.

In some areas the Methodists worked under a fraternal arrangement with the Congregationalists. The Reverend and Mrs. Rudolph Zerbucken, missionaries in Korea, came to work in Hawaii. Numerous young people attended Mills School and later the Mid-Pacific Institute. Among the Filipinos, such work as the Filipino United Church (now Aldersgate Methodist Church) was carried on jointly for years. At Lahaina the Reverend B. T. Makapagal gave a long life of service to the people of his country. He came from the Philippines in 1912.

Since many of the Korean arrivals had been Methodist, the Korean Compound School was established under the leadership of Dr. Syngman Rhee, who had been denied readmission to Korea by the Japanese government. Dr. Rhee's protégés became not only leaders in Hawaii, but after 1945 leaders for the new nation of Korea. Dr. Y. C. Yang of Honolulu became Korean ambassador to the United States.

The identification of the Methodist Church with the Oriental workers was to produce strong leadership for the church in the present, but in the earlier years it brought disaster to individual churches. After the 1919 strike, the Aiea church was closed for two years when the Reverend Utanosuku Fujishiro and most of his congregation had to leave their plantation-owned homes. At Kahuku all the Japanese lost their jobs and were replaced by Filipino workers. The Kahuku Methodist Church had to begin a new program. Many of the workers moved to Honolulu and became members of Harris Memorial and Wesley Memorial churches.

Although they established no grade or high schools, the Methodists were active in education work. They promoted Japanese-language schools with Christian emphasis. They established the first Vacation Bible schools in the territory. Christian hostels were built for young people who left the plantation camps to work or study in Honolulu. The Goodwill Industries, encouraged by Methodist support, were established in Honolulu. The Reverend Euicho Chung is director of the Goodwill Industries.

The Methodist contributions to community and church leadership have been great. The career of United States Senator Daniel K. Inouye is but a heightened expression of scores of others who found in the churches the incentive for leadership. Not least is the career of Dr. Harry S. Komuro. Born on the mainland, he grew up in the Harris Memorial Church where his father was pastor. After his study for the ministry, a year of teaching in Japan, and further pastoral work, he became the pastor at Harris Memorial, and then in 1955 he became the head of all Methodist work in Hawaii. In 1964 Dr. Komuro became the National Executive Secretary for the Methodist Board of Special Ministries. The former pastor of the First Methodist Church, Dr. Frank Butterworth, succeeded him as superintendent of the Hawaii District. The Reverend Lawrence Hinshaw, pastor at First Methodist Church, became superintendent of the Santa Barbara District in 1968.

The Methodist churches had been largely ethnic-language churches. Now they are English-speaking churches. Filipino United Church was renamed Aldersgate Methodist; First Korean was renamed Christ Methodist; Hilo Korean was renamed Hilo Community; and Wahiawa Korean was renamed Olive Methodist. Churches such as Wesley Memorial and Christ Methodist sought for new ways of service in the church neighborhood. Aldersgate, with its basic Filipino congregation, found challenges in the Mayor Wright Housing area among all racial groups, and developed work among the Samoans. Working at Aldersgate, the Reverend Faafouina Iofi and Mr. Vaiao Alailima are leaders among the Samoans.

Island-born Methodists have given effective leadership outside their church. The Reverend David Harada, after being chaplain at Hawaii State Hospital, served as chairman of a study project on mental health for the State of Hawaii. The Reverend James Misajon, who served for years as a business manager of the Hawaii Mission, resigned to serve the Peace Corps training center in Hilo.

One major project in which the Hawaii Mission worked is Camp Kalani, a retreat and conference center on Kailua Bay. Another is Pohai Nani, a retirement home which is one of the Pacific homes operated under supervision of the Methodist Church. The Susannah Wesley Home phased out its orphanage work and, as the Susannah Wesley Community Center, has initiated preschool and other social work. It operates a "Head-Start" program and other service programs at Kuhio Park Terrace, a high-rise housing project for low-income families. As such, it is now primarily an Aloha United Fund project. The Wesley Foundation at the University of Hawaii has had an effective student program since 1957 under the direction of the Reverend Robert McCullagh. A special worker, the Reverend Hilo Himeno, is minister to international students at the East-West Center.

The Hawaii Mission is now the Hawaii District of the Southern California–Arizona Conference of the Methodist Church. The conference voted in 1960 to grant such status before 1964, but the details were not all settled so the Quadrennial Conference of 1968 marked the beginning of the Methodist Church standing as a self-supporting district.

Methodist Church has seven thousand members in thirty churches. Fifteen of these are mission churches receiving aid from the Hawaii Mission, and a few others receiving aid for special projects, but all churches give to missionary support.

Because of its worldwide missionary contacts, the Methodists in Hawaii have brought a number of ministers to Hawaii from overseas mission stations. These include the Reverend Serapio Afalla and the Reverend Melanio Loresco from the Philippines, the Reverend Taiji Takahashi of Japan, and the Reverend Dae Hee Park of Korea. Ministers of Korean ancestry are the Reverend Samuel Lee, the Reverend S. W. Kim, and the Reverend Harry Y. Park. The Reverend James Y. Terauchi and the Reverend Jiro Mizuno, who are of Japanese ancestry, have served for years with the Hawaii Mission.

In 1968 the United Brethren Church and the Methodist

Church united to form the United Methodist Church. The first meeting of the Western Jurisdictional Conference of the united denomination was held in Honolulu in July 1968.

The Wesleyan Church, a conservative offshoot of Methodism, has sent a worker to Hawaii but has not built a church.

9. A memorial for Dora Rice Isenberg.
Lutheran Church, Lihue, Kauai.

10. The Lutheran Churches

Hackfeld and Company of Hamburg, Germany, established a store in Honolulu in 1849. This firm later started a sugar plantation at Lihue, Kauai. A number of Germans came to Kauai to work on the plantation. These Germans insisted that they had to have a church where German was used and a German-language school for their children. Paul Isenberg, a partner in Hackfeld and Company, persuaded the Reverend Hans Isenberg, a relative, to come to the Islands to take charge of the school and to conduct the services in German. German remained the language used until 1917.

The German Lutheran Church of Lihue was built in 1881, and for twenty years it was the only Lutheran Church in the Islands. For part of that time it was affiliated with the Hawaiian Evangelical Association, and Pastor Isenberg was granted the status of a corresponding member.

In 1899 the Reverend Shim Yin Chin, a Lutheran minister from China, started a church in Kula, Maui. Since the other Lutheran work was in German, the church at

Kula was transferred to the Episcopal Church and the minister received Episcopal ordination. The church now exists as St. John's Episcopal Church of Kula.

In the late 19th century Germany became active in the Pacific, taking over a portion of Samoa. After the Spanish-American War, Germany acquired all Spanish Pacific islands except Guam. More Germans came to Hawaii.

From time to time Pastor Isenberg conducted services in German in Honolulu, and in 1899 organized the Honolulu Lutheran Church. Hackfeld and Company contributed generously for a building, and the congregation called the Reverend Willibald Felmy as pastor. He arrived in time for the dedication of the church in 1901. The Reverend Emil Engelhardt was the next pastor, and as a member of the German army he returned to Germany in 1914 for active duty. The church then decided to obtain an American pastor, and in 1916 Dr. Arthur Hormann of Watertown, Wisconsin, became pastor.

The entrance of the United States into World War I brought difficulty to the Germans in Hawaii. Many of the Germans born in Hawaii had grown up and married Hawaiian girls or had become Hawaiian citizens, even before annexation. When the Alien Property Custodian sought to take over Hackfeld and Company, the American citizens who owned stock were able to preserve their interests. On July 4, 1918, the name of the company became American Factors, and the name of their store Liberty House. The same shift from German took place in the church. Pastor Hormann used English instead of German for the services, and church ties with Germany were cut.

After 1918 Pastor Hormann was the only Lutheran minister in the Islands, and the church was an independent Lutheran Church. During the Second World War the church worked with representatives of the United Lutheran Church of America in the work with servicemen, and in 1946 the church became part of the United Lutheran Church. The United Lutheran Church sent men to aid in the Lutheran work and established three additional congregations on the island of Oahu: St. Paul's in Kaimuki, St. John's in Kailua, and the Lutheran Church of Pearl Harbor.

In 1941, just before the attack on Pearl Harbor, the Lutheran Church—Missouri Synod began laying the groundwork for a Service Center, which was used by military personnel throughout the Second World War. Pastor Adolph Meyer, who was called to this work in 1944, organized Our Redeemer Lutheran Church in Honolulu the following year (1945). Since that time eight other congregations and preaching stations have been established by the Missouri Synod on the islands of Oahu, Hawaii, and Maui.

The Evangelical Lutheran Church (now the American Lutheran Church) arrived in the mid-1950's to begin work in the Honolulu area, where there are now four congregations. The most recent of these is the Prince of Peace Lutheran Church in Waikiki, which is situated on the top floor of the Lutheran Senior Citizens' Home (Laniolu).

Now the three Lutheran groups, comprising eighteen congregations and preaching stations and a combined baptized membership of about five thousand, are working toward a unified Lutheran witness and strategy in the Islands. In January 1967 work was initiated in forming a Lutheran Council of Hawaii to make pulpit and altar fellowship possible for the three participating groups. This goal was realized in 1968.

In 1954 work was undertaken by the Lutherans in the Wailuku-Kahului area on Maui, and it continues today. Lutheran work in Hilo began in 1953. Christ Lutheran Church was organized there in 1954.

EVANGELICAL FREE CHURCH

Norway, Sweden, and Denmark had State churches, all Lutheran, so most Scandinavians are Lutheran. In each country small groups left the State churches. When these groups came to America, they grew into regular denominations. One, the Evangelical Free Church, is predominantly Norwegian in background. Workers from the Free Church have been in Hawaii, and a congregation exists, although a church has not yet been built.

11. The Baptist Churches

Baptists in America from the time of Roger Williams to the present have believed in separation of church and state to preserve the independence of the church. This insistence on church independence has resulted in many Baptist groups.

A Southern Baptist layman, Mr. J. C. McDonald, began Baptist work in Hawaii. From 1926 to 1934 he conducted a Sunday school in Wahiawa. As he met other people of Baptist background, he aided in the organization of a Baptist church in Honolulu. In 1930 they founded an independent Baptist church named Calvary Baptist.

Later this church voted to affiliate with the American Baptist Convention (Northern) and was renamed the First Baptist Church. The Baptists purchased the old Makiki Church at Kinau and Pensacola, and in 1957 they built a modern church plant at this location. Since World War II three other American Baptist Convention churches have been built, named First Baptist Kailua, First Baptist Pearl Harbor, and First Baptist Ewa Beach.

Jackson College was loosely affiliated with the First Baptist Church when organized but later became completely independent, and then it merged with Honolulu Christian College to become Hawaii Pacific College, a nondenominational school.

The American Baptist Association consists of churches termed Missionary Baptist. Historically these churches had left the Northern Baptists over the issue of sending missionaries. The first Missionary Baptist Church was started in Kailua in 1950. Other missionary Baptist churches are in Kaimuki, Kaneohe, and Wahiawa.

There are numerous independent Baptist churches. The first was the Mount Zion Baptist Church in Kalihi, now located in Maili. The Reverend Ivory W. Collins was pastor of Negro churches before he came to Hawaii in 1942 as a wartime civilian employee. During the war years he held services for Negro civilian employees and Negro servicemen. Mount Zion Church was organized as a Negro Baptist church. Now it is interracial and Mr. Collins is still its minister.

The Reverend James R. Cook organized the International Baptist Church after a series of evangelistic meetings held at the Honolulu International Center. The church was organized in March 1966 and is located in Nuuanu Valley.

An independent fundamental Baptist church has been built on Moanalua Highway near the Tripler Hospital entrance and named Fellowship Baptist Tabernacle. Mainland Baptist sects such as Free Will Baptist (Waipahu), Conservative Baptist (Kailua), and Primitive

Baptists (Pauoa Valley) work in Hawaii.

On Maui the Hawaiian Islands Mission of the Denbigh Missionary Fellowship, a project of Independent Baptist churches with Dr. Edward Todd the director and ten workers, maintains the Doris Todd Memorial Christian Day School at Paia, Maui, and does youth, camp, and church work.

Most of these churches were organized by mainland people who wanted their type of church in Hawaii, or by evangelists working independently or with mainland support personally developed.

SOUTHERN BAPTISTS

The Hawaii Baptist Convention (Southern Baptist), however, is a denominational enterprise. Mr. J. C. McDonald's Wahiawa Sunday school became organized as the Wahiawa Baptist Church in 1934 with the Reverend W. H. Wooten as pastor.

Later the church received denominational support to work with Baptists stationed at Schofield Barracks. Southern Baptist missionaries bound for China and Japan visited Hawaii and suggested Hawaii become a mission field. In 1940 Miss Hannah Plowden, appointed a missionary to China in 1921, was in Hawaii returning to China when the Southern Baptist Foreign Mission Board decided not to send her back to China but have her work in Hawaii. The Reverend Victor Koons came the same year. He organized Olivet Baptist Church in 1941. Miss Plowden was founder and first principal of the Baptist Bible School. The Foreign Mission Board sent Japanese-speaking missionaries to Hawaii. During the war many Issei, with no Buddhist or Shinto services, attended Japanese services at the Baptist Missions. Dr. Malcolm Stuart, a long-time mission worker, is now a state denominational worker. At one time, forty-nine regularly appointed foreign missionaries were assigned to Hawaii.

Dr. Victor Koons, as field secretary of Foreign Missions, led in the organization of the Hawaii Baptist Convention in 1949 and became the first executive secretary of the Convention.

Money to aid local congregations and build beautiful churches came from the Foreign Mission Board. Some churches received as high as ninety-five per cent of their budgets. Missions soon became churches with such aid. In 1959 the Foreign Mission status was changed, and Hawaii was designated a "Pioneer State" to receive aid in decreasing amounts. Dr. Stanton H. Nash came in 1959 to carry out this program; in 1963 he was succeeded by Dr. Edmond Walker.

Twenty-five years after Dr. Victor Koons began work as a missionary, the Hawaii Baptist Convention was the third largest Protestant denomination in the Islands, with twenty-seven churches, seventeen missions, and six related ministries. The Hawaii Baptist Academy had developed from the Baptist Bible School. There were Baptist student centers for university students both at the Manoa and Hilo campuses. Thirty-nine ministers serve as pastors, with a dozen more in various positions.

The Convention is now divided into six associations: Hawaii, Maui County, Kauai, Honolulu, Windward

Oahu, and Central-Leeward Oahu. One achievement of the Hawaii Baptist Convention has been its enlistment of local youth as ministers. Over one-third of the pastors working in Baptist churches were born in Hawaii, and the Reverend Dan H. Kong is pastor of its largest church—Olivet.

The Pearl Harbor Baptist Church with over eight hundred members is almost one hundred per cent military. The Puu Kahea assembly grounds at Waianae is used for

10. Pearl Harbor Baptist Church,
Salt Lake Boulevard, Honolulu.

conferences and retreats. The Hawaii Baptist Academy now has over five hundred students.

In 1967 a new headquarters building was built at 1225 Nehoa Street, adjacent to the Academy. The Baptist Book Store was transferred from downtown to this new location.

Mrs. Susan Nishikawa, associate director in the Cooperative Church Development Division for the Hawaii Baptist Convention, has written the Mission study book *In Aloha Land,* which was used as the 1969 adult study book in the entire Southern Baptist Convention.

12. The Presbyterian and Reformed Churches

THE UNITED PRESBYTERIAN CHURCH
OF THE UNITED STATES OF AMERICA

The American Board of Commissioners for Foreign Missions, although predominantly composed of New England Congregationalists, was not denominational. The General Assembly of the Presbyterian Church in 1812 declined to organize a Board of Foreign Missions but expressed its support of the American Board. In the same year the American Board expanded its membership to include four Presbyterians, including a former moderator of the General Assembly, Eliphalet Nott. Beginning with the Second Company, many of the missionaries to Hawaii were Presbyterian. Graduates of Princeton Seminary included such missionaries as the Reverend Charles S. Stewart, the Reverend William P. Alexander, the Reverend Lorrin Andrews, the Reverend Richard Armstrong, the Reverend Cochran Forbes and his son the Reverend Anderson O. Forbes, and the Reverend Peter Gulick. The Reverend and Mrs. Charles Stewart had with them as a teacher Miss Betsy Stockton, a Negro woman who was a member of the Presbyterian Church in Princeton. Auburn

Seminary graduates are exemplified by such outstanding leaders as the Reverend Lorenzo Lyons, the Reverend Sheldon Dibble, the Reverend Titus Coan, the Reverend Harvey Hitchcock, and the Reverend Lowell Smith. After his medical training, Dr. Dwight Baldwin took work at Auburn and was ordained. Indeed, so many of the missionaries on Maui were Presbyterian that the island association on Maui was first termed the Presbytery of Maui.

Later two graduates of Lane Seminary of Cincinnati came to Hawaii: the Reverend Claudius Andrews, founder of Maunaolu, and the Reverend John F. Poque, one of the early secretaries of the Hawaiian Board.

One of the great Presbyterian missionary stories is that of Dr. Marcus Whitman and the Oregon Territory. When the first church was established in the Pacific Northwest by the Reverend Henry Spalding and Dr. Marcus Whitman, two Hawaiians, Mr. and Mrs. Joseph Maki, were charter members by letter from Kawaiahao Church in Honolulu. These Hawaiian Christians were workers with the Hudson's Bay Company in the Oregon Territory.

The Reverend Timothy Dwight Hunt resigned from the mission in 1848. He went to San Francisco and organized the First Presbyterian Church. This influence from Hawaii is commemorated in a stained-glass window in the chapel of the San Francisco Theological Seminary.

When in 1837 the Presbyterians decided to organize an official Board of Foreign Missions, most Presbyterians in Hawaii continued work under the American Board. After almost a century, a belief arose that the Presbyterians promised the Congregationalists that no Presbyterian work would be done in the Islands. Actually, when the American Board withdrew in 1863, the Hawaiian Evangelical Association formed "was henceforward to consist of all native and foreign Congregational and Presbyterian clergymen on the Sandwich, Micronesian and Marquesan Islands."

This acceptance on an equal basis of Congregational and Presbyterian clergymen led to many Presbyterian clergymen working in the Hawaiian Evangelical Association. John F. Poque, Charles McEwen Hyde, O. H. Gulick, and J. Leslie Dunstan have been secretaries of the Hawaiian Board who came from Presbyterian backgrounds. For years members of Presbyterian churches fitted just as easily into Island churches.

However, many Presbyterians in the Islands did want a church, and the Presbytery of Los Angeles, after a survey in 1957, established the First United Presbyterian Church of Honolulu in 1959. The Reverend William Phifer became the first pastor and the Reverend Philip Lee the associate. Mr. Lee was raised in the Presbyterian Church of China. The congregation met in the Y.W.C.A. of Honolulu until a building was erected at Nehoa and Keeaumoku Streets and dedicated in 1961. In 1961 plans were made for the establishment of Christ Presbyterian Church in Kailua. The congregation was organized early in 1964, and the church building dedicated in 1967. The Reverend Warren G. Studer and the Reverend Abraham Dohi are the leaders of Christ Presbyterian Church. And now a third Presbyterian church at the new suburban town of Mililani has been started.

THE CHRISTIAN REFORMED CHURCH OF HAWAII

The state church of Holland is the Reformed Church. Beginning in 1834, some people in Holland left the state church to form a Conservative Calvinistic Church. In the United States they took the name the Christian Reformed Church. Many members of this church settled in Michigan, and the missionary offices are in Grand Rapids, Michigan. In June 1963 a Mr. and Mrs. Jack Carlman called together a Bible study group. In September 1965 the Reverend Mike Vander Pol was sent to organize a Christian Reformed Church in Honolulu.

The home mission office provided the funds to purchase the Cornelius Von Hamm home at 2875 Pacific Heights Road. Dr. Melvin D. Hugen arrived in October 1967 to become the installed pastor. The Von Hamm home is not only the church, but a place for servicemen to stay.

Besides the people of Dutch ancestry, there are in Hawaii people of Indonesian ancestry. When Indonesia became independent, Indonesians who wished could choose Dutch citizenship. Thousands of people, many racially mixed, went to Holland. Not liking the climate, a significant number have come to Hawaii, and some are members of the various churches of Hawaii.

THE KOREAN CHRISTIAN CHURCHES

The two Korean Christian churches are Presbyterian in organization. Dr. Syngman Rhee, the first president of the Republic of Korea, was the founder of these churches. Dr. Rhee was a man who had endured prison for his convictions. His strong unswerving personality was powerful to lead but also developed opposition. After working with the Methodist Church in Hawaii for some years, he resigned and became the organizing head of the Korean Christian Church in 1915. A lovely building with Korean-type architecture was built on Liliha Street. When Dr. Rhee left the Republic of Korea and came to Hawaii, he resumed his attendance at this church. Visiting Koreans have referred to the Korean Christian Church as the Republic of Korea Church.

After Dr. Rhee became president of Korea, and during the Korean conflict, there were serious disagreements in the church that led to civil court action. The faction loyal to President Rhee won.

When Dr. Syngman Rhee died, a funeral was held at the Liliha Street Church, and his body was then flown to Korea. Millions of Koreans paid tribute to the man, who in forty years of exile nurtured the dream of an independent Korea and during the Korean conflict led a determined people. Yet more years of Dr. Rhee's manhood were spent in Hawaii than in Korea, and he both received and gave to the spiritual strength which exists in Hawaii.

The Reverend Richard C. Kimm, long-time pastor, is a member of the Presbytery of Seoul and of the Presbyterian Church of Korea. The Reverend Philip Kwan was a pastor at Wahiawa during the 1950's, and the story of Mrs. Kwan is almost one of Christian martyrdom.

Young and beautiful, Miss Yong Hee Lee was preparing to go to the United States for study when the Korean conflict began in 1950. The Communists captured twenty-five Christian students who had studied or were going to study in America. They were offered freedom if they would work with the Communists. One joined the Communists but twenty-four held firmly to their Christian faith. In the subsequent brainwashing and slow starvation, eighteen died, refusing to renounce their faith. When the Americans recaptured Seoul, Miss Lee was one of the six still living. She was so close to death that it was six months before she could walk. When she recovered she went to America to take up the studies she had planned. In America she met a young Korean minister, Philip Kwan. They were married and came to the Wahiawa Christian Church. The year of hardship had left a weakened body, and Mrs. Kwan spent over a year in Leahi Hospital. When she speaks of her experience she says very simply: "I expected to die. I do not know why the Communists did not kill me. Yet I knew I could never deny my faith."

13. The Religious Society of Friends

The Society of Friends (Quakers) has witnessed "concerns" for over three centuries. When the "concerns" relate to socially sensitive causes, the Quakers have exerted an influence upon the consciences of people of many other faiths. Three centuries ago, the founder, George Fox, stated that he lived by a covenant of peace that was before wars and fighting were. So the Quakers' protest against war is not a result of Vietnam but part of their continuous concern.

The first mention of a Quaker in Hawaii was in 1835. A Mr. Daniel Wheeler conducted a religious service on Christmas Day 1835. Queen Kalama attended the service and sent Mr. Wheeler a gift of five barrels of potatoes, five turkeys, five chickens, and a hog.

A century later, in 1935, this visit of Mr. Wheeler was remembered when some members of the Society of Friends gathered to commemorate that event and see about organizing themselves. At that time Mr. Thomas Kelley was teaching at the University of Hawaii. Thomas Kelley, whose *Testament of Devotion* is a very successful book with its combination of devotion to the Quaker "Inner Light" and commitment to Quaker "concerns," was in Honolulu only a year, but apparently was able to locate enough members for meetings.

Dr. and Mrs. Gilbert Bowles, for 48 years missionaries in Japan, brought vital witnesses when they retired to live in Honolulu. Dr. Bowles led in relief work for Korea and other projects.

The Honolulu Meeting of the Society of Friends was established November 28, 1937, by the Fellowship Council of the Friends World Committee. Some of the early members were Catherine Cox, Dr. and Mrs. Gilbert Bowles, Dr. and Mrs. Herbert Bowles, and Mr. Suga Ozaki.

When the Pacific Yearly Meeting was established on the West Coast, the Honolulu Meeting became affiliated. The Meetings were held at the Y.M.C.A. or the Church of the Crossroads until 1956, when a house was purchased at 2426 Oahu Avenue and remodeled to serve as the meeting place.

The Quaker services are held on Sunday, with fifteen minutes of singing after which the traditional service of silence begins. The members sit "listening" to the inner guidance of God's spirit. Certain ones may feel an inward urging to share his thoughts and will do so. After an hour the service ends.

There is no hired minister or pastor, so committees do the work. An Overseers Committee has general charge of membership and weddings while the Worship Committee is concerned with the spiritual life. Like most other Meetings, the Honolulu Meeting has a Peace Committee.

Dr. David Bassett is chairman.

Reinhold Keislick is the clerk in charge of the monthly business meeting. University of Hawaii Professor of Art Ben Norris was the clerk for some years. A resident couple live at the Meeting House.

A number of people who are not members of the Meeting are sympathetic to their work, especially the peace effort. One such person is Miss Fumiye Miho, graduate of Yale Divinity School, who worked for the Society of Friends in Japan.

The people of Honolulu have witnessed the centuries-old beliefs of the Quakers in dramatic fashion. In 1958, the ketch *The Golden Rule* sailed into Honolulu on its way to protest against nuclear testing in the Marshall Islands. Albert Bigelow was the leader. He and two others of the crew of four were Quakers, and in court tests reaffirmed the Quaker right to have a concern and to express that concern even in defiance of government decrees. These men served a jail term in Honolulu and they made the entire community aware of the teachings of the Society of Friends.

14. The Hawaiian Mission of Seventh-day Adventists

The Adventist ideas of the immediate Second Coming of Christ agitated many people in New York State in the 1830's and 1840's. A missionary teacher on Kauai shared these Adventist ideas, but remained a worker with the American Board. Later some people holding these Adventist beliefs formed the Seventh-day Adventist Church. Religious writings supporting the Adventist beliefs were in a barrel of clothing which a ship gave to the Pitcairn Islanders. Without a missionary they became Seventh-day Adventists, and their story brought missionaries to the Pacific.

Seventh-day Adventists first came to the Hawaiian Islands in 1883 when Abraham LaRue and Henry Scott arrived from San Francisco, California, to sell Adventist literature on Oahu. On December 27, 1885, Elder William H. Healey, with his wife and ten-year-old daughter, was sent to Honolulu by the General Conference of Seventh-day Adventists. Elder Healey began evangelistic meetings on January 15, 1886, in a fifty-foot tent pitched near Fort and Vineyard streets. When he left Honolulu four months later, there was a company of nine baptized believers.

A. J. Cudney followed Healey to Oahu, and on July 22, 1888, he organized the nine charter members in Honolulu as the first Seventh-day Adventist Church in Hawaii. A few days later, July 31, 1888, Cudney left Honolulu on a sail boat to go to Pitcairn Island, but his ship and all on board were lost at sea. Since his tragic death occurred before he had the opportunity to report the organization of the church, the church was not officially recognized by the General Conference of Seventh-day Adventists until its reorganization in 1896. One of the charter members was Mr. John McKeague, whose son Robert was the first Hawaiian to become a Seventh-day Adventist elder or minister.

On November 19, 1891, while en route to Australia on the ship *Alameda,* the founder of the Seventh-day Adventist Church, Mrs. Ellen G. White, and a party of five stopped briefly in Honolulu. She spoke to a large audience in the Y.M.C.A. Chapel. The sizable attendance was largely the fruit of the efforts of Elder G. B. Star and his wife, who had arrived six weeks earlier, prior to going on to Australia.

In 1895 E. H. Gates arrived, and in February 1896 he reorganized the church in Honolulu. Mrs. Gates taught a small church school in her home. About this time Dr. Preston Kellogg opened a sanitarium in downtown Honolulu, but it was short-lived. Also in 1895 H. H. Brand and his wife opened a school for Chinese boys, and later, in 1897, a boarding school known as the Palama Chinese School, which later became the Anglo-Chinese Academy.

In June 1897 the Brands went to Hilo on the island of Hawaii, where they opened the Hilo Chinese School.

In 1908, during the administration of C. D. M. Williams, the first Seventh-day Adventist Church building was erected on Kinau Street near Ward Street.

In 1912 Elder Robert McKeague began his ministry on Maui. In the 1920's a broadcasting program began in which McKeague conducted the Hawaiian broadcast and Elder Shohei Miyake had the Japanese portion.

The first permanent elementary school in the Islands, known as the Bethel Grammar School, was begun in 1914; with the addition of secondary grades, this school developed into the present Hawaiian Mission Academy. It has a special English department and has continued through the years to be a strong and important part of the educational work in Hawaii.

In 1929 Hawaii became a part of the Pacific Union Conference. Prior to that time it had been a detached mission, administered by the Foreign Mission Board of the General Conference of Seventh-day Adventists. In 1963 Castle Memorial Hospital opened its doors to serve the windward side of the island. This Seventh-day Adventist hospital has also furnished employment to many people and is currently a 72-bed general hospital, serving all the areas of the medical field.

In the membership of the Hawaiian Mission of Seventh-day Adventists are found people of the varied races of Hawaii. Elder Shohei Miyake, born in Japan, had considerable influence on some Issei families during World War II, and the Japanese Seventh-day Adventist Church is flourishing. One conversion was notable, that of Saburo Shingaki. Shingaki was a Japanese civilian on Saipan who became a member of a guerrilla group after the American capture of Saipan during World War II. Shingaki was condemned to death in 1946 for taking part in two murders. His sentence was commuted, but since he was a civilian he was sent to Oahu Prison. Elder Miyake changed Shingaki's bitter hatred into Christian forgiveness. In 1954 Shingaki was released to return to Japan, where he studied for the ministry and went to Okinawa in 1961 to work.

The years since World War II have brought continued growth to the Seventh-day Adventists. The Central Adventist Church was relocated on Piikoi Street. The Reverend Don L. Mulvihill is the present pastor. The Reverend Hideo Oshita, long-time worker in Hawaii, became pastor of the Central Japanese Seventh-day Adventist Church of Los Angeles. The Reverend Richard Among, a Hawaiian minister, serves the churches at Waianae and Waipahu. The Reverend A. G. Streifling is the present president of the Hawaiian Mission of Seventh-day Adventists.

15. The Salvation Army

In the days of the whaling ships, the Seamen's Bethel started work with the underprivileged, especially with the children of mixed ancestry. When the Bethel burned and the congregation merged with Fort Street Church to form Central Union Church, the special social work for the underprivileged changed. Since most of the work was by racial churches, the poor of mixed racial ancestry were neglected. Central Union Church started work at Palama, and a member of Central Union, Mr. C. R. Sturdevant, decided that the Salvation Army would be the agency to do this work.

However, the Salvation Army declined to send workers unless the work was under their sponsorship. So Central Union Church continued the work at Palama, but Mr. Sturdevant had collected enough funds to guarantee support for the Salvation Army workers for a year. Seven Salvation Army workers, led by Captain and Mrs. John Milsaps, arrived on September 13, 1894. Their first service was held out of doors on the steps of the Opera House on Union Street.

The business community began its pattern of financial

support which has continued to the present Aloha United Fund. Within a few months Captain Mary Zoomers had started work in Hilo, and Captain Henry Langride on Maui. David Lyman, part-Hawaiian grandson of the founder of Hilo Boarding School, joined their work, and for years he directed the Salvation Army on Kauai.

Since the Kakaako area was an area of great need, the Citadel Corps moved there, and welfare work was emphasized. The Kauwela Corps had supervision over the Men's Home and over the industrial work to reclaim discarded articles.

Mr. Samuel Wilcox gave forty acres of land to establish a farm home for neglected boys in the Kaimuki area. Commandant Rachel Payne established a home for girls in Manoa Valley, and to train girls the Waioli Tea Rooms were started. The Wilcox farm was sold in the 1950's for over a million dollars and the money used to rebuild both the boys' and girls' homes. Working with the Aloha United Fund, these homes have become rehabilitation homes for disturbed children.

The welfare work of the Salvation Army has been outstanding. When the Korean conflict meant the evacuation of American civilians and military dependents from Korea, the Salvation Army set up a service to aid these people. Perhaps nothing has dramatized their fine work more than the response to the 1960 tidal wave disaster which struck Hilo. Roused from bed after midnight, the Salvation Army workers had a planeload of clothing, blankets, and food on the way to Hilo by nine o'clock in the morning.

PRESENT-DAY LEADERS

The widespread urban changes since 1950 have caused many changes in Salvation Army work and facilities. The Booth Memorial Home has been relocated at 3624 Waokanaka Street in Nuuanu Valley. Almost a thousand inquiries a year are made to the Booth Home, and 122 young women were admitted in 1967. The Men's Social Service Center, formerly on Vineyard Street, was relocated at 806 Iwilei Road, with rehabilitation (usually from alcoholism), housing, and work opportunity. Facilities for children were operated at the Waioli cottages. The practice of the earlier days, when girls of the Waioli cottages were trained as waitresses at the Waioli Tea Rooms, has been discontinued. The tea rooms became so popular that they became a full-time commercial venture separate from the work with children.

The Salvation Army conducts its work on all islands and, besides its Social Service work, has Corps community centers with religious services and youth work. The headquarters is located at the Citadel Corps, with additional work at the Aiea, Kauluwela, Liliha, Pearl Harbor, and Kaneohe Corps.

Brigadier Frank Moss is in charge of Salvation Army work in Hawaii. Youth Commissioner Robert Stillwell conducts a wide variety of youth programs, including that at Camp Homelani. The Christmas program is a popular part of Salvation Army work: over 25,000 individuals were assisted at the 1967 Christmas season. Additional types of service are the Bureau of Missing Persons and the Emergency Disaster Aid.

The Salvation Army officers are rotated in assignments so few remain longer than a few years. Brigadier Frank Moss served previously as Youth Secretary. The record of service by the Salvation Army is one that merits the praise it receives.

16. The Christian Church

Some churches in Hawaii, like the First Chinese Christian Church and Lihue Christian Church, which are members of the United Church of Christ, took the name Christian as members entered from Oriental religions. However, a number of indigenous American churches arose on the American frontier calling themselves Christian and stressing that only the Bible should be the standard for faith. At first there was an antidenominational emphasis, and some groups have remained loosely organized. Others have organized into regular denominations. The largest of these uses as an official title, Disciples of Christ. Alexander Campbell was the initiating leader of the Disciples. A Presbyterian, he renounced the credal requirements of Presbyterians and stressed baptism by immersion and communion every Sunday, believing that without creeds Christians could come to a common faith based on the Bible.

The Reverend Thomas Garvin, a pastor in San Francisco in 1894, made a survey for a possible Christian church in Hawaii. He found in Central Union Church people of this religious faith. Two Honolulu businessmen, William Lewers Hooper and Walter C. Weldon, had married young women who had been raised in Washington, Pennsylvania, where Alexander Campbell had lived. Mrs. Weldon's father had been a co-worker with Campbell. On July 27, 1894, the First Christian Church of Honolulu was organized with Mr. Garvin as pastor. In a few months a major revival tent meeting started, lasting from November 16 to Christmas Day. One convert was the Reverend Eric Lewis, a clergyman of the Church of England and former missionary. A church was built on Alakea Street and dedicated on November 24, 1895. Mr. Garvin returned to California after eighteen months of work.

In 1899 a Mr. Lathrop Cooley of Cleveland gave $5,000 for Foreign Missions' work in Hawaii. The Reverend and Mrs. Abram E. Corey came as missionaries, but found the Christian Church without a pastor. Mr. Corey served both as pastor and as missionary. He founded three missions for Oriental families: the Lathrop Cooley Mission at Gulick and Beckley Street, the R. L. Sloan Mission, and the R. L. Sloan Mission branch in Moiliili. The Coreys soon left as missionaries to China. Later he was elected president of the International Convention of the Christian Church. The missions he founded in Hawaii continued for some time. Mr. Eu Oi Farm was one of the first converts and for a long time was active in the work for the Chinese. The church on Gulick Street was sold to a Pentecostal church. Work flourished in Chinatown near Hotel and Smith streets but later moved to School Street (the Golden Wall Theater site). The Reverend Stephen Mark from China had become leader of a group of young Chinese Christians, and when they moved to Queen Emma Street and built the Community Church, the School Street Mission merged with the Community Church.

The Reverend David C. Peters came as pastor of the downtown church in 1911. In 1914 the church was offered a good price by a business firm wanting the downtown location. A visitor from Denver gave $10,000 for a new church. Mr. Peters directed the building of the new church on Kewalo Street, and the congregation met in the Y.M.C.A. until the new church was completed. The design of the new church brought Mr. Peters the additional task of designing the King's Daughters' Home in Kaimuki. Mr. Peters became a Y.M.C.A. worker during World War I. The First Christian Church has provided fine leadership for many community projects. Oren E. Long, a long-time elder of the Christian Church, was a teacher, principal, superintendent of Public Instruction, secretary of state, and territorial governor in his long life of service, which culminated with his being elected one of the first United States senators from Hawaii.

Miss Edith Noffsinger, a missionary in the Philippines, came to work in the church during World War II. Expert in Dr. Frank Laubach's methods of teaching illiterates to read, Miss Noffsinger took charge of the Department of Public Instruction's adult education work for Filipinos when thousands came to Hawaii in 1946. The Reverend Emilio C. Yadao, educational worker for the I.L.W.U, and Miss Noffsinger established the Wahiawa Christian Church.

Since World War II, the longest pastorates at First Christian have been those of Walter Griswold and George Jacobs. In 1967 the congregation rebuilt the church at the Kewalo location. Other churches are Windward Christian and Wahiawa Christian Church. In 1966 the Reverend Alan Cole became the state executive secretary for the denomination.

CHRISTIAN CHURCHES

A number of Christian churches are not members of the Disciples of Christ. The oldest one is the Kaimuki Christian Church, which began in 1909 when a member of First Christian began a Sunday school. For a number of years this was held in Liliuokalani School. A church was organized in 1922, and afterwards a church was built at Kokohead and Harding avenues. The present pastor is the Reverend Harold E. Gallagher. Other churches are at Wahiawa (Central Oahu Christian Church), Sunset Beach, Maile, Kaneohe, Kalihi, and Palolo Valley. These churches all cooperate with the Disciples of Christ in such enterprises as an Annual Labor Day Convention.

CHURCH OF CHRIST

Since Congregational churches united with the Evangelical and Reformed Church to form the United Church of Christ, there has been confusion with the older Church of Christ. In the protest against denominationalism which led Alexander Campbell to start the Christian Church, there were those who insisted that no denominational type organization should be formed, so each Church of Christ is independent and there is only a loosely held association among them. Even the claim that there are twenty thousand churches and one million members has no denominational reports to substantiate the number.

The local congregation began during World War II. In October 1944 they purchased a home at Keeaumoku and Dominis streets, which served as church and parsonage. In 1954, under the ministry of the Reverend F. B. Shepherd, a new church was constructed at the site. A similar church in Kailua had the Reverend Ben Guillermo as pastor. Other churches are at Wahiawa, Pearl Harbor, and Waipahu.

A CHURCH WITHOUT A NAME

In protest against denominationalism, Mr. and Mrs. David Christie became Gospel workers trying to recreate the early New Testament church. As part of their faith they have no organization, no church building, and, in fact, no official name, lest people become loyal not to Christ but to the organization or denomination. Miss Beatrice Mookini is a dedicated worker in this faith, and the majority of the congregation is part-Hawaiian. Meeting in homes, the twelve servants work on all the islands.

17. The Revivalistic Faiths

John Wesley was the founder of modern mass evangelism. Mass evangelists used to use a blend of reason and psychological persuasion in convincing people to make a religious commitment. But somewhere in the development of mass evangelism in America, the emphasis came to be on psychological persuasion of a very emotional nature. From Jonathan Edwards and George Whitefield in colonial America to Billy Graham of the present day, most of the Protestant churches of America have cooperated with mass evangelist programs. However, denominational differences led some evangelists, notably D. L. Moody, to emphasize what they termed the simple Gospel message and to tend to look upon conversion under highly emotional mass persuasion as the standard of true Christian experience. Moody's successors tended to operate outside the churches and to develop their own temples or tabernacles as independent of denominations. These resulted in the formation of new denominations. For example, Aimee Semple Macpherson's Angelus Temple in Los Angeles became the headquarters for the Full Gospel Mission. This pattern of independent evangelists who set up independent churches has had a two-fold effect in Hawaii. The mainland groups have established branches in Hawaii, and independent evangelists have started their own independent groups.

John Wesley also had a conviction that a person truly converted would be Holy. The attainment of Holiness was not only possible but a proof of true believing. John Wesley's followers in the Methodist churches tended to emphasize the possibility of Holiness, and some emphasized the possession of Holiness as proof of genuine discipleship. The latter group left the Methodist Church to form the Holiness Church.

Hence, in the revivalistic churches in Hawaii there are three groups, those who stress the conversion experience only, those who add the test of Holiness, and those who are Pentecostal.

Historically, the day of Pentecost marked the beginning of the Christian Church. The Holy Spirit came upon the Apostles and disciples at Pentecost. All Christian faiths acknowledge the historical importance of the day. The Pentecostal churches insist upon the personal meaning of Pentecost—each disciple today can receive the Holy Spirit exactly as the first Christians did. Most Pentecostal churches distinguish between the experience of salvation and the baptism by the Holy Spirit with its attendant speaking in tongues and other phenomena associated with the first Pentecost.

THE CHURCH OF THE NAZARENE

In 1908 three Holiness groups met jointly in Kansas City
and organized the Church of the Nazarene. Revival meetings, an insistence upon the proof of Holiness through
tithing, and the observance of prohibitions, which still
included a ban on commercial entertainment, made the
Nazarenes a fast growing church in the Western states.

During World War II a Nazarene serviceman, G. J.
Woodridge, wrote to his pastor, the Reverend Leo Baldwin, about his disappointment in finding no Nazarene
Church in Honolulu. In June 1946 the Reverend and
Mrs. Leo Baldwin arrived and began work, holding
services in the Japanese Holiness Church. Soon afterwards
the Reverend Cecil Knippers organized the Hawaii District of the Church of the Nazarene and served as first
superintendent.

The Church of the Nazarene quickly established mis-
sions in most of the larger communities on all the islands.
There are ten churches in Hawaii. The Reverend W. Lee
Gann is the present superintendent. The Nazarenes established interracial appeal with such ministers as the Reverend Solomon Kekoa, a Hawaiian, and Reverend Kaichi
Yamamoto. Although Yamamoto attended a Nazarene
Mission School in Japan, he was violently anti-Christian.
When a fellow student said he would allow his hand to be
cut off rather than relinquish the Bible, Yamamoto drew
a sword across the student's hand. The student, with hand
dripping blood across the Bible, forgave Yamamoto, who,
out of the experience, became a Christian.

Another minister is the Reverend Nelson Tuitele, pastor of the Aiea Samoan Church of the Nazarene.

HOLINESS CHURCH

The Japanese Holiness Church was near King Street and University Avenue. Work was begun before World War II by the Holiness Conference of North America, and the missionaries from the mainland were Japanese. The ministers of this Holiness Conference are all of Japanese ancestry. The church is now named the Honolulu Holiness Church, and the church has two pastors. The Japanese-speaking pastor is the Reverend Mikio Ishino, and the English-speaking pastor is a mainland Nisei, the Reverend I. Bill Hara. The new location for the church is at 2207 Oahu Avenue.

ASSEMBLIES OF GOD

The First Assembly of God of Honolulu was started by the Reverend and Mrs. Eldon Vincent, who were sent from the Foreign Missions Department of the General Council of the Assemblies of God, headquarters in Springfield, Missouri.

The first meeting was held on February 23, 1947, in the Lincoln School on a Sunday afternoon, seventy-four people being in attendance. Property was secured at Lunalilo and Victoria streets. The lanai and living room of the old house on the property was the place where the services were held for over a year. The present church was started in 1949, but a number of modifications were made over the years.

The Aloha Bible Institute has trained church workers of all types, and the enrollment at times has been close to a hundred students.

The Assembly of God Church in Hilo was the independent Glad Tidings Church, established before World War II. It became associated with the other Assemblies of God after denominationally appointed workers came to Hawaii.

Assemblies of God exist on all the islands, and they have become the largest Pentecostal group in the Islands, with twenty-five churches. The First Assembly of God has served as headquarters for a number of Evangelistic campaigns, such as the one conducted by Oral Roberts. The Reverend Woodrow Yasuhara was the first resident to be ordained and now serves as district superintendent for Hawaii. The Reverend Eldon Vincent, still pastor of the church he established, has been a leader throughout the years.

THE CHURCH OF GOD *(Headquarters: Cleveland, Tennessee)*

A tent meeting on Noeau Street led by members of the Church of God in the armed forces culminated in the organization of a Church of God on January 30, 1944. The Reverend and Mrs. Grier W. Hawkins came as co-pastors in April 1945. A church was built at 822 Coolidge Street and dedicated in 1948.

Since then the Church of God has grown to seven churches: four on Oahu, two on Maui, and one in Hilo. The state overseer is the Reverend Robert E. Fisher. The Church of God maintains a servicemen's representative in Hawaii. Each year they hold a state convention and camp meeting.

THE CHURCH OF GOD *(Headquarters: Anderson, Indiana)*
This Church of God began its work in Hawaii in 1955 when Mr. and Mrs. Curtis Loewen came to Hawaii to attend the University of Hawaii. They found other members in the armed forces and began holding services at private homes. In July 1956 the Reverend and Mrs. Carl Riley arrived to be pastors of the Aina Haina congregation, and services were held in the banquet room of M's Ranch House.

A church was built and dedicated at Hind Iuka Drive and Mona Street, which has also served as denominational headquarters. The Reverend Brice E. Casey is the present pastor.

THE CHURCH OF GOD IN CHRIST
This church is under the leadership of Bishop W. H. Reed, and there are two congregations on Oahu and one in Kauai. In 1960 the Reverend Clennon King on Kauai ran for president on the Afro-American ticket. He preached what would now be termed "black nationalism," proclaiming "a new world would come of one creed, one class and one race,"[1] for World War III would kill off all whites.

Conflict developed between Bishop Reed and King, and King went to Jamaica, which deported him as a Communist agitator.

INDEPENDENT PENTECOSTAL CHURCHES

In Hawaii many of the Pentecostal churches are independent of any mainland denomination. In 1919 evangelist Thomas MacGuire started a Glad Tidings mission and organized a Pentecostal church. The congregation was Hawaiian and Spanish. In 1928 the Hawaiian congregation became the *Hawaiian Pentecostal Church* and relocated at Gulick and Beckley streets. The members insisted upon the use of the Hawaiian language. The present pastor is the Reverend Solomon Wainee. The present name of the church is the Hawaiian Pentecostal Full Gospel Assembly, but it is completely independent. The Reverend Solomon Naauoa, who was affiliated with this church, conducted a Haven of Rest Mission.

The *Door of Faith* churches are also Pentecostal. The Reverend Mildred Brostek came to Hawaii as a young woman and held evangelistic services in a store building on King Street near Middle Street. The meetings grew and now there is a large church at 1161 Young Street. The Door of Faith workers went to the other islands, and it is now a statewide denomination. Most Door of Faith ministers have been women; one of the tragedies of the church was the murder of Mrs. Elizabeth Trager, who conducted a storefront mission in Wahiawa.

The *Samoan Pentecostal Church,* the *Puerto-Rican Pentecostal Church,* and a Filipino Pentecostal Church with the name *The Way of Salvation* are all independent churches. The *Kalihi Community Church* came into being after the split of the *Pentecostal Faith Assembly,* which was also started by Thomas MacGuire.

Other churches have developed from the pattern of an evangelist who conducted services. The *Four Square Gospel Mission* and the *Full Gospel Mission* are active. The Full Gospel Mission has its headquarters and the Hawaiian Bible Institute at 2464 North School Street.

The most successful of these churches is the *Apostolic Faith Church*. In 1925 the Reverend and Mrs. Charles Lochbaum came to Honolulu and set up a tent near King and Middle streets. Later a church was built at this location, and a branch established in Kaimuki and another in Lahaina. These churches are often called by the names of their large electric signs. The Middle Street Church and the church in Lahaina are sometimes referred to as "Jesus Coming Soon Church," and the Kaimuki Church as "Jesus, the Light of the World." There is also an Apostolic Faith branch on Molokai.

At the death of Mrs. Lochbaum, Mr. Lochbaum transferred the title of all his property to the congregation. He served as pastor emeritus. The Reverend William M. Han is the head pastor. Mr. Gustavus Sproat, one of the leaders, became a pastor when he retired from his position as clerk of the Supreme Court.

The many evangelistic centered churches are in large part small congregations, but some have come to positions of prominence. *Kaimuki Community Church,* organized in 1947, began with the part-time service of its pastor the Reverend Byron D. Boone, who was a police officer.

A new church has been built at Kaimuki and Seventh avenues. The congregation maintains a mission station in Jahore, Malaysia, Miss Adeline Char being in charge.

The Kapahulu Bible Church, established in 1949, is a member of the Christian and Missionary Alliance and has a strong program. The Reverend Gordon Fowler is pastor.

Dr. Theodore Richards supported a mission project named the Kakaako Mission. Nondenominational and fervently evangelistic, Kakaako Mission operated much like rescue missions in large cities. The Kakaako area became industrial with a zoning for industrial purposes only. The last evangelist at Kakaako was a Reverend Don Rohrs of the Missionary Church Association, and the trustees of Kakaako Mission transferred the mission with its assets to the *Moanalua Gardens Missionary Church.*

Many of these evangelists belong to evangelistic groups which have become semidenominations. The Church Missionary Association has seven workers besides Pastor Rohrs. Evangelists connected with the *Independent Fundamental Churches of America* established the Maile Bible Center in 1947 and have centers in Palolo Valley and Makaha. Grace Chapel of Honolulu, which began in the old Lutheran Church on Beretania near Punchbowl, belongs to a group which is called the *New Testament Church.*

BRETHREN

In the Reformation period the Anabaptist movement sought to make radical changes in the church, especially in its relationship to the state. Persecuted by both Catholics and Protestants in Germany, many groups with Anabaptist antecedents came to America. The Amish and Mennonite groups still live according to the pattern of two centuries ago.

The Moravians settled in Bethlehem, Pennsylvania, and the Brethren in Germantown, Pennsylvania. The Church of the Brethren became the largest of these German churches in America. In 1883 a split took place in the Church of the Brethren, and the more conservative group termed itself the Brethren Church. Some Brethren churches use the name Grace Brethren, and this group is in Hawaii.

Like many other churches, the work of the Grace Brethren Church began with a dedicated serviceman. In 1953 Technical Sergeant and Mrs. Edwin Jones persuaded the Brethren Foreign Mission Office to send two missionaries; the Reverend and Mrs. Foster Tresise. The Brethren now have churches at Waimalu and in Waipio, both areas with many service families.

While differing in its origin, the Brethren Church is quite similar to the other Fundamental Evangelistic groups.

1. Mimeographed letter No. ten of the Church of God in Christ, Kapaa, Kauai.

18. Jehovah's Witnesses

The belief in the second coming of Christ was a major doctrine of the 19th century. American optimism emphasized the coming of a millenial age, a thousand years of peace in which Christ would personally rule.

Emphasizing this millenial viewpoint, the Reverend Charles Taze Russell organized the International Bible Student Association in 1872. Among his followers was Judge Joseph F. Rutherford, who succeeded Pastor Russell and adopted the name Jehovah's Witnesses. In 1942 Dr. Nathan Homer Knorr became the leader. The legal title to all corporation property is held by the Watch Tower Bible and Tract Society of Pennsylvania, and at times Watch Tower is used as equivalent to the term Jehovah's Witnesses.

Judge Rutherford, during the first world war, had a celebrated lecture which was given all over America. This lecture, entitled "Millions Now Living Shall Never Die," was translated into Hawaiian—"Miliona e Ola Mai aole loa e Make." The translation into Hawaiian was made by W. J. Coelho. This was about 1920, but there is no evidence that any successful work was started in Hawaii at that time.

In 1934 the Hawaii Branch of the Watch Tower Bible and Tract Society was established. Mr. Donald Hasslet directed the work in Hawaii until 1948, when he went to Japan. Appointed were Mr. and Mrs. Keith Stebbins, who were responsible for the major growth of the Jehovah's Witnesses. Differing from the millenialists in other Christian churches, the Jehovah's Witnesses proclaim that only those dedicated to the Kingdom of God shall survive in the destruction of the world. All others will be destroyed, not sent to Hell. Hell does not exist, say the Witnesses. The second emphasis is that Jehovah alone is God. Jesus Christ is high priest and perfect man, but not God. Emphasizing that Christ preached of the Kingdom, they reject the present churches, both Catholic and Protestant, and call their religious edifices Kingdom Halls. Outstanding are their conventions, usually held in summer. About 1,500 Jehovah's Witnesses have attended these summer district assemblies.

People of all racial groups in Hawaii have become Jehovah's Witnesses. Mr. Eugene Paoa is leader of the Kaimuki Kingdom Hall. Miss Patricia Nakayama attended the Watch Tower Bible School of Gilead, New York, and was sent to Japan as a missionary. The branch director who succeeded Mr. Keith Stebbins is Mr. Robert K. Kawasaki.

The Jehovah's Witnesses are not pacifists but regard all present government as evil. Since all members of Jehovah's Witnesses are ministers, they claim exemption from the draft. In Hawaii the draft boards are unwilling to exempt all members as being ministers or as members of a pacifist church. One youth who had not registered for the draft was charged with draft evasion, and he enlisted to avoid the charges; but in the main the draft boards in Hawaii have not made an issue and have granted exemption.

There are about twenty Kingdom Halls in the state, and many young people are engaged in the tasks of visitation and selling of Watch Tower literature.

19. The Independent Hawaiian Churches

There are a number of independent Hawaiian churches. Some of these have branches and are listed as denominations in the book *The Religious Bodies of America*. Others are more expressions of family religious unity than ecclesiastical organizations.

These churches have various origins. Some were early mission churches that did not join the Hawaiian Evangelical Association. Others were offshoots, for a number of reasons, of the Congregational Church. A third group came into being as part of some other religious activity such as revival meetings.

MISSIONARY-RELATED CHURCHES

The church in Niihau is an example of the first type. The Reverend George Roll, an early missionary, organized the church on Niihau, and the church today maintains the pattern which was common in Hawaiian churches a century ago. When the Hawaiian Evangelical Association was formed, the missionary pastor at Waimea, who also supervised the Niihau Church, did not enter the Association, and both churches became independent.

The Waimea Church had two language congregations, Hawaiian and English. The English-speaking congregation was organized as the First Foreign Church and is still independent. The Hawaiian congregation of Waimea joined the Hawaiian Evangelical Association. The isolated Niihau Church has its own pastors. The Reverend John Kaohelaulii is the present pastor. The Sunday services are usually an all-day community sharing. The Reverend Ella Wise Harrison of Honolulu is a frequent visitor, and the present ties of Niihau are with the church Ka Makua Mau Loa rather than the United Church of Christ.

THE FAMILY CHURCHES

Most Hawaiians have a strong family loyalty, which has been both the strength and weakness of a number of independent churches. One group has a common history. In the Kalahikiola Church in Kohala, Hawaii, a factional feud developed which led to the establishment of an independent church by the Reverend J. H. Poliwailehua in 1853. Some years later some of this congregation moved to Oahu. The Reverend John Kekipi Maia was pastor, and the name of the church is Ke Alaula Oka Malama-lama Hoomana Naauoa O Hawaii (The Bright Morning Rays of the Church of Reasonable Service of Hawaii). The church building at 910 Cooke Street was built in 1897. As branches developed, the name Hoomana Naauoa O Hawaii was used as the denominational name.

Following John Kekipi Maia as pastor was his son, then his son-in-law and daughter, the Reverend and Mrs. Andrew Iaukea Bright, Sr.

The Bright family was large, and the sons and daughters, learning to sing Hawaiian in church, became outstanding Hawaiian entertainers.

The Reverend Moses K. Piohia is the pastor of the Cooke Street church and also president of the denomination. A number of descendants of the Reverend James Kekela, Hawaiian missionary to the Marquesans, are members of Hoomana Naauoa, and the Reverend David Kekela is pastor in Hilo. The Daniel Kaopuiki family have been leaders on Lanai. The Hoomana Naauoa branch at Koae near Kapoho was destroyed in the 1960 volcanic eruption.

Some years after the building of the Cooke Street church, twelve members left the church and established a separate church—The Church of the Living God (Hawaiian title, Ka Makua Mau Loa Ho'omana O Ke Akua Ola). A church building at Mokauea and Kaumualii streets was dedicated in 1911. This was replaced in 1947. In 1937 the long-time pastor the Reverend John Wise was succeeded by his daughter, the Reverend Ella Wise Harrison. The church has faith healing as one of its tenets, and all pastors and secondary pastors *(hopekahu)* use services of healing in which ancient Hawaiian ideas are united with Biblical material. Five branches exist on the other islands. Located near Oahu Prison, the church has carried on work in the prison.

In 1948 some members left the church to establish Ka Hale Hoano Hou O Ke Akua. The full English name of the church is The Hallowed House of God, King of Kings and Lord of Lords. Lieutenant Commander W. H. Abbey

led in the early days, but the Reverend Edward Ayau of
Molokai became the spiritual leader. A church was built
in Kalihi in 1954, but the church on Molokai is the main
church.

Another family type church is Kealaokalamalama (The
Way of the Light) in Kailua-Kona. A great spiritual
leader among the Hawaiians was the Reverend Akaiko
Akana, pastor of Kawaiahao Church from 1918 to 1933.
He was from Kona, and after his death a church was built
in his memory. His brother, the Reverend Francis K.
Akana, Sr., was the leader. The church was organized in
1935, and a temple was dedicated on July 17, 1936. The
present pastor is Francis K. Akana, Jr. A Honolulu branch
is located at 1207 Prospect Street.

OTHER INDEPENDENT CHURCHES

Some independent Hawaiian churches came into being
because the looseness of Congregational ties gave no
denominational loyalty or control. The Hawaiian Church
at Koloa, Kauai, was an early missionary church. Today
the congregation is an Assembly of God Church, although
the property does not belong to that denomination.

A woman from Ka'u, Hawaii, Mrs. Edith Auld, had a
gift of healing, and many came to her for help. Just before
World War II she established a church at Houghtailing
and Vineyard streets with the name The Gospel of
Salvation. A new church was constructed in 1959. Mrs.
Auld died in 1959, but members of the family continue as
leaders. The church does not enroll members and emphasizes the services of healing and prayer.

Other churches came into being as an evangelist or religious worker came to Hawaii, made some converts, and then left. The little group of converts organized a church and became an independent group. The Hawaiian Pentecostal Church on Gulick Street is an independent church with services in Hawaiian. Lanakila Church at 10th Avenue and Maunaloa Avenue was built in 1946 by a group which used the title The Church of the Gospel of Jesus Christ. Under the leadership of Pastor Ryan Y. Dung, the Lanakila Church is largely Hawaiian.

The True Jesus Mission of the Latter Rain is led by James P. Awana. The Hawaiian branch has become independent but is aware of mainland ties.

At Haleiwa a branch of Ka Makua Mau Loa, under the leadership of Joseph S. Kuni, became independent. The name today is Kealiiokamalu (Prince of Peace).

No complete list of these independent Hawaiian churches is possible. Often a grandmother has gathered her grandchildren for Sunday school teachings, and the family worship *(ohana)* supports a vital religious life. These independent churches have fostered a family type sharing with services in Hawaiian. Belatedly, some are using English.

20. Faith and Health

In the past century medical science has made tremendous advances in theory and practice. The first discoveries that definite diseases had definite causes and could be prevented by a definite treatment gave the hope that diseases could be entirely eliminated. The medical emphasis came to be upon definite physical causes and effects, often ignoring the psychosomatic relationships of mind and body.

Consequently, both in medicine and in religion, persons dealing with the psychosomatic had considerable success. The patent medicine vendor at a county fair and the faith healer in a tent were dealing with a fact in human existence that scientific medicine in the 19th century discounted—a person's physical health is directly related to that person's emotional and spiritual health.

Today when mental health institutions provide clinical training for clergymen, and denominations (such as the Episcopal with their St. Luke's Society) support the type of spiritual ministry once termed faith healing, it is difficult to realize the chasm that existed between religion and medicine in this area a century ago.

Two generalizations are possible: medical teaching (as distinct from medical practice) dealt with patients as physical problems; religious groups which emphasized a faith and health relationship made significant contributions to religion.

CHRISTIAN SCIENCE

The largest and most successful of the groups which sought health through faith is Christian Science. Christian Science had a view of life which related mind and body with a theology which supported that view. Mary Baker Eddy was the founder of Christian Science. A woman of neurotic nature, she was healed apparently through hypnotic suggestion. She combined the method of psychological suggestion with religious motivation. She published her ideas in the book *Science and Health* in 1875, after having practiced and taught the ideas for a number of years. The Christian Scientists were formed in 1875, but it was 1882 before the Church of Christ Scientist was formed in Boston.

The Christian Science healings have been many, but today, as when Mrs. Eddy founded the church, the cure still depends upon the degree to which the mental and emotional state can affect the physical state of the patient.

Religiously, Christian Science recognized the age old dilemma of Christianity—if God is all powerful and God is all good, why is there evil in the world? The traditional Christian answers relating to this dilemma, such as Original Sin, the Atonement of Christ, and redemption, were dismissed. Mrs. Eddy resolved the dilemma by denying the existence of evil as a reality; to her evil was an error of mortal mind. The simplicity of this solution appealed to many whose American optimism could no longer accept the logic of Calvinism, which had solved the dilemma through the unregenerate nature of man.

Christian Science came to Hawaii through Mrs. Helen Whitney Kelley, granddaughter of the pioneer missionary Samuel Whitney. She held meetings in her home beginning in 1898. In 1902 a larger meeting place was secured and regular Sunday services and lectures were held, and a church was built in 1909 when the group of twenty-six organized as a church and applied to the Mother Church for a charter. The charter was received in January 1910 for the First Church of Christ Scientist, Honolulu. The present structure at 1508 Punahou Street was built in 1923 and is significant as the first religious structure in Hawaii designed to relate to its Hawaiian environment. The Christian Science Church maintained work for servicemen, and the Aloha Chapel in the Pearl Harbor area served as church and meeting place. Other centers were established in such places as Wahiawa and Kailua on Oahu, Hilo, and Kaunakakai.

For years the church has maintained reading rooms in downtown Honolulu and in Waikiki. Since one aspect of Christian Science is the treatment by practitioners, there is a Christian Science office in the Ala Moana Building, 1441 Kapiolani Boulevard, where three practitioners are available. Others are available through the various church centers.

NEW THOUGHT—UNITY

Mrs. Mary Baker Eddy had a follower and co-worker, Mrs. Emma Curtis Hopkins. Mrs. Hopkins left Christian Science and became a lecturer, emphasizing mental, emotional, and spiritual health with its effects in physical health and success. Mrs. Hopkins founded no church, but her ideas influenced a number of others who founded such organizations as the Unity School of Christianity, Divine Science, and the Church of Religious Science. These new thought groups all emphasize that health and prosperity can be yours if your thinking is right.

In the 20th century, Norman Vincent Peale echoed many of their ideas while remaining in a regular denomination, but in the 19th century, when revivalism emphasized the lostness of man, man's inability to help himself, and man's need of repentance, the new-thought advocates left the churches to propagate their ideas.

THE UNITY CHURCH

The Unity Church began with the work of the Reverend Charles Fillmore, a Methodist minister in Missouri who did not regard Unity as a new denomination but as a movement to emphasize the importance of faith in mental health and healing. The Unity School of Christianity and a publishing house printing Unity literature existed long before Unity incorporated itself as a denomination.

The Reverend Marie Handley founded Unity Church of Hawaii in 1937, and for years conducted a reading room as well as church services at 240 Lewers Road. This is still a reading room and meditation center. The Reverend Philip Pierson led the church in a building program at 3608 Diamond Head Circle. The present pastor is the Reverend V. Stanford Hampson.

THE CHURCH OF RELIGIOUS SCIENCE

The Church of Religious Science was founded by Dr. Ernest Holmes, who stated that "Religious Science is a correlation of laws of science, opinions of philosophy, and revelations of religion applied to human need and the aspirations of man."[1]

The definition of God in Religious Science is not different from that of the majority of Christian churches. Dr. Holmes emphasized a Universal Mind and that through its operation the sick can be healed and persons can control conditions. Consequently, the services of Religious Science are very similar to the liberal Protestant churches.

Persons interested in the Church of Religious Science held meetings in a Waikiki hotel and obtained a charter for a church in 1954.

The Reverend Lillian Caldwell came in 1959 and soon found a location for the church on Lewers Road. After some years the lease ended, and the church conducted services at a number of locations, including the Seicho no Ie Church at 1333 Matlock Avenue. The faith and health teachings of Religious Science are quite similar to those of Seicho no Ie. In 1968 they obtained the former Pentecostal Holiness Church at 225-A Hualani Street in Kailua.

The poet Don Blanding was a member, and after his

death the name became the Don Blanding Memorial
Church of Religious Science.

DIVINE SCIENCE CHURCH

Members of Divine Science churches came to Hawaii, and
the International Federation of Divine Science Churches
decided to organize a church in Honolulu. Recently the
church was established with thirty charter members. The
Reverend Marjorie Goslin is pastor, with offices and a
teaching center at 342 Lewers Street.

I AM ACTIVITY

The I AM faith had a totally different origin from new
thought, yet the emphasis upon spiritual thought resulting
in physical health is the same.

Saint Germain of France is accepted as one of the
Ascended Masters who govern earth, whose influence
helped in the drafting of the Declaration of Independence
and the Constitution. In 1932 Saint Germain brought the
light of the Mighty I AM Presence through a messenger,
Mr. Guy W. Ballard. Prayers became decrees, such as
that which the Ascended Master Jesus gave: "Be ye
perfect." This affirmation becomes, "Some day you must
cleanse, purify, perfect, illumine and raise the physical
body into the Electronic Body of your beloved Mighty
I AM Presence when you become the ascended being."[2]

The I AM Sanctuary in Honolulu is located at 3745
Claudine Street. Their work began in 1938. Mrs. Eva
Boyd is the present leader in charge of the Honolulu
Sanctuary.

THE CHURCH OF SCIENTOLOGY

Modern man believes but also distrusts his technological civilization. Many modern men feel all would be well if man had both wisdom and technical competence, and the Church of Scientology has this appeal. Scientology is a Western continuance of many earlier forms of wisdom— the Vedas, Tao, Gautama, the Hebrews, Jesus, and philosophers from the Greeks to Freud. This wisdom needs a technology called Dianetics. All religion has seen that self-appraisal or confession is the first step. In Scientology the confessional is called Auditing, and a 20th-century electrometer is used as a confessional aid. Mr. Ron Hubbard has developed a training system by which Scientologists can advance to the highest levels— there are about sixteen levels—half by training in the theory and practice of Scientology and half by becoming an auditor or counselor. The highest level are in England, where Hubbard now lives.

The reported successes of Scientology are as diverse as improved I.Q.'s, improved musical ability, the overcoming of fits of depression, the stopping of use of drugs, the cure of chronic stomach pain, the improved training of horses for obedience trials, and the providing of a new sense of responsibility. So Scientology promises the answer to every problem which man has in our computer age.

The Church of Scientology in Hawaii has its headquarters in Aina Haina at 142 Nenue Street.

1. Quoted on Sunday service programs of the Church of Religious Science.
2. *The Purpose of the Ascended Masters I AM Activity*, Saint Germain Press, Santa Fe, New Mexico, n.d., p. 51.

21. The Unitarian Fellowship of Hawaii

At the same time the American Board sent the first missionaries to Hawaii, the churches of New England were in the midst of the Unitarian controversy. Numerous congregations in New England became Unitarian—that is, while still believing in God they rejected the Trinitarian concept. The fervent missionary zeal which sent men to Hawaii was Trinitarian, but when the missionary families sent their children back to New England to school, some returned with Unitarian ideas.

Sanford B. Dole, president of the Republic of Hawaii and first governor of the Territory of Hawaii, was a life-long attendant of Central Union Church, but never a member. He held to Unitarian ideas. Charles Reed Bishop, banker husband of the princess Bernice Pauahi, contributed to every good cause, religious and educational. He was not a member of Central Union, although chairman of the Board of Trustees. In later life Mr. Bishop became a member of the Unitarian Church of San Francisco, and later he became a member of the Berkeley Unitarian Church. Dole, Bishop, and a number of other

prominent men in Honolulu at the time of annexation
had beliefs which were Unitarian.

However, no attempt was made to organize a Unitarian
church. A number of Unitarians were active in such
churches as the Church of the Crossroads. In 1953
Dr. Frank Ricker, field secretary of the Unitarian
Association, visited Hawaii, and a Fellowship of Unitarians was started. The Fellowship asked Dr. Ricker to
return as pastor. The Fellowship held Sunday services at
the Hawaiian Mission Academy. In 1961 they purchased
the former Cooke home at 2500 Pali Highway, which is
now their church.

Traditionally the Unitarian Church has been intel-
lectually oriented. Some Unitarian churches have held to
Biblical and Christian emphasis interpreted liberally.
Others were humanistic, denying any theistic belief. But
both groups felt that religious belief required rational
examination. The second pastor, the Reverend Gene
Bridges, became a controversial figure. In the church,
where many members prided themselves upon being
intellectual, Bridges introduced political activism and
sensitivity training. The control of the church passed to
the supporters of Bridges, and the older members talked
of establishing a second Unitarian church.

An almost forgotten incident at the Unitarian Church
shows the multiplicity of influences in Hawaii. Mrs.
Madelyn Murray, a self-proclaimed atheist, came to
Hawaii to avoid arrest in Baltimore. Without resources
she and her family were sheltered at the Unitarian
Church. During her stay in Hawaii she announced she

would found an Atheistic Society but left when the State of Maryland prepared to extradite her.

22. The Filipino Churches

The major faith of Filipinos is Roman Catholicism. There are Filipino Catholic priests in Hawaii, and the Filipino Catholic clubs are active in many parishes. The Catholic Social Service has long recognized special problems in regard to the Filipinos in Hawaii. Typical was the importation in 1946 of five thousand laborers. These men had been recruited hurriedly just before the independence of the Philippines stopped free access of Filipinos into the United States. Five thousand men, either unmarried or with wives who remained in the Philippines, were social problems, and all community agencies, including the churches, have sought to solve the problem. Isolated from many community contacts, some of them found contacts with churches other than the Catholic. The Pentecostal Gospel of Salvation Church at Kalihi and Beckley streets is mostly Filipino.

A number of Filipinos have become religious workers and preachers for such churches, and the street preachers who appear in downtown Honolulu are mostly Filipino. In religion they have found a meaning. There are a few Filipino groups which require special discussion.

COMMUNITY CHURCHES

The Congregational and Methodist churches had cooperative work with Filipinos, bringing some Protestant workers from the Philippines. One was a Methodist worker, the Reverend N. C. Dizon. After some years, Mr. Dizon left the Methodist Mission and established the First Filipino Community Church at 838 Kanoa Street. Later, work was started in Hilo, and in 1960 a church was dedicated in Wahiawa. The Reverend Joseph H. Dizon is now pastor of the Honolulu church. These churches are an independent denomination, congregational in government.

MONCADO FOUNDATION OF AMERICA

General Hilario Camino Moncado, whose qualifications ranged from being a five-star general of Philippine guerrillas during the Japanese occupation to being an international golfer with a handicap of three, was the founder and president of the Filipino Federation of America. The Federation operated mostly in California and Hawaii. A small subdivision in upper Kalihi Valley was named Moncado Village as a Filipino center. After the general's death, his wife, Mrs. Diana Moncado, established the Moncado Foundation of America with offices at 1534 Kalaepaa Drive. Mrs. Moncado was a singer who had sung with operatic companies in Europe and America.

General Moncado had written that "man's moral concept is but man's great divine power to achieve all things on earth."[1] Thus the Federation had religious appeal without being a denomination. In 1957 Mrs. Moncado visited the Shrine of Our Lady of Guadalupe in Mexico and brought to Honolulu a reproduction of Our Lady of Guadalupe. This was placed on the altar in the Foundation Hall, which was designated Guadalupe Church. Although persons belonging to the Moncado Foundation may be of any faith, Guadalupe Church has Sunday services followed by Sunday school. On August 11, the Feast of Our Lady of Guadalupe, the Moncado Foundation has a procession with special prayers and devotion. Guadalupe Church is Roman Catholic in basic belief, and in the future it can become a lay organization of Filipinos within the Catholic Church or an independent, separate denomination.

Mrs. Diana Moncado died in 1964, and her son, Mr. Mario Moncado, is now head of the Moncado Foundation.

THE PHILIPPINE INDEPENDENT CHURCH

The Roman Catholic Church leaders in the Philippines for centuries had been Spanish, and even before 1898 the struggle against the Spaniards had religious overtones. This resulted in various religious expressions in the Philippines, one of which was the Philippine Independent Church, a modified Catholicism. This church, with bishops, was recognized as being in fellowship with the Anglican churches of the world.

Missionaries of the Episcopal Church cooperated with the Philippine Independent Church for years before the denomination came to Hawaii. In August 1959 a cooperative venture with the Episcopal Church was developed. The Philippine Independent Church has its own congregations, but they meet in Episcopal churches whenever possible. Ten preaching stations were developed with three priests. The Reverend Timotheo P. Quintero is the priest in charge. The work is supervised by the Episcopal bishop, although the denominational work is directed from Manila. The report indicates that there are about seven hundred communicants.

FULL GOSPEL MISSION

The Full Gospel Mission in Hawaii is interracial, but the district superintendent provides an example of religious change and leadership among the Filipinos. The Reverend E. C. Liberato left the Philippines in 1926. In Los Angeles he became a member of Angelus Temple while Aimee Semple Macpherson was still the leader. In 1936 he came to Hawaii and established the Full Gospel Mission. He is now the district superintendent of the Hawaii District, which has eighteen branches in Hawaii and over a thousand members. The Full Gospel Tabernacle at 2464 North School is also the site of the Hawaii Bible Institute. Mr. Liberato also helped found and still assists in the Philippine District of the Full Gospel Mission.

1. Part of the inscription on the base of the statue of General Moncado in front of Guadalupe Church.

11. A menorah designed by Edward Brownlee.
Temple Emanu-El, Honolulu.

23. The Jewish Faith

Two mysteries highlight the first Jewish arrivals in Hawaii. A sailor on a whaling ship, Ebenezer Townsend, records that on August 19, 1798, King Kamehameha came on board and "he also brought a Jew cook with him."[1] No list of names of foreigners associated with King Kamehameha reveals a name that might have been Jewish, so this is either a mistake or an unsolved mystery.

The second mystery concerns Elijah Abraham Rosenberg, who became a friend of King Kalakaua. Although the rabbinical lists do not contain his name, he called himself a rabbi and had a magnificent Scroll of the Law (Sefer Torah) and an elaborately carved silver pointer used in reading the Scroll. He presented these to King Kalakaua, and after his stay in the Islands he disappears from history. The Scroll has been lost, but the pointer was presented to Temple Emanu-El and is now used in the services.

Jewish people were in the Islands at various times throughout the 19th century, but the first indication of any Jewish services was an authorization of Layman Elias

Pech to conduct Jewish weddings. In 1901 a Jewish Benevolent Society was organized and a Jewish cemetery was established. The group estimated that there were about one hundred Jews in Hawaii then, including those who did not practice the Jewish faith. Holy Day services were held in private homes or rented clubrooms.

The number increased, although most of the Jews came only on short-term contracts or as members of the armed forces. To care for Jewish personnel in the armed forces, the National Jewish Welfare Board sent Mr. and Mrs. Alexander Linczer to Hawaii in 1923. Jewish residents of Honolulu attended the services at the Jewish Welfare Center, and in 1938 they formally organized the Honolulu Jewish Community. There were about forty families in this community, and they did superb work for Jewish refugees from Europe and on projects with personnel of the armed forces.

In 1950 the National Jewish Welfare Board closed its work. The congregation of the Honolulu Jewish Community reorganized itself as a religious body, and Temple Emanu-El came into being. Barnett Sapiro was the first president, and in 1951 Rabbi Francis Hevesi, formerly chief rabbi of Budapest, became the first rabbi of Temple Emanu-El.

Under the leadership of the second rabbi, Alexander Segel, the temple became associated with Reformed Judaism, joining the Union of American Hebrew Congregations. Temple Emanu-El held services first in the chapel at Fort DeRussy. In 1951 they purchased a home in Manoa Valley and converted it into a temple. In 1959 they sold the home. For a year they held Sabbath services at the Church of the Crossroads. In 1960 they dedicated the permanent temple on the Pali Highway.

Architect Edward Sullam designed Temple Emanu-El to fit its location in Nuuanu Valley. The sanctuary is a blend of traditional Jewish aspects with a modern emphasis. "Strong vertical accents emphasize the finite stature of man as he confronts God."[2] The Ark containing the Scrolls of the Law is the center of Jewish worship. On the doors of the Ark are teakwood tablets symbolizing the tablets of the law. Incised upon them are the letters which begin the Ten Commandments in Hebrew. Suspended from the ceiling above the Ark is the Eternal Light, a bronze lamp with winged symbolism. This lamp is dedicated to the millions of Jewish martyrs who died in World War II.

Temple Emanu-El was built under the leadership of Rabbi Roy A. Rosenberg and attorney Bernard Levinson, who was president of the congregation. Mr. Levinson, who served from 1950 to 1960, is now a justice of the Supreme Court of Hawaii. Nathaniel Felzer and Alex Schaffer followed as presidents of the temple. In 1966 Rabbi Robert Schenkerman came as the spiritual leader.

Temple Emanu-El has the usual auxiliary organizations most churches have: the Sisterhood, men's club, and youth activities. They also have a special program—the Institute for Adult Jewish Studies—which people of the community as well as members of the congregation may attend.

The traditional Jewish confirmation training which

leads to the Bar Mitzvah (for boys) or Bat Mitzvah (for girls) is still a major part of the religious school.

For many years the armed forces have arranged to have a Jewish chaplain stationed in Hawaii. Temple Emanu-El has cooperated with the Jewish personnel, especially at the times of the Jewish Holy Days.

1. Dedication booklet of Temple Emanu-El, Honolulu, 1960.
2. Brochure for Temple Emanu-El, Honolulu, 1966.

24. The Military Chapels

The chaplains of the military services have enriched the religious life of Hawaii. These men of God in the service of their country have found time to participate in the community and in the religious faiths to which they belong. The examples of their courage and faithfulness inspire all who know them. Numerous clergymen of the community have served as chaplains in the armed forces. The Reverend Hiro Higuchi and the Reverend Masao Yamada, who served with the 442nd Regiment during World War II, are typical of these dedicated men. The first chaplains to die in World War II died on December 7, 1941, in the attack on Pearl Harbor. Chaplain Aloysius Schmitt was on the U.S.S. *Oklahoma,* and the Fleet Chaplain, Thomas Kirkpatrick, still lies entombed with the men of the U.S.S. *Arizona.*

All the major military establishments in Hawaii have chapels. Most were the wooden cantonment chapels of World War II. St. Roch's Church at Kahuku was a cantonment chapel and was moved to its present location when the army installation became surplus after World

War II. The first chapel erected was the old Post Chapel at Schofield Barracks, built in 1915 with funds that came from civilian communities as well as the military. The air force has erected a permanent chapel at Hickam Air Force Base, and the army erected one at Schofield Barracks, magnificent structures which show the value of religious faith to the military.

The chapels of the military services are designed to be used by all faiths, and a fine cooperation exists between religious faiths. For example, Tripler Army Hospital has three small chapels for Jewish, Catholic, and Protestant use, with one large chapel which can be used by any of the three. This hospital chapel also has two paintings by a former patient portraying the work of the Catholic and Protestant chaplains in the South Pacific during World War II.

The most spectacular of the religious establishments associated with the military no longer exists. Italian prisoners of war captured in North Africa in World War II were brought to Hawaii. In a prisoner-of-war camp directly opposite the Wheeler Air Force Base, these prisoners erected a shrine. Astori Rebato of Venice, an architect, designed the shrine with classic pillars. It was dedicated to Mother Cabrini, the Italian-born American saint. Artists among the prisoners portrayed her life.

When the prisoners returned home, the camp, except for the shrine, was abandoned. Built over an irrigation well, the concrete shrine began to crack, and vandals visited the isolated place. The paintings were removed and placed in the Catholic Diocesan Chancellory, and the army demolished the building, but the memory remains as a gesture of aloha from the Italian prisoners of war to Hawaii.

12. Mother Cabrini Shrine, Italian prisoner-of-war camp, Wahiawa, Oahu. ARCHITECT: ASTORI REBATO, VENICE.

13. *Buddha*—driftwood carving by Fritz Abplanalp,
exhibited at Seattle World's Fair.

25. Buddhism

BUDDHA

A short survey of Buddhism is necessary for an understanding of Buddhism in Hawaii. Siddhartha Gautama was born in Nepal 2,500 years ago. Japanese Buddhists use the name Shakamuni (Sakyamuni in Sanskrit, meaning the teacher of the Sakya clan). He lived a carefree and happy life, completely isolated from any pain and sorrow. Suddenly becoming aware of disease, old age, and death, he left his home to find the meaning of existence.

Siddhartha Gautama accepted the Hindu concepts of reincarnation and karma. He sought for release from the fate of endless reincarnations. When he discovered the Four Noble Truths in an experience of enlightenment, he became the Buddha, or the Enlightened One.

These are the Four Noble Truths of Buddhism:

1. Life is pain and unhappiness.
2. Pain and unhappiness come from desire, from selfish craving.
3. This desire or craving can be overcome.
4. The way of overcoming is through the eightfold path:

Right (or correct) understanding
Right purpose
Right speech
Right conduct
Right vocation
Right effort
Right alertness
Right concentration

Two major forms of Buddhism developed. The earlier form was known as Theravada, or "the way of the elders." This is the Buddhism of the Southeast Asian countries. Mahayana Buddhism (the second form) applies the name of Hinayana, or "the lesser vehicle," to this form of Buddhism.

MAHAYANA BUDDHISM

Mahayana Buddhism, "the greater vehicle," developed in India and spread to China and Japan. It is the Buddhism of Hawaii. Mahayana Buddhism showed great variety in its growth. One of its first developments was the conviction that a person who had attained potential Buddhahood, and so was prepared to enter Nirvana, would work to aid mortals and even after death would refuse the bliss of Nirvana to remain a compassionate spirit aiding the unfortunate. These compassionate beings were termed Boddhisattvas. The greatest of these Boddhisattvas was named Kwan Yin in China, and Kannon, the Goddess of Mercy, in Japan. Kwan Yin's infinite compassion and helpfulness are symbolized in figures with many arms. The Soto Mission Temple has a thousand-year-old statue of the Goddess of Mercy, predating the founding of the Soto Sect. The Chinese Temple at River and Vineyard streets is primarily a temple of Kwan Yin.

A second development of Mahayana Buddhism is the belief in Amida Buddha. Early in Buddhism many believed that Gautama Buddha had a divine existence previous to his birth as a mortal. Faith developed in other manifestations of this divine Buddha, among them Amida Buddha. To some, Gautama Buddha was one earthly appearance of Amida Buddha. In Japan, faith in Amida Buddha's infinite compassion became the most popular form of Buddhism. Amida was said to have such great compassion that any who trusted in Amida and had faith would go to the Pure Land. In the Pure Land their souls would receive the cleansing that would permit entrance at last into Nirvana. Most of the Buddhists in Hawaii believe in Amida Buddha. The more conservative pray to Amida as a being of such compassion that they have but to pray and their needs will be fulfilled. More modernistic Buddhists feel that Amida is the symbolic representation of the compassion of all Buddhas.

Zen Buddhism is the form of Buddhism that has aroused the greatest interest among Westerners. Zen is a psychological discipline in which intuitional enlightenment is sought. Since most religions feel that intuitional knowledge is part of religion, the disciplines of Zen attract even Christian thinkers, who seek to use its techniques without accepting its impersonal theology.

THE JAPANESE IN HAWAII

Although some Buddhist influence came with the early
Chinese to Hawaii, the first organized Buddhist work
came when the first Japanese laborers came to work on
the plantations of Hawaii in 1887. The Reverend Ejun
Miyamoto was the first missionary from Japan, and in
1888 the Reverend Soryu Kagai was appointed by the
Nishi Honganji as its official representative. Later other
Buddhist groups came to Hawaii. Most Shinto and Buddhist groups expanded to build temples and start ethnic-
language schools. In 1920 there were about 20,000 students in 163 Japanese-language schools. These schools
were usually held in the late afternoons. The 1920 plantation strike and the existence of these schools led to laws
(later declared unconstitutional) to curb them. In 1934
there were 41,192 children in the schools. Ethnic-language
schools were religious. Some were conducted by Christian
churches, but most were Buddhist. With the outbreak of
World War II, all were closed, and many of the teachers,
particularly those Buddhist priests who had been in the
Islands a short time, were taken to internment camps. The
Japanese in Hawaii grew concerned as the leaders in the
ethnic-language schools, temples, and shrines were ar-
rested and subjected to internment. In many cases Hawaiian Japanese donated the schools to some organization. On Kauai "everyone of the 22 Japanese-language
schools, all of the 14 Japanese cultural associations, and
even eight Buddhist temples and Shinto shrines" were
dissolved and "donated to agencies such as the Red Cross,

Y.M.C.A., Veterans' Trust Fund or specific community purposes."[1]

The Nisei led in this panic dissolution of temples, shrines, and schools. The older Japanese resented this and after the war compelled many of the younger generation to seek ways of restoring what they had abandoned under the stress of war. This was complicated by the return of the internees, embittered by their wartime imprisonment. Some of these returnees insisted upon complete loyalty to Japan, even to the extent of avowing that Japan had won the war. The Seicho no Ie Sect had members who insisted upon the victory of Japan for several years, even when their sons who had been in the American army returned home.

Buddhism has impressed itself upon the consciousness of Hawaii in many ways. Dr. Wilhelm Hillebrand of Germany purchased land at Nuuanu and School streets in 1855 and started planting tropical plants from all over the world. Kamehameha V sent him on trips to China and India to get laborers, find out various treatments for leprosy, and obtain seeds and plants. Dr. Hillebrand became interested in Buddhism and shared his interest with his friends Captain and Mrs. Thomas Foster. The Fosters purchased the Hillebrand home and gardens when Dr. Hillebrand returned to Germany. Mrs. Foster also kept an interest in Buddhism. She contributed to the excavation of the ancient site near Benares, India, where Gautama Buddha was enlightened, and she was the largest contributor to the memorial built in honor of Gautama. She gave her home and gardens to the City of Honolulu as a botanical park.

Within the gardens, appropriately, is a statue—a six foot reproduction of the Great Buddha of Kamakura, given by Governor Bungo Tsuda of Kanagawa Prefecture to the City of Honolulu to commemorate the centennial of the first Japanese immigration to Hawaii.

Commercial cemeteries have also stressed the structures of Japanese Buddhism. The Kyoto Gardens along Nuuanu Stream have a replica of the Gold Pavilion of Kyoto, and on Windward Oahu the Valley of the Temples features a replica of the Byodoin Temple of Kyoto. Over two and a half million dollars were spent for this temple of a commercial cemetery.

The Honolulu Academy of Arts has some outstanding Buddhist art, including a statue of Sakyamuni Buddha from the T'ang dynasty.

In large part the future of Buddhism has been determined by the Americans of Japanese ancestry who fought in the American armed forces. The resurgence of Buddhism led by the returning veterans is the greatest religious phenomenon of the postwar years. Shinto, more closely identified with Japan, received the continued support of older people, but it is the younger, American-born second and third generations who furnish the growing membership for the Buddhist groups. Buddhism has also attracted many of other racial groups. Most Buddhist temples conduct services in the English language, and the orientation has been increasingly to American culture. However, the newer Japanese faiths, with strong ties to Japan, have grown through the reinforcement of the ties to Japan, while the older Buddhist groups were emphasizing American ties in the years since World War II.

BON DANCES

Bon Dances are a colorful feature of the religious life of Hawaii. Although the exact date is July 15, the various Buddhist groups arrange their schedule so that a Bon Dance is held almost every weekend from late June through August. These are as much an expression of Japanese culture as Buddhist religion. The following explanation of the Bon Dance is given by the Young Buddhist Association connected with the Hompa Honganji Mission:

During the time of Shakayamuni [sic] Buddha, a disciple, Mogallana, attained to a degree of insight which enabled him to see into the depths of existence and found his mother suffering in the hell of hungry demons. In front of her was displayed a variety of food, but whenever she picked up something to eat, the food burst into flames. It was the retribution for her greed and selfishness while she lived on earth. Mogallana sought a way whereby he could relieve his mother's torments. On the advice of his teacher, Shakayamuni [sic] Buddha, he offered a huge feast in honor of the Buddha's disciples on the occasion of Varshika, which is the last day of the summer retreat. This day of reflection and resolution fell on July 15.

It is said that because of Mogallana's dana, or selfless giving, his mother was emancipated from hell and delivered to a place of higher comfort. When he learned this he was overjoyed and he and his friends celebrated the occasion with dancing and by making offerings to the priests and to their teacher, Shakayamuni [*sic*] Buddha.

What than is the modern significance of O-Bon practices? We would like to think that is a time for us to remember, honor, respect, and cherish our loved ones who have passed away. We express this feeling with reverence and joy. Reverence is an expression of honor and respect and is manifested in the hearts of those who believe in and live with Buddhism. Joy, as found in the O-Bon Dance and its festival atmosphere, expresses our happiness for what has been given to us and our happy gratitude to the Buddha and his teachings.[2]

THE BUDDHIST CALENDAR

WESAK (Buddha's Birthday)	April 8
BUDHI (Enlightment)	December 8

A public service is often held in Kapiolani Park or another location on the Sunday closest to Wesak or Budhi Day.

PARINIRVANA (Buddha's Death)	February 15
BON FESTIVALS (Late June through August)	July 15
OHIGAN (Services for the dead)	March 21
	September 22

Any of the three days before or after the equinoxes.

1. Andrew W. Lind, *Hawaii's Japanese,* Princeton University Press, 1946, published in cooperation with the American Council Institute of Pacific Relations, Inc., p. 135.

2. Young Buddhist Association of Honolulu, *Bon Dance* program leaflet, July 7, 8, 1967.

26. Buddhist Groups

TODAIJI HAWAII, BEKKAKU HONZAN

Todaiji Hawaii, Bekkaku Honzan, is the Separate Main Temple of the Kegon Sect in Hawaii. When Buddhism entered Japan, it was first established at Nara. Emperor Shomu and Empress Komyo felt that so gentle a faith needed protection and invoked the protection of fierce guardian gods. At the Hawaiian temple there are statues of these guardian gods, as well as those of the emperor and empress.

The temple and its worship is the most Japanese of any form of Buddhism in Hawaii. The temple at the corner of Jack Lane and Luakini Street is set in a magnificent Japanese garden. Central in the garden is a statue of the bishop, Mrs. Tatsusho Hirai, who, it is claimed, is the only woman Buddhist bishop in the world.

The story of Todaiji in Hawaii is mostly the story of its bishop. She was born into a family of rich religious life and graduated from a private high school. In Japanese fashion, a marriage was arranged for her. She came to Hawaii to marry the son of Japanese immigrants. Her husband was a second-generation Japanese and cared nothing for the ancestral faith which was so dear to her. The marriage failed and she was returned to her parents. Since Mrs. Hirai had wished to be a nun in her younger days, she was permitted to enter the Todaiji Temple at Nara. After years of study and preparation, she was appointed the first missionary of the Todaiji.

Her work has been successful. The temple is colorful and clean, and it is a rare privilege for visitors to attend any of the many services. The temple has carved figures of warrior gods to protect the temple. A black figure enveloped in flames is the God of Wisdom and is over 1,130 years old. There is an altar for the ceremony of cleansing by fire on the fifteenth and twenty-eighth of each month. This temple does not hold Bon Dances, but a special ceremony is held each summer. Each family builds two little boats, each about thirty-six inches long—one in honor of the husband's ancestors, the other for the wife's ancestors. About July 16 the boats are brought to the Ala Moana Park and decorated with flowers and lanterns and gifts of food. After a service by the bishop, the boats are launched and float away with their offerings of love.

Bishop Hirai is fond of conducting the tea ceremony, and her graciousness imparts a spiritual quality to a ceremony which is usually regarded simply as training in etiquette. Bishop Hirai's nephew (adopted as her son), Ryowa Hirai, is assisting her in the ceremonies.

SHINGON MISSION — TRUE WORD MISSION

Kobo Daishi founded Shingon in A.D. 806. As one of the

oldest of Buddhist Sects, it is conservative in adhering to Japanese forms.

The Shingon faith came to Hawaii in the 1900's, and the headquarters temple, at 915 Sheridan Street, was built in 1917. The services are held on the tenth and twenty-first of the month. The Shingon Mission has five branches on Oahu, five churches on Hawaii, two churches on Maui, and one church on Kauai. There are also additional meeting places besides the temple buildings. The present bishop is Bishop Tetsuei Katoda.

JODO MISSION OF HAWAII—PURE LAND MISSION

A Chinese priest named Hui-yuan (Zendo in Japanese) saw that it was impossible for most people to attain Buddhahood. Zendo, while insisting upon helping others as a requirement, taught that faith in Amida Buddha would help. Without denying the ultimate goal of Nirvana, a concept of the Pure Land came into the teaching. In Japan, Honen was the founder of Jodo. The Hawaiian headquarters temple, on Makiki Street by the freeway, has on its altar the central figure of Amida Buddha, with the figures of Honen and Zendo at the sides.

The Jodo Mission began work in Hawaii in 1898. It made adaptations to Western forms—services on Sunday as well as daily services and a broadcast of its services to followers on the other islands. The Reverend Kodo Matsunami has stated the goal of the Jodo Mission in this way:

No one can foresee the future Buddhism of Hawaii, but it will no doubt be up to us who will create our own destiny not as an inheritor of Japanese Buddhism which was brought by our predecessors but as designer of an independent Hawaiian Buddhism which is suitable to us and yet transcend our time and environment.[1]

The Jodo Mission has two other temples on Oahu, two on Kauai, three on Maui, and eight on Hawaii. For years it maintained student dormitories for members who came from the other islands to attend the University of Hawaii. The present bishop is Bishop Kyodo Fujihana.

Each year during the Bon Festival, an eight-foot skiff is constructed. After services at the temple it is taken to Kewalo Basin and towed out to sea, where it is left to float away with lanterns and other gifts for the departed. The United States Coast Guard, after frantic sea and air rescue missions arising from telephone messages saying a boat aflame or with flashing lights was adrift at sea, now requests the Jodo Mission to give advance warning of the Bon Festival.

HOMPA HONGANJI

The strongest Buddhist group to work in Hawaii is the Hompa Honganji Mission of the Jodo-Shinshu Sect, or simply Shin Sect. The Shin Sect is also the largest Buddhist denomination in Japan. Honen, the founder of the Jodo Sect, believed man was saved by faith, although ritual and working for others helped. Shinran Shonin, one of his followers, taught that man is saved by faith alone. For salvation and assurance of going to the Western Paradise or Pure Land, one needs only faith in Amida Buddha.

The Shin Sect in Hawaii has become the most Westernized of the Buddhist faiths and has formulated a creedallike statement for use in English services in Hawaii. This creed in part is: "We rely upon Tathagata Amita Buddha with our whole heart for the enlightenment in the life to come, abstaining from all sundry practices and teachings, and giving up the trust in our powerless self."

Honganji Mission founded the first Japanese-language school in the Islands at Hilo. Bishop Honi Satomi was sent from Kyoto in 1894. In 1900 Bishop Yemyo Imamura founded the Young Men's Buddhist Association, which maintains its headquarters across the street from the temple. An English night school existed before the Japanese-language school began in Honolulu. In 1907 Ryusaki Tsunoda, later head of Columbia University's Oriental Library, founded a high school with instruction in Japanese. The congregation founded an English school for the elementary grades in 1948.

Until World War II the Shin headquarters in Kyoto controlled appointments. During the war all ties were severed with Japan and the English-speaking members of the congregation elected the bishop. At present the congregation elects a bishop for a three-year term; however, the desire to keep cultural ties with Japan has usually led the congregation to vote for a bishop from Kyoto. Two recent bishops were the Right Reverend Chitoku Morikawa and Dr. Shojitsu Ohara, the latter who resigned to return to Japan in 1967. In 1967 the congregation elected the Reverend Kanmo Imamura of Berkeley, California. The Reverend Imamura, the first American-oriented

14. Hompa Honganji Temple, Honolulu.

bishop, served in Hawaii from 1934 to 1941. Then he went to Berkeley, where he was director of the Berkeley Buddhist Ministers' Training Center. He is the son of Bishop Yemyo Imamura, who served from 1899 to 1932. A statue of the first Bishop Imamura is in front of the main temple.

The temple on Fort Street is the main center of work. There are seven branches in Honolulu, besides work on every island. Since the count is by families and there are over two thousand paid members, which means heads of families in most cases, the Honganji Temple has the largest Buddhist congregation in Honolulu. There are over eleven thousand households associated with Honganji in Hawaii.

The temple is Byzantine architecture as it was brought by the Mogul invaders to India, the combined Byzantine-Indian architecture providing a distinctive place of worship. This temple has pews, pulpit, and a choir; the great drum of earlier worship has been replaced by an organ. Hymns and anthems are sung.

At Hompa Honganji, the resurgence of Buddhism after World War II was led by Japanese born and educated in America. The first president of the revived Young Buddhist Association was Mr. Ralph Honda.

The congregation functions much as any American congregation functions, with Sunday school, a director of religious education, youth service, Boy Scout troops, women's auxiliaries (one for Japanese-speaking and one for English-speaking women), and a choir.

The Moiliili Temple of Honganji, near University Avenue and King Street, was erected in 1960 and is a spectacular addition to the temple architecture of Hawaii.

Honganji has been fortunate in having strong, Island-born leadership. Mr. Sunao Miyabara was the executive secretary of the Young Buddhist Association for years. The Reverend Tsumika Maneki, a University of Hawaii graduate in 1922, was with the University's Agricultural Extension Service for years. In 1953 he decided to enter the Buddhist ministry, and after training in Kyoto he became principal of the Honganji Mission School. He has translated a novel about Shinran Shonin, the founder of the Shin Sect. The Reverend Yoshiaki Fujitani, born on Maui, attended the University of Hawaii and received advance degrees from the University of Chicago. He is Director of Buddhist Education for Hawaii. The Reverend Kay Tagami of Hilo, Hawaii, is the first Hawaiian-born woman to be a minister; she studied Shin Buddhism at Ryukoku University in Kyoto, Japan.

JIKOEN HONGANJI

The Jikoen Honganji Temple at the corner of School Street and Likelike Highway is a temple for Okinawan Buddhists. Although associated with other Honganji groups, the temple membership is almost all Okinawan, and there is a special Okinawan Hall for cultural and social affairs of the Okinawans in Hawaii.

The first Jikoen Temple was built in 1938 on Houghtailing Street near King Street, at a cost of $20,000. The new temple cost over $400,000. Warren Higa was the chairman of the building committee and has emphasized that any Okinawan organization can use the hall. The Reverend Jikai Yamasato was the minister who led the rebuilding program.

HIGASHI HONGANJI

Like the Hompa Honganji, the Higashi Honganji is part of the Shin group, but it is not as Westernized in its concepts or its program of work. Its old temple headquarters at 1128 Banyan Street is a strong center of Japanese activity in the Palama area. The new temple for the Moiliili area is in Palolo Valley and was built in 1961. This is a temple combining Japanese and Indian tradition and is a modernized form of architecture. Abbot Kosho Otani came from Kyoto for the dedication.

Bishop Tenran Mori was in charge of temple building work for Higashi Honganji. The first temple of this group was established in Waimea, Kauai, in 1899 by the Reverend Sazanami. There are now six temples of this group, four on Oahu, one in Hilo, and the one in Waimea, Kauai. The one on Kauai was the first organized Buddhist temple in Hawaii.

The Reverend Shugen Inouye, a Buddhist priest of Higashi Honganji, was only twenty-nine when he died, but he had received national recognition for his work in ceramics, including a one-man show at New York's Museum of Contemporary Crafts.

The present bishop is Bishop Ryoichi Shirayama.

ZEN BUDDHISM

The Zen Sect is different from the above Buddhist groups, which are related to each other. Zen emphasizes not faith, good deeds, or ritual, but the intuitional experience termed the Zen experience. Only those who have had the Zen experience can understand Zen teachings.

Yet, in spite of this, Zen Buddhism is most eager to teach. One of its leaders was the Reverend Ernest Hunt, a former Christian who became a Buddhist and was active in the war years, emphasizing that Buddhism was a universal religion and not an alien enemy cult, its property subject to seizure.

SOTO MISSION

The Soto Mission started its work in Hawaii in 1913 by order of the head of the Zen Sect in Japan. The Venerable Hosen Isobe was the first leader, and the temple was located at School and Nuuanu streets. In 1934 ground was purchased for a new temple, but only classroom buildings were erected. Finally in 1952, under the direction of Bishop Zenkyo Komagata, the new temple was built, at a cost of a half million dollars. At the dedication, Archbishop Rosen Takashina of the Zen Sect came from Japan.

Architecturally, the Soto Temple emphasizes the Indian origins of Buddhism. The altar has the distinctive figures of Mahayana Buddhism. The largest figure is Amida Buddha. The seated Buddha is the historical Gautama, and other figures are representations of Boddhisattvas. Back and to the sides of the altar are the figures of founders of Zen—Josai Daishi (Keizan Jokin) on the left and Joyo Daishi (Dogen Kigen) on the right.

The Soto Mission in Hawaii has become quite Westernized. Sunday school instruction is in English. Weddings are held in either English or Japanese, with a service much like the Christian ceremony. Bon Dances are held every summer. The bonsai garden, the sand garden, and the water garden are beautifully Japanese.

The Soto Mission headquarters and temple on Nuuanu Avenue enlists a great number of Zen followers, including Caucasians. There are four other branches on Oahu, two on Hawaii, and one on each of the other islands. The community acceptance of Buddhism as a faith of many groups was well demonstrated at the eighty-eighth birthday testimonial dinner given for the Reverend Ernest Hunt.

DIAMOND SANGHA

The Soto Zen Temple has many elements of popular Buddhism that do not appeal to some Western minds.

Diamond Sangha (Sangha, Sanskrit for brotherhood) was organized by Robert Aitkin in October 1959. Aitkin had been a civilian worker on Guam before World War II. Captured and interned, he learned something about Zen, and later he made postwar trips to Japan. The Aitkin home in Manoa Valley became the headquarters of Diamond Sangha, which is registered as a religious organization, and the Aitkins have purchased land on Maui near Pauwela for a retreat. The emphasis is on *zazen*, the "sitting Zen" which trains the mind to consider a single object.

A monk, Eido Shimano, came to instruct the group in Zen discipline. The Venerable Hakuun Yasutani, a leading Zen teacher in Japan, has also been in Hawaii to conduct retreats. A place for retreats has been purchased at

Pupukea. A typical all-day retreat begins at 4:00 A.M. There are 25-minute periods of zazen, lectures, and personal interviews with the teacher.

THE NICHIREN MISSION

The only Buddhist sect to take the name of its founder was the Nichiren Sect. Nichiren studied deeply the Buddhist scriptures, especially the Lotus Sutra, which teaches that the original Buddha is omnipresent, eternal, and infinitely compassionate. By his stern moral character, Nichiren set an example for his followers.

The temple was located on Barron Lane near School Street and Nuuanu Avenue, and a Bishop Takaki came from Japan to build the temple. The present temple was built just off the Pali Highway at 3058 Pali Highway. The temple, lacking the usual Boddhisattva figures, emphasizes the sutras as the basis of Buddhist belief.

The present bishop is Bishop Kanjitsu Iijima.

SOKA GAKKAI

Soka Gakkai is the post-World War II movement that has made the greatest impact on modern Japan. It claims its membership covers fifteen per cent of the entire population of Japan. Its membership swelled from 1,300,000 households in 1960 to 5,600,000 in 1966. The spectacle of 30,000 white-uniformed young people marching with discipline has resulted in Soka Gakkai being likened to the Nazis. Soka Gakkai's success in politics has created concern in Japan. Yet Soka Gakkai insists that it is only the lay organization of centuries-old Nichiren Shoshu Buddhism. Claiming that Soka Gakkai is the faith which has inherited the true teaching of Nichiren Daishonin, Nittatsu Shonin (the sixty-sixth High Priest of Nichiren) has maintained the traditional Buddhist ceremonies of the past along with the modern expressions of Soka Gakkai. Soka Gakkai had its beginnings in 1930 when Tsunesaburo Makiguchi and Josei Toda organized a Creative Value Education Society, the members of which were mainly school teachers. Dr. Makiguchi wrote a book entitled *Philosophy of Value*. The society was opposed to the militarism of Japan in the 1930's and, at the outbreak of the war, was suppressed. Mr. Makiguchi died in prison, and in 1951 Josei Toda reorganized the society as the Value Creation Society (Soka Gakkai) and did not restrict its activities to teachers. Toda died in 1958, and in 1960 Daisaku Ikeda became the third president. The ultimate goal of Soka Gakkai is to revive the spirit of true Buddhism —emphasizing mercy and peace. It has become the largest religious organization on earth avowing pacifism. With its first president a martyr of militarism, the society now is engaged in worldwide pacifism. Whereas the Buddhist interpretation of peace in the past meant personal, inner peace, the Soka Gakkai emphasizes world peace with what seems at times a militant pacifism.

The headquarters of Soka Gakkai is in Tokyo, with printing presses and all the modern methods of mass influence, but the head temple, Taisekiji, is at the foot of Mt. Fuji. Here the path through the 250-year-old Sanmon (temple gate) leads by low guest houses to the Meido Temple. Since Soka Gakkai was organized, multistoried dormitories housing fifteen hundred persons each, a grand lecture room seating five thousand, and a grand reception hall have been built.

Yet Nichiren Shoshu remained much the same in its worship. Every midnight the 700-year-old service (*ushi-tora gonyo*) is conducted. In Tokyo, ten thousand teen-age girls have competed in Fife and Drum Band contests.

This blend of ancient Buddhism and modern life quickly spread to areas outside of Japan. American servicemen, especially those with Japanese wives, were apparently the first members to come to Hawaii. The earliest leader in Hawaii was Mr. Wataru Kawamoto, who held the title of Shi-bucho. Organized with thirty-two members in October 1960, Nichiren Shoshu Soka Gakkai claimed six hundred members by 1964. Branches were organized militarily. The immediately interested group contained United States service personnel married to Japanese.

Because Soka Gakkai is political and social in Japan, the local organization has dropped the name Soka Gakkai and uses only the Buddhist designation Nichiren Shoshu, insisting that they are the only true followers of Nichiren. The Hawaii Kaikan of Nichiren Shoshu is located at 2729 Pali Highway, and claims that over five thousand members have enrolled since the founding of the Hawaii Kaikan. In August 1968 a conference including delegates from Japan and mainland America was held with about twelve thousand people in attendance. Sleeping facilities for delegates were at pier eight, and although it was a conference of Nichiren Shoshu, the emphases were those of Soka Gakkai.

MYOKOJI MISSION

The Honolulu Myokoji Mission is an independent Nichiren temple near Nuuanu Stream on a lane beginning at 2003 Nuuanu. Like other Nichiren sects it honors the historic Gautama. In 1967 a beautiful Temple of Peace was erected. This temple is said to have some of the ashes of Gautama Buddha.

AN INDEPENDENT NICHIREN SECT

An independent Nichiren priest in Hawaii is Shaka Provoo. John D. Provoo became interested in Buddhism when eleven years old. His family lived near a Buddhist temple in California. Later in the United States Army he was stationed in Hawaii and studied Buddhism. Sergeant Provoo was at Corregidor when it fell. When the Japanese learned he was a Buddhist, he received favored treatment. After the war Provoo was accused of collaborating with the enemy and was convicted of treason. Ten years later, in 1955, he won his freedom. He later studied in Japan and became a member of the Nichiren Sect. He has a small altar in his home which he terms the Temple of the Eternal Buddha.

OTHER BUDDHIST GROUPS

There are numerous branches of the main Buddhist sects in Hawaii, and there are also a few independent groups. These groups represent emphases existing in Japan before the modern era combined the Japanese religions into registered denominations. The following are located in Hawaii:

1. *Shinshu Kyokai Mission,* 1641 South Beretania Street, is an independent congregation with beliefs of the Shin Sect. They maintain a dormitory for students and young men working in Honolulu. Because of the location, the Bon Festival of this temple is popular with tourists.

2. *Palolo Kannondo,* 3326 Paalea Street, is a temple to Kannon (the Goddess of Mercy) rather than Amida Buddha. A statue to the Boddhisattva who was the patron and protector of fishermen was placed between the Blowhole and Haunama Bay. Not only Japanese but other racial groups used to stop at the shrine for good luck. After December 7, 1941, the statue was broken and dropped over the cliff into the sea. Some fishermen found the statue and took it home and cemented the broken parts together. Although the shrine still exists, the statue was not returned to its former place but now stands in the dooryard of the Kannondo Temple.

3. *Chowado Henjokyo,* 1757 Algeroba Street, is discussed under the New Faiths of Japan, yet its Buddhist approach marks it also as part of Buddhism.

4. *Koboji Shingon Mission,* 1223 North School Street, is a typical Shingon temple but is independent of the Shingon headquarters.

5. *Bodaiji Mission,* 1251 Elm Street, has rebuilt its old temple. This temple is not associated with any of the major Buddhist sects but has drawn most of its ceremonies from popular Japanese practices in Hawaii.

1. Kodo Matsunami, *A Short History of Buddhism in Hawaii,* (mimeographed pamphlet of the Jodo Mission), p. 8.

27. Shinto

Shinto was the religion of ancient Japan, a polytheistic nature worship. Its name comes from the Chinese phrase *shen* (god) *tao* (way) and has the derived meaning "The Way of the Gods." Shinto is a conglomerate of ancient beliefs and practices. The myths of Shinto relate the story of the origin of Japan. The Shinto word *kami* is usually translated god or deity but seems more like the Polynesian word mana, the indwelling power. At places like groves, mountains, rivers, rocks, *kami* was present, and a shrine or temple was built where *kami* had a habitation. Translators who write of Fuji, whose *kami* exists, can say "divine Fuji" or "God Fuji," but the meaning of the English is different from that of the Japanese.

In Shinto mythology, the Sun Goddess Amaterasu-o-mi-Kami established the Imperial family. In the establishment of State Shinto in 1882, the Emperor was recognized as a direct descendant of the Sun Goddess. However, before State Shinto, shrines dedicated to the Sun Goddess had existed. Before World War II the Japanese government recognized thirteen major Shinto sects, which can be divided into five classes. The pure Shinto sects maintained the Shinto of early Japan, The Confucian sects emphasized the teachings of Confucius. The Mountain sects grew out of the early belief in the mountains as gods or abodes of the gods. The Purification sects had some Buddhist ideas. The Faith Healing sects like Konkokyo and Tenrikyo were classed by the government as Shinto. This restrictive classification requiring every sect to belong to one of the thirteen was abolished in 1945, but sects were still required to register. By August 1950, 206 Shinto sects had registered.

The symbol of a Shinto shrine is the gatelike structure called a *torii*. Worship at all Shinto shrines is an individual matter. There are no congregational services, and even a family matter like a wedding will have only the main participants. Since Shinto is the way of the good spirits, the atmosphere of every shrine is bright and gay. Early Shinto was lacking in any idea of personal sin.

Although there was no idea of sin, there was a feeling of evil spirits. Strips of cloth were tied to trees about the shrines to scare away the evil spirits. The strips, now made of paper, represent prayers against the forces of evil. Strung along the rope that is part of the torii, these prayer strips give the impression that evil is left outside when one enters the area of the shrine. Near the gate is a washbasin, and in the physical act of washing one's hands and rinsing one's mouth with water, one symbolizes the spiritual preparation for approaching the shrine. There is a bell to ring. The hands are clapped reverently. Often an offering is given and the person makes his prayer, and leaves. More often in Hawaii than in Japan, the priest in charge conducts a brief service. At some shrines prayer sheets have been prepared which are given to the worshiper.

SHINTO IN HAWAII

The first Japanese arrivals in Hawaii probably brought objects as well as ideas relating to Shinto. The first Shinto shrine was built in Hilo in 1898. Two of the officially recognized Shinto sects came to Hawaii—Shinto (Honkyoku) and Taishakyo.

The Daijingu Temple belonged to the Shinto (Honkyoku) Sect. The Reverend Kinai Ikuma was its priest for over forty years. The Daijingu Temple on Liliha Street was built in honor of Amaterasu, the Sun Goddess. Prominent in the worship of the Sun Goddess was the emperor's birthday and special services of dedication of children to the Sun Goddess. Immediately after the attack on Pearl Harbor, the temple was closed and then confiscated by the Alien Property Custodian.

After the war ended, a shrine was established at 2307 Young Street by Bishop Kinai Ikuma, then eighty years old. A law suit was instituted, and after years the principal assets of the Liliha temple were recovered. Meantime, the bishop had died, and his son-in-law, the Reverend Kagoe Kawasaki, had become bishop. He relocated the temple at 61 Puiwa Road near the Queen Emma Home. Bishop Kawasaki has prepared an excellent description of the temple. He defines *kami* "as an all embracing heavenly central Divine Spirit. . . . We believe that everything that exists is a part (i.e. manifestation, appearance, or revelation) of this Divine Kami." Bishop Kawasaki says that the mirror and the round ball are the traditional Shinto symbols of perfection and harmony.

The Izumo Taishakyo Mission of the Taishakyo Sect was established in Honolulu in 1906. In 1923 the mission brought a master temple-builder from Japan, and a temple was built on Leleo Lane. This temple was built in the ancient manner, without use of nails, and was highly prized by the Japanese. To avoid its confiscation under the Alien Property Act, the members donated the temple to the City of Honolulu. After the war the Mission fought a long court battle to recover the temple and finally succeeded in 1961. However, the area containing the temple had been condemned by the Honolulu Redevelopment Agency. The temple was saved as a cultural heritage and rebuilt at a location near Nuuanu Stream.

Meantime, another Izumo Taishakyo Temple had been located at 1916 Young Street. Traditional Japanese weddings are held at the temple. The present priest is the Reverend Shigemaru Miyao.

The Hawaii Ichizuchi Jinga, 2020 South King Street, is a Shinto sect which was in existence before the Japanese government restricted the shrines to thirteen main sects. The Reverend Shina Miyake founded the sect in 1913 on Alapai Street; it was relocated at the South King Street address in 1918. In 1963 the temple was rebuilt, at which time three shrine builders came from Japan. The shrine is identical with many in Japan.

The Wakamiya Inari Shrine is at 2132 South King Street. The main deity of the shrine is Shoichii Shi Sha,

15. Kotohira Jinsha Temple, 1045 Kama Lane, Honolulu.

and little attention is now given to deities which are common to the Inari shrines of Japan. The Reverend Yoshio Akizaki, who studied in Tokyo in 1912, founded the shrine. His son, the Reverend Takeo Akizaki, has been in full charge since the founder died in 1951. The present priest says that many things have changed. Whereas his father sat and waited for people to come to the temple, he goes to hospitals and homes. In his father's time many of the worshipers were content to come to the shrine without seeing the priest. However, the younger people born in Hawaii expect the priest to counsel and help with their problems. Consequently, the hours of worship services are posted for both morning and evening, and the Reverend Takeo Akizaki has more hours of counseling and worship services than the average Christian clergyman has.

The Kotohiro Jinsha Temple of Hawaii is at 1045 Kama Lane. Although the temple is next to the freeway, the entrance is on North King Street at Kama Lane. The Reverend M. Isobe is the priest. It has a large, modern hall, and receptions after weddings and the dedication of children are held at the shrine. The temple has all the traditional things of Japanese shrines: torii, lions, lanterns, and prayer ropes.

28. The New Faiths of Japan

The pluralism of ancient Shinto made the acceptance of Buddhism easy in Japan. Over the centuries an adjustment of the two faiths took place, so no one thought of belonging to one to the exclusion of the other. A child was dedicated or a marriage ceremony was held at the Shinto shrine. A death, especially the memorials which followed, brought Buddhist services at Buddhist temples. This was also true in Hawaii. The first generation Japanese went to both Shinto and Buddhist shrines and most households had both a *butsudan* (Buddha shelf) and a *kamidana* (Shinto shelf).

But in Japan new varieties of faith were developing, many of them cults with faith-healing practices. Since World War II these have multiplied, and estimates indicate there may be as many as five hundred new cults or varieties of other cults in Japan today. Some of these cannot be classified as either Buddhist or Shinto; they have Buddhist, Shinto, and Christian elements. Japan's defeat turned many Japanese to these new cults. The military had used State Shinto to promote loyalty to a divine emperor. Buddhism was used to some extent so that soldiers would accept death in battle as an assurance of a finer re-incarnation. People turned to new modes of spiritual expression. Some, like Soka Gakkai, were an ancient faith in a strikingly modern form. Others like Tensho Kotai Jingu did not even exist before World War II. These faiths are also successful in Hawaii, for they are modern and they link their followers not to some ancient ancestral form, but to a modern contemporary Japan.

TENRIKYO

Tenrikyo is the oldest of these faiths which has come to Hawaii. Tenrikyo was founded in Japan in 1838 by a woman, Mrs. Miki Nakayama. The foundress was born on April 18, 1798. She lived to be 90. The most common prayer was "Namu Tenri-o-no-Mikoto." Tenri-o-no-Mikoto is most usually translated as Lord of Divine Wisdom.

A kindly and capable person, Mrs. Nakayama sought to help other people. One of her teachings is: "If you daily do your best in the service of others, you may set your heart at peace."[1]

So effective did she become in helping women to have an easy childbirth, that she became known as the goddess of easy delivery. In the Japanese concept of divinity, some were to identify Mrs. Nakayama with God the Parent.

Tenrikyo's foundress stressed that sickness is caused by mental actions. In the teachings of the Tenrikyo, eight kinds of mental dust are named—miserliness, covetousness, hatred, self-love, enmity, anger, avarice, and arrogance. The spirit of contentment sees everything as the expression and goodness of God the Parent, so a determination results to live a joyous life. Tenri City near Nara is the headquarters in Japan. There is the great thousand-bed hospital where significantly the treatment is both spiritual and medical.

Tenrikyo came to Hawaii in 1929 when the Reverend Sakiyero Ueno set up a small temple in a Smith Street apartment. Later headquarters was established on King Street, but in 1964 the headquarters was moved to a new church designed by the Reverend Kaneki Honda, a Nisei priest, at 2920 Pali Highway, across from the Queen Emma Museum. The Reverend Yonekuni Saito is the pastor of the King Street church. The Tenrikyo Kalihi Church in Kalihi-kai maintains a Japanese-language school, and the Honolulu-ko Church on Judd Street has judo instruction.

Tenrikyo has about thirty-five churches and branches in the Islands. There are about forty priests. Many members have journeyed to Japan and participated in the program at Tenri City. Two hundred and eighty-two members made a special journey to Tenri City in January 1966 to mark the eightieth anniversary of the death of the foundress. Of the three thousand members in Hawaii, more than half are second and third generation Japanese.

KONKOKYO

The Imperial Japanese government in the 1930's required all religious groups to register. The thirteen main Shinto sects included faith-healing groups. Konkokyo and Tenri-kyo were classified as major Shinto sects although both were monotheistic. The founder of the former, Bunjiro Kawate, started Konkokyo on October 21, 1859, teaching that he was a manifestation of God in life. The name he used for God was Tenchi-Kane-no-kami. Konkokyo, like Shinto, is a religion of joy. Konkokyo, emphasizing one God instead of many *kami,* and having worship services for a congregation, still is closer to Shinto than the other faith groups. Konkokyo has two groups of followers—*kyoto* or confirmed followers, and *Shinto,* or ordinary believers.

Konkokyo was the first of these independent religions from Japan to come to Hawaii, arriving in 1913. Its head-quarters temple has been at 1728 Liliha Street for years, and the old temple was replaced in 1968 by a modern tem-ple. The clear brightness of the place of worship is like Tenrikyo and Shinto temples. The Reverend Masayuki Kadama is the priest in charge of the temple, which has six branches in the state.

SEICHO NO IE

Seicho no Ie (literally, House of Growth) is one of the faith cults. Its founder, Dr. Masaharu Taniguchi, was edu-cated in English Literature at Waseda University and worked for some years as a translator for an English oil company. He writes and speaks in both Japanese and En-glish. He wrote a semi-atheistic novel entitled *Judging God.* The novel was put on sale on the day of the great Kanto earthquake and fire, and all copies were destroyed. Soon after this Dr. Taniguchi had a mystical experience in which he realized he had been mistaken in judging God. The world, known through the five senses, is merely a production of our minds. "The real world, the world of reality, is God's world or Buddha's domain." The denial of outward reality and the affirmation of the inward spirit led to a religion with some similarities to Christian Science and the Church of Religious Science. He emphasized that Buddha and Christ alike meant that man was originally Buddha and a son of God and sinless. Consequently, the "truth movement" emphasized mental health because man's disease was due to sin-idea.[2]

Dr. Taniguchi founded Seicho no Ie in 1930. The first teacher appeared in Hawaii in 1938. The outbreak of World War II brought the closing of the regular Buddhist and Shinto temples. Thousands of Issei were without spiritual support and turned to other faiths, and consequently Seicho no Ie flourished in Hawaii.

There seems nothing in Dr. Taniguchi's books that supports the idea that a person who has the right mental attitudes can heal or protect someone else. Yet this became a very important aspect in Hawaii. Dr. Andrew W. Lind reported: "According to the leader of the largest group of believers in Honolulu, some 1,283 photographs of A.J.A. (Americans of Japanese Ancestry) soldiers were brought to her by their parents, and owing to her ministrations and the faith of the parents, not one was killed."[3]

Seicho no Ie had the appeal of an intellectual leader, and it is a faith which brought healing or protection with appeals to both Christ and Buddha.

Today Seicho no Ie is well established in Hawaii. Mr.

Sanji Katayama is in charge of the headquarters at 1333 Matlock Avenue. There are about twenty-five units, and membership reports over a thousand households. Youth membership is on an individual basis, and an active youth organization holds statewide summer conferences. Miss Helen Abe of Hilo was the 1967 youth president.

TENSHO KOTAI JINGU KYO

World peace through personal purification is the mission of Tensho Kotai Jingu Kyo. The leader, or Ogamisama (the Godly One), was Mrs. Sayo Kitamura. The teaching is that Ogamisama was a present-day incarnation of God, and a phrase (now seldom used) described her as God's only daughter.

Mrs. Sayo Kitamura was a vigorous and capable farm wife. Her future mother-in-law arranged before harvest time for her son to marry a strong, capable girl, who was forced to work long and hard during the harvest. The first girl was not able to endure the work, and the marriage was broken and at the next harvest another arranged. It took real strength of both mind and body to overcome such a start in married life, but Mrs. Kitamura, the sixth bride, succeeded. In her hard working life she had no time for religion. She suspected someone burned her barn, and she went to a temple where a priest told her that if she prayed she would learn who burned the barn. She began praying and became absorbed in religious matters. She found a way of peace, and in 1945 came the revelation that through her God spoke. Using the analogy of the radio, she said she was the transmitter of God's voice. The movements she makes of rhythmical ecstasy caused Japanese reporters to give her the name of the Dancing Goddess.

This faith was registered as a religious sect in Japan in 1947. Mr. and Mrs. Tsune Nishimura of Hanapepe, Kauai, heard about Ogamisama and went to Tabuse, Japan, to seek help for their son, Hiroshi. The Nishimuras invited her to Hawaii. This first visit, in May 1952, received no publicity except among the Japanese. Ogamisama established branches on Oahu, Maui, and Hawaii and a second home was built for her in Lihue, Kauai. Mr. Takeyoshi Hirai is in charge in Honolulu at 2716 South King Street. Branches exist on the major islands.

A study made of this faith was presented for a Master's Degree thesis at the University of Hawaii.

Ogamisama returned to Hawaii in 1955, in 1960, and at the conclusion of a world tour in 1965. This last visit was part of a world tour in which she visited branches of this faith wherever Japanese immigrants were located. In Hawaii she visited followers in Kealekekua, Pahala, Hilo, Paia, Lahaina, and Lihue. On this last visit, her worldwide prominence brought her a motorcycle escort and an official visit to the governor of the State of Hawaii.

The services in the various branches usually have a tape-recorded sermon of Ogamisama, as well as prayers and hymns. An example of Ogamisama's preachings is this: "After having gone through all animal embodiments, humans are born in this world to polish and refine their souls, not to make love, to accumulate fortune or to succeed in life."[4] Self-purification is the way to world peace.

Mrs. Kitamura died on December 28, 1967.

CHOWADO HENJOKYO MISSION

"Chowado" means the Road of Harmony.

The founder of this Buddhist-based health sect was the Reverend Reisai Fujita. Fujita studied with Hosho Funaoka, head of the Buddhist Academy in Tokyo and later chief abbot of a Shingon Sect. Fujita became a semi-invalid, addicted to drinking. Fujita found in Zen Buddhism and other Oriental disciplines certain breathing exercises which led to his complete cure.

Fujita came to Hawaii in 1929 and remained for three months. He insisted upon adherence to the teachings of Buddha, but most of his followers came because of the physical exercises. "Physical health is the basis of everything in this world" was his teaching. Following World War II, he came to Hawaii to live permanently.

At first the meeting place was in the Liliha area. Then a contractor donated a lot at 1757 Algaroba Street in McCully. The two-story building provided a large second-floor room used for religious and health-training purposes. The services are Buddhist with chanting of Buddhist sutras. However, there are hymns composed by the priest on the theme of health.

SHINREIKYO

Among the faith-healing cults of Japan is one which established the Metapsychic Scientific Institute, which has published its teachings in English. Master Kanichi Otsuka has made worldwide tours promoting his ideas and selling his book *Divination and Power: An Eastern Science and Teachings of Master Kanichi Otsuka*.

A branch of this faith—Shinreikyo Hawaii Shibu—was established in Hilo in 1963, with Mr. Kameo Kiyota as its leader.

SEKAI KYUSEI KYO (THE CHURCH OF WORLD MESSIANITY)

World Messianity is the English name of this pacifist, mental, and spiritual health organization. Definitely rejecting the idea that it is a faith-healing cult, Sekai Kyusei Kyo had a disciplined practice called *johrei,* which seeks purification through the Divine Light of God. Through this purification; pain and suffering may be alleviated, and consequently the practice of johrei may mean healthier individuals.

The founding teacher of Sekai Kyusei Kyo, Mr. Mokichi Okada, began the discipline of johrei in 1919, and slowly developed his teaching. The aim of that teaching—to establish Paradise on earth—caught the Japanese mind in the despairing years following World War II. When Mr. Okada died in 1955, the faith was well established. The present leader is his daughter Mrs. Itsuki Fujieda. She visited Hawaii in 1968 for the dedication of the new Church of World Messianity.

The Church of World Messianity established its Hawaiian work before the death of its founder. The leader is a woman, the Reverend Mitsu Toshimi, whose husband was killed during World War II while serving in the Japanese Army. The Reverend Shokei Iwamori is her assistant, and nine branches have been established with 1,300 members.

After fifteen years' work in Hawaii, the Church of World Messianity built a $500,000 temple at the junction of Nuuanu Pali Drive and the Pali Highway. Besides the branches, the church maintains a vegetable garden at Waimanalo. Believing that chemical fertilizers and insecticides put poisons into the human body, the vegetables are given to members as part of their spiritual-physical health living. In every way, the emphasis is that spiritual and physical health are interconnected.

1. *Ofudesaki II,* Tenrikyo, March 26, 1967, p. 28.

2. Masaharu Taniguchi, *Divine Education and Spiritual Training of Mankind,* Seicho no Ie Foundation, 1956, p. 164.

3. Andrew W. Lind, *Hawaii's Japanese,* Princeton University Press, 1946, published in cooperation with the American Council Institute of Pacific Relations, Inc., p. 208.

4. *The Road to Heaven* is an English compilation of Ogamisama's teaching. This quote is from mimeographed portions distributed in Hawaii.

29. The Chinese Religions

For centuries the Chinese religions were Buddhism, Taoism, and Confucianism. A typical Chinese was seldom known as a Buddhist, Taoist, or Confucianist, but was rather a mixture of all three. This is true also in Hawaii.

Of the three, Buddhism is the most formal and pure. There are gold statues of Buddha, prayer books and beads, and simple offerings of incense, water, fruits, and flowers.

Taoism is a form of mysticism, and adulteration of the aesthetic teachings of Lao Tzu. It is a mixture of folklore and magic. Elaborate ceremonies are often practiced to keep harmony between man and nature.

Confucianism is less of a religion. It is rather a sense of ethics, a way of life. The thoughts of Confucius who lived 2,500 years ago are found in numerous books and are still used as a guide to daily life.

CHINESE BUDDHISM

To the Chinese belief in many spirits, both gods and demons, the Buddhist belief in Boddhisattvas simply added more gods, and in many temples the exact religious origin of a particular god is unknown. Most of the Chinese who came to Hawaii did not distinguish between Buddhism and the other Chinese religious ideas. Buddhism brought to China, however, a definite ritual, an emphasis upon meditation, and a priesthood.

When the Chinese immigrants prospered, the children went to private schools. If the school was Catholic or Episcopal and required or expected all students to be baptized, the children were baptized. The second and third generations found that in Hawaii they were expected to have a religion, and since the lack of religious designations in China was confusing, many Chinese simply said they were Buddhist. There were no organized Buddhist groups and no membership requirements as Christian churches had. The temples were privately owned or existed in connection with Chinese societies. As the Japanese Buddhists built temples which related them to Japan, so the Chinese began to emphasize the Buddhist part of their multiple religion.

The Chinese had been in Hawaii for over a century before Chinese Buddhism had an organization. In 1953 a number of prominent Chinese decided to form a Buddhist Society and bring Buddhist priests from Hong Kong. The Communists of Red China forced all Buddhist monks to leave the monasteries and go out to work. A number fled to Hong Kong, and some of the Chinese in Hawaii wanted their friends selected. Another group wanted the Chinese Buddhist Association in Hong Kong to make the selection so as to have qualified priests. The Hawaii Chinese Buddhist Society was organized, meeting above the

Tang Chinese Herb Store on Maunakea Street. Mr. Tang was the leader. The other group led by Mr. Henry Chun-Hoon asked the Hong Kong Association to send a qualified monk, and Abbot Sic Tse Ting arrived in January 1956 to be the spiritual head of the Chinese Buddhist Association.

The Hawaii Chinese Buddhist Society leased the old Beretania Street United Church of Christ. They arranged for Buddhist monks from Hong Kong. When the urban renewal program forced them from the Beretania location, they purchased the old Nuuanu Congregational Church at 1614 Nuuanu Avenue. The present priest in charge is Reverend Chuen Wai, and the name of the temple is the Tan Wah Chi Temple.

The Hawaii Chinese Buddhist Society emphasizes that its altar images are related to historic Buddhism, whereas the images of the unorganized Chinese temples of Hawaii are a conglomeration of Buddhist and Taoist deities. The main altar figures are: center, Omito (Japanese, Amida; Indian, Amitabha) the immortal Buddha of Infinite Light and Life; right, Kwan Yin (Japanese, Kannon; Indian Avalokitesvara); left, Tay Chong Wong (Indian, Nahasthomaprapta), the God of Wisdom.

In front of Amitabha is a small seated figure of Sakyamuni, the historical Gautama Buddha. There is also a small image of Gautama as an infant, which is used once a year on his birthday.

Just inside the doors of the temple is a statue of the Boddhisattva Wei Ton, sometimes called God Wei Ton, sometimes General Wei Ton. General Wei Ton was the head general of thirty-two generals of Indra's four deva kings, and was asked by Buddha to protect Buddhist teachings. Thus Wei Ton is the guardian of the gate and protector of the temple and of the Buddhist disciples.

In 1955 the Chinese Buddhist Association established the Chinese Buddhist Church in the house they had purchased at 42 Kawananakoa Place. They erected a memorial hall where family memorial tablets were kept and where memorial services were conducted. The images and furnishings were brought from Hong Kong, including a ten-foot Buddha made of camphor wood and covered with gold leaf. Around the walls were panels depicting the life of Buddha, beginning with his premortal existence.

Other priests came to Hawaii. Monk Fat Ming who had escaped from Communist China was one.

In 1966 the Hawaiian Buddhist Association began the erection of a new church. An outstanding example of Chinese traditional architecture, it cost $250,000. The Chinese Buddhist Church has doors on all four sides with shrines. The main figures on the altar are the same as those of the Chinese Buddhist Society, but at the rear entrance is an altar in back of the main altar, where there is a statue of Kwan Yin depicted not as the serene figure of the main altar, but as a multi-armed figure in Indian style. The many arms are symbolic of the manifold ways in which Kwan Yin shows compassion.

CHINESE TEMPLES

The Chinese people in their primitive faith developed the principle of Yin and Yang: opposites have complementary characteristics, either of which can be good or bad. The religious teachings that came later have not replaced the basic pragmatism of the earlier faith. This pragmatism can be learned from the story of the bad boy, which is used to inculcate respect for parents. The mother takes her little bad boy to the temple and tells the story of Choy Sun Tung Ji, who discovered too late his mother's love. Then the mother takes the little boy's slippers and places them at the feet of the Choy Sun Tung Ji image, then burns incense and goes home. The next day the little boy has to go back alone for his slippers. Then, he is good.

Men of Chinese ancestry who are active members of Christian churches often belong to Chinese associations in which Chinese practices having religious significance are part of the ceremonies. However, many of the practices which had religious significance in China are now kept simply because they are traditional or "because they bring no harm." New Year's Eve in Honolulu is a display of fireworks. The noise and fire hazard arouse suggestions of curbing the use of the fireworks. The greatest objection to any restrictions is that it is an interference with religion. This use of fireworks may have religious meaning in China, but in Hawaii fireworks at the dedication of a new building or the opening of a Chinese play is no more than a quaint custom.

The great concepts of Confucianism and Taoism motivate many Chinese in Hawaii as well as elsewhere, but the expression of the Chinese temple religion in Hawaii is rarely intellectual. The few Chinese temples are polytheistic and contain figures of a number of gods. The petitioner who desires the help of some god goes to the temple and burns incense or oil or has a prayer said. To purchase the oil or incense, it is necessary to exchange money for temple currency, which is then burned in the temple incinerator. These incinerators are the mark of every Chinese temple.

Chinese family shrines probably existed from the days of the first Chinese arrivals in Hawaii. In 1878, a Chinese monk, Leong Dick Ying, brought to Hawaii two gold-leafed figures—the Taoist Kwan Tai and the Buddhist Kwan Yin. These were placed in a temple somewhere in the Chinatown area. Later he built a Kwan Yin temple at Kukui and River streets. This was later moved to an upper-floor temple at River and Vineyard streets, to be replaced after the rebuilding of Vineyard Street by the present resplendent Kwan Yin Temple. Monk Leong had entrusted the Kwan Tai figure to a Taoist priest, Ching Sup Yat, who had a temple in Chinatown. This temple was destroyed in the great fire of 1900. The Kwan Tai temple was rebuilt on College Walk.

A number of other temples were located on College Walk and in the area between School and King streets. The Wanda Miu on College Walk, near the School Street bridge, was attended by an old priest who lived long past eighty. This entire area has been placed under an urban renewal plan, and only the major temples survived. The records of the urban renewal show that the temple furnishings in many cases were placed in storage or disposed of in other ways.

A Chinese school with special Chinese disciplines combined with religious meditation was located near Beretania and Smith streets. This was not relocated when the area came under urban renewal in 1969.

KWAN YIN TEMPLE

The Kwan Yin Temple (officially, Koon Yum Temple) is now the most significant structure of the traditional Chinese all-inclusive religion. Supported by the Chun Hoon family, the temple has an important part in the life of many older Chinese, among whom are still a few women whose feet had been bound in childhood. A full description of the temple may be of help in understanding the complexities of Chinese religion.

The Kwan Yin Temple has been in its present location since 1921; however, the present Chinese-styled structure was built in 1961. The temple advances the teachings of Buddha, Confucius, and Lao-tzu.

The business of the temple is governed by a board of trustees; and a Buddhist nun, Sakya Liu-Chi, acts as its agent. Sister Liu-Chi, as she is often called, is a vegetarian and a celibate, and has been in Hawaii since 1958, having come from the Tung Po Tao Cloisters in Kowloon.

The temple is dedicated to Kwan Yin (known to Japanese Buddhists as Kannon and to Indians as Avalokitesvara). The Goddess of Mercy is to all Chinese followers the "pure, sweet, and most sincere" Divinity. Originally she was depicted as a male figure in India and ancient China and Japan, but she gradually came to be represented as a woman. Often she sits meditatively on a lotus blossom, symbolic of good rising from evil. Sometimes she is the goddess of a thousand eyes and arms, who reaches out in response to the sufferings of mankind. Her compassion encompasses all.

As you enter the temple, the dominating central figure is the Goddess of Mercy, Kwan Yin, flanked by the Dragon Maiden on her left. The Dragon Maiden holds a pearl proffered to Kwan Yin. On the right is the Deity of Kindness, Sin Choy, who is the Helper Saint of fifty-three deities and is also known as the Deity of Spiritual and Material Wealth.

The altar to the right holds the statues of Sakyamuni Buddha, accompanied by the Saints Wei Tor and Li Ju; the former holds a wooden wand which dispels evil, disperses the teachings of Buddhism, and protects the students of Buddhism; the latter is one of the famous Eight Immortals, Deity of Medicine and Healing.

The altar to the left holds the statues of Kwan Tai (center), legendary military hero of the Three Kingdoms period, also known as Kei Liarm Po Sat; Mun Cheong (right), patron saint of scholars and Deity of Knowledge; and Wah Tor (left), legendary medical scholar of the Three Kingdoms.

To the extreme right of the front door is the altar containing statues of Mun Kwun, guardian of the gate, and Di-Ju, guardian of the property.

Separate from the main temple stands a miniature structure housing the statues of Tu-Di, guardian of the Earth and Hades, and a statue of Choy Sun Tung Ji, the little boy figure who represents the idea of filial piety.[1]

WONG TIN TIN HOO TEMPLE

Wong Tin Tin Hoo Temple was one temple relocated from its College Walk location. It was started during the Second World War at 1430 College Walk. It was relocated at 688 North Kuakini Street in 1967. The special appeal of the temple during World War II was a memorial statue to Mau Hoong Sun Sung of Canton, a Chinese air force pilot shot down in fighting against the Japanese. Families came to burn incense and have prayers said for their own sons in military service. This has continued during the Korean and Vietnam fighting.

The central figure on the altar is a statue of Kwan Yin, made of concrete by Honolulu craftsman Harry Lai and presented to the temple. Most of the other figurines came from China and are similar to those in the Kwan Yin Temple. There are the Eight Immortals and the Seven Sisters. The Festival of the Seventh Sister has prominence in mid-summer.

Another object of distinction is a lacquered chandelier carved of wood, ornamented with kingfisher feathers and then lacquered.

Miss Wong Yung is the priestess in charge.

OTHER TEMPLES

An example of how a Chinese temple came into being is the Hou Wong Miu, just above School Street on upper Fort Street or what is now the Pali Highway. A Chinese woman, Mrs. Chow Shee, gained a reputation for healing, which she claimed came through her god, Hou Wong, or

Duke King. A shrine was built for the patron god, but soon other shrines, such as the Bad Boy Shrine, were added. The present owner is Mr. Albert K. K. Chow, and with the busy traffic of the Pali Highway making access difficult, the temple has few visitors.

There are a number of Chinese temples in Honolulu. One was on School Street between Holy Trinity Episcopal Church and St. Theresa's Catholic Church, but in 1967 it was taken down.

Besides these, there are shrines belonging to societies. The See Yup Society had a temple, Kuan Ti Miu, above its lodge hall, but the temple had ceased to be used even before it was torn down. The Lum Sai Ho Tong built a new hall in 1953 on River Street. Upstairs is the Ku Po Miu. This was the only temple to survive the renewal program. The chief image is that of the ancestress of the Lum family.

THE CHINESE CALENDAR

Chinese festival days are semi-religious. They follow the Chinese Lunar Year. Chinese New Year, which comes in late January or February, is the time of much activity in the temples. Many Chinese festivals are transferred to the Western calendar New Year, but the temples still observe the Chinese New Year. In the spring the Chinese clean graves and hold memorial services. The correct date for this Tsing Ming (or Ching Ming) observance is on April 4 or 5, fifteen days after the spring equinox, but in Hawaii this may extend over several weeks.

The seventh night of the seventh moon in late summer is

the festival when Chinese girls pay tribute to the Weaver Maid, the seventh daughter who finally married the man she loved.

The Chinese Moon Festival, fifteenth day of the eighth month, is a Harvest Moon Festival with round moon-cakes. The Chinese temples also observe the Winter Solstice.

The Double Ten (October 10) anniversary of the founding of the Republic of China is an important political date.

1. Information sheet from Kwan Yin Temple.

30. Baha'i

A Persian, Siyyid Ali Muhammed, born in Shiraz, Persia, October 20, 1819, started the Baha'i faith. On May 23, 1844, he announced that he was the Gate (*Bab*) of a universal faith which was to supplant Islam. He sent a proclamation to some of the leading men of Persia. After almost six years of imprisonment, he was executed. One of his followers tried to assassinate the shah, and the movement was put down with numerous executions.

One leader to whom the Bab had sent a proclamation by his first disciple was Mirza Husayn Ali, son of one of the shah's ministers. This nobleman alone of the ones to whom the proclamations were sent accepted the cause. He never met the Bab in person, but the Bab sent him personal items such as the Bab's writings and seals. The nobleman took the name Baha'u'llah. He was the only one of the imprisoned followers of the Bab not executed but exiled.

In Bagdad he began his teaching but was imprisoned by order of the Turkish government, and after a time he was sent to Palestine to be imprisoned. Shortly before his imprisonment he stated that he was the one whom the Bab prophesied would come. Until the end of his life, he remained technically a prisoner. But he was so revered by those in charge of the prison that when he decided to live in a cottage on Mount Carmel, he was allowed to do so. The British ambassador to Persia had interviewed the Bab, and some interest had developed in this new faith in England. This was renewed when some people visited Baha'u'llah. At the World Congress of Religion, held at the World's Faith of 1893 in Chicago, a speaker presented some information about the spiritual strength of this mystical religion now termed Baha'ism.

Baha'u'llah died the following year. His son, Abbas Effendi, took the title of Abdul-Baha. This son had been born in Teheran the very day, May 23, 1844, when the Bab had announced the new faith. He became the interpreter of the faith.

At the Congress of Religions, a statement of Baha'u'llah showed the vision of his faith:

> That all the nations should become one in faith, and all men as brothers, that the bonds of affection and unity between the sons of men should be strengthened, that diversity of religion should cease and differences of race be annulled . . . Let not a man glory in this, that he loves his country; let him rather glory in this that he loves his kind.[1]

Shortly after Baha'u'llah's death, a group of Americans came to Haifa to learn more of this faith. Soon American organizational ability was promoting Baha'i, not only in America, but all over the world.

The Baha'i faith was first brought to Hawaii in 1902

by Miss Agnes Alexander, daughter of the president of Punahou, William DeWitt Alexander, and granddaughter of the missionaries Baldwin and Alexander. Friends joined her in study of this faith. On Maui her cousin, Mrs. Katherine Baldwin, was active. Mr. Kawachi Yamamoto was the first Japanese Baha'i and Mrs. May Fenton was a Hawaiian follower. Miss Alexander also interested Charles Reed Bishop, who had moved to California, in the movement.

The first public lecture was in the Alexander Young Hotel in 1909, and a delegate went to the Baha'i convention in 1912, but it was not until 1927 that a definite meeting place was established in Mrs. Samuel Baldwin's cottage.

Miss Martha Root, a national lecturer for Baha'i, made a world tour but became ill and died in Honolulu. She was buried in Oahu Cemetery.

In 1940 Mr. and Mrs. Jon Freitas and Mr. and Mrs. Joseph Marques donated land on McCully Street by the Ala Wai Canal, and the next year a center building was built. In 1960 this site was sold, and a seventeen-room house at 3264 Allan Place in Nuuanu Valley became the headquarters. The International Headquarters in Haifa, Palestine, known as the Universal House of Justice, gave instructions for the community to divide into seven assemblies with other separate jurisdictional sections on the neighboring islands. So in 1964 the National Spiritual Assembly for the Hawaiian Islands was formed, with Mrs. Elizabeth Hollinger as secretary.

1. Emeric Sala, *This Earth One Country*, Humphries, 1945, pp. 156–57.

31. The Faiths from India

For years the Watamull family of Bombay has had stores in Honolulu. The family members are American in thought and orientation, and there has been intermarriage with other racial groups. If some of the families observe Indian practices containing Hindu religious ideas, it is more cultural than religious.

However, Hindu religious ideas have entered Hawaii in many ways. The East-West Philosophers Conferences have usually had one notable expositer of Indian thought, and lecturers and exchange professors from India have been at the University of Hawaii. With the establishment of the East-West Center, a considerable number of Indians who observe Hindu dietary rules and religious practices have come to Hawaii, so the faiths of India exist in Hawaii.

For a number of years the sculptor Mariozzi was a member of the Vedanta Society, which reflected the teachings of the Indian thinker Krishnamurti. Without being a formally organized group in Hawaii, they promoted understanding of Indian thought. In 1958 a teacher from India making his first contact with the Western world took part in a Y.W.C.A. discussion with Buddhist and Christian speakers. The audience was small, but ten years later the same teacher drew capacity audiences. In those ten years the Maharishi Mahesh Yogi had become world famous as the "guru of transcendental meditation" and had enlisted the Beatles and others of the entertainment world as his followers. He has followers in Honolulu, and an International Meditation Center has been organized with meetings held at the Y.W.C.A.

32. Religious Architecture and Art

Christian architectural forms came to Hawaii in various ways. Byzantine architecture from Constantinople influenced all Eastern architecture. The Byzantine dome exerted its influence in the Honganji Temple on the Pali Highway, for the Moslems adapted it for their mosques. Later the Buddhists used the dome in limited measure.

The Romanesque, using the round Roman arch as the basis for design and structure, has modernized Romanesque in St. Patrick's Church in Kaimuki.

The Gothic design, with its pointed arches and stained glass, had a revival in Europe and America in the years when Hawaii was building many of its older churches. St. Andrew's Cathedral was designed in Gothic style. The transepts were never built, and the 1958 rebuilding used a modernized Gothic, which harmonizes amazingly with the older Gothic forms. The Church of the Epiphany in Kaimuki is also Gothic, and a number of churches such as Sacred Hearts Church in Hawi, Kohala, and Kaumakapili Church on North King Street have Gothic windows and other features.

Iolani Palace is a Renaissance palace with emphasis upon proportion, balance, and symmetry in outward design. No churches in Hawaii are completely Renaissance, but Central Union and Kawaiahao are New England Colonial, which was a blossoming of Renaissance architecture in America. The Cathedral of Our Lady of Peace is Renaissance with the Spanish influences evident. In use of symmetry in a formal setting, the Mormon Temple at Laie used a modernized form of Renaissance architecture.

The various national groups in Hawaii have sought to maintain something of their homeland. Makiki Christian Church on Pensacola Street drew its architecture from a medieval Japanese castle. First Chinese Church on South King Street has the loveliness of Chinese design. The Korean Christian Church on Liliha Street and St. Luke's Episcopal Church on Judd Street stress Korean forms. The Samoan Congregational Church of Jesus Christ, with its inlaid wooden ceiling, is a marvelous example of Samoan woodwork.

The Buddhist and Shinto temples are mostly Japanese, and some of the Shinto shrines might be in remote Japanese villages. The Chinese Buddhists use the brilliant color of China. The Soto and Jodo temples sought to establish relationship to India in their architecture. The Soto Zen temple on Nuuanu Avenue has Indian aspects with a design which might be called an adaptation to Hawaii.

In Japan the centuries-old temple designs are being replaced by modern Japanese design. A blend of this modern design with some traditional temple features are apparent in the Church of World Messianity just off the Pali

Highway, and the Konkokyo Temple on Liliha Street. Modern architectural design with just a hint of Chinese influence characterizes the Community Church of Honolulu at Nuuanu Avenue and Wyllie Street.

It is modern architecture which is contributing the most to Hawaii's architecture today. Modern architecture insists upon certain criteria for buildings. A church in Hawaii should have a design suitable for Hawaii, not simply a transfer of New England, Spanish, or Oriental designs. The first church to be designed for a Hawaiian setting was the First Church of Christ Scientist on Punahou Street.

The second point in building design is uppermost, and that is freedom from the restrictions of masonry. With steel, concrete, and glass, it is not necessary to build in earlier forms in which design was restricted by the materials used. The Latter-day Saints Tabernacle at Beretania Street and Kalakaua Avenue was the first use of striking modern design.

Third, modern architecture insists that a building should be designed for a certain function, that is, worship. The Congregationalists built identical churches at Kapaa and Hanapepe, using a simple yet effective worshipful design.

In the fourth place, modern architects seek to express in a building something of the meaning of a church, its faith and convictions.

The modern architect asks first—what does this congregation believe that should be expressed in its place of worship? Second, how can the building express that

belief and be built functionally in support of the belief
of the church? Third, how should the church relate to its
environment?

The First Methodist Church is a completely modern
church which has embodied all of these features. Since
Hawaii is built of coral and lava, these were the building
materials. The very structure of the church carries out the
purpose of the church to show love to God and love to
one's neighbor. The open sides of the church are an expression of the idea that love to one's neighbor extends to all
the world. It must be admitted that this splendid concept
ignores the fact that wind and rain are also features of
Hawaii. This is also true of the Church of Our Lady of
Good Counsel in Pearl City. The First Presbyterian
Church combined an openness of view with a wall of
plate glass to provide air conditioning.

Now almost every church being built in Hawaii has
modern design or at least an awareness of these principles
of modern design. Lava rock, open design, and views of
beauty show the visitor that the church was designed for
Hawaii. Good design and simplicity of lines distinguish
these modern churches. The Church of the Holy Nativity
in Aina Haina received an award. Saint Pius X Church
in Manoa Valley, Waiakeola Church in Waialae-Kahala,
the many chapels of the Latter-day Saints, and a host of
others have a modern design.

A number of churches are very successful in creating a
point of focus for the total design. The United Church of
Christ on Judd and Liliha streets has an abstract window
design of the cross with red panels symbolizing the wounds

of Christ. Perhaps the most striking of these modern churches are on Kauai, where Father John McDonald enlisted the work of Hawaii's outstanding artists. The results are St. Catherine's Church at Kapaa, St. Sylvester's Church at Kilauea, and St. William's Church at Hanalei.

The Second Vatican Council was a most significant event for Roman Catholics. The renewal of the church affects architecture as shown by Chaminade College Chapel. The emphasis upon the Mass as participation and the Fellowship of Believers with one another and with Christ has led to a semicircular arrangement of pews, in a circular chapel.

Closely allied with architecture is the religious art in churches. In one of the most unusual art treasures in Hawaii, it served as a substitute for architecture. The Painted Church at Honaunau is a tourist attraction but also is a memorial to Father John of Belgium. Father John (born Joseph Velghe) began his missionary service in the Marquesans and worked with Brother Michel Blanc, a carpenter and builder who provided art for the churches he built. Father John came to Hawaii in 1899 and was assigned to Honaunau. Soon after his arrival, a new church was built, a small rectangular box. Father John decided he wanted the Gothic Cathedral of Burgos and painted the interior to provide the illusion. The flat wall behind the altar was painted to picture the Gothic apse in perspective. Along the walls were painted pictures: The Temptation of Jesus, The Appearance of the Cross to St. Francis, Cain and Abel, and A Good Death, mostly copies of religious art Father John had known in Europe.

The one of the Prophet Daniel and the handwriting on the wall has Hawaiian words for the usual Hebrew.

Father John also painted murals in the old church of Maria Lanakila, which had been built in 1860 and was destroyed in the 1950 earthquake. Father John returned to Belgium in 1904. Twenty years later he gave instruction in drawing and painting to a student who, as Father Evarist, came to Hawaii in 1927 and was pastor of churches on Hawaii, Maui, and Lanai. Father Evarist had a publication, *Le Cathechisme en Images,* and painted the interior of the Star of the Sea Church at Kalapana. He did not try to imitate a cathedral interior but did place on the barrel vault of the ceiling Roman arches for his major pictures. One, Christ the King, is dated November 6, 1930.

These painted churches are art treasures, and they manifest the extent of the European artistic dominance.

In contrast, artist DeLos Blackmar, in 1940, sought for complete Hawaiian identification in painting for the Church of the Holy Innocents in Lahaina. Above the altar the painting portrays a Hawaiian Madonna and Child with red ti-leaf halos. The panels on the front of the altar portray the Hawaiian staffs of life—breadfruit, fish, and taro. Artist Juliette Fraser painted a Hawaiian nativity for St. Catherine's Church in Kapaa, Kauai.

Highly influential upon the art of Hawaii was Jean Charlot, who had been a mural painter associated with the great muralists of Mexico. A Roman Catholic, Jean Charlot had a broad appreciation of all Hawaii's religious background. Fascinated by the spiritual quality of ancient

Hawaii, Charlot wrote plays in the Hawaiian language as well as painting murals for the University of Hawaii, portraying the spiritual concepts of ancient Hawaii. The Waikiki Branch of the First Hawaiian Bank commissioned Charlot to do a fresco of Hawaii's history. Charlot included a scene portraying the elated excitement of the Hawaiians as the first words ever printed in the Hawaiian language came off the press. Charlot's most striking religious painting is over the altar at St. Catherine's Church in Kapaa.

The Catholic artists of Hawaii have made religious art significant in a Hawaiian setting, sponsoring exhibitions and contests (one on a Madonna theme drew over two hundred entries). Catholic schools as well as most parish churches have modern religious art created in Hawaii. Some art may be stylized in the forms of the Stations of the Cross, but much of it is modern in design and concerning Hawaii.

Sculpture has been significant in Hawaii's religion. In Catholic churches, much traditional ecclesiastical art exists—crucifixes, Madonnas, and saints, such as can be found in thousands of churches in Europe and America. But some of the more recent churches have work of artists resident in Hawaii. Swiss born Fritz Abplanalp carved the crucifixes for Our Lady of Good Counsel Church in Pearl City and St. Anthony of Padua Church in Kailua.

The statue of Father Damien now placed in the National Statuary Hall in Washington, D.C., has been controversial. The one selected was designed by New York artist Marisol Escobar. Inspired by a photograph of

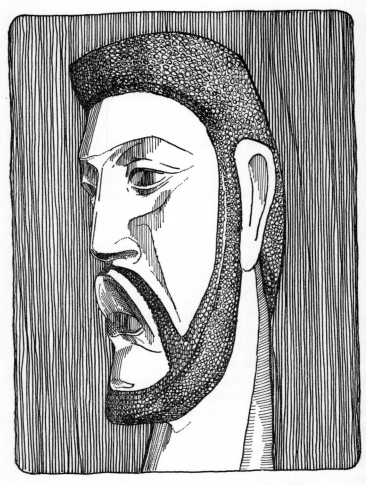

16. *The Prophet*—woodcarving with Monel
Metal and bronze, by Fritz Abplanalp.

Father Damien taken a few months before his death, the statue left no doubt as to the sacrifice that Father Damien had made in serving the leprosy exiles at Kalaupapa. The acceptance of this statue shows a maturity of artistic judgment that augurs well for the future of art in Hawaii.

For centuries stained glass has had major importance in ecclesiastical art. The first major use of stained glass was in the old Central Union Church at Richards Street. Arranged in geometrical design, the windows had no ecclesiastical significance. St. Andrew's Cathedral had the first stained-glass window with Biblical themes. Numerous other churches—Church of the Epiphany, Kaumakapili, Holy Rosary in Paia, Maui, and St. Patrick's Church—have traditional windows.

In its 1958 reconstruction, St. Andrew's erected almost the entire West wall of stained glass. Centered over the entrance are the symbols of the trinity. South of the center, the life of Christ is depicted. The north portion outlines the history of the Christian message from its beginning to the coming of the Episcopal Church to Hawaii, even remembering the termites which caused the rebuilding of the church.

St. Augustine's Church in Waikiki is outstanding both as modern architecture whose upward sweep rivals the Gothic in aspiration, and for its stained-glass windows made in Austria. The first window with a Hawaiian theme pictures the arrival of the first Catholic missionaries in 1927. The second shows the Maui Catechist Helio, who reputedly had five thousand people prepared for baptism before the first Catholic priests arrived on Maui. A third pictures Father Damien at work in Kalaupapa, and the fourth shows Bishop Sweeney being presented with the new St. Augustine Church.

Sister Anne Pierre, C.S.J., was a teacher of art in Catholic schools and a capable artist who painted in fresco the altar mural for Sacred Hearts Church in Waianae. Tseng Yu-Ho (Mrs. Gustave Ecke) did a fresco of St. Francis Xavier for St. Catherine's Church in Kapaa, Kauai. Mrs. George McLaughlin sculptured the Stations of the Cross for St. Pius X Church while Helene and Marciel Calliet painted the gesso panels for the Stations of the Cross for Holy Trinity Church. Mrs. Henry Stanford Persons sculptured the designs for the Twelve Apostles, which are being cast in bronze for St. Andrew's Cathedral.

Madge Tennent's marvelous paintings of Hawaiian women are sometimes classed as Madonnas. Juliette May Fraser's *Ke Anuenue* is a book of illustrations of ancient Hawaiian legends; her most famous religious art was done for a chapel on the Greek Island of Chios.

Maurice Kidjel has two distinctive murals—one *The Footsteps of the Fathers* in Temple Emanu-El, and the other *The Coming in Glory* for the dome of the Apostolic Faith Church. Benjamin P. Whittle has painted a traditional head of Christ on black velvet. St. George's in Waimanalo has a wrought-iron crucifix designed by John Lochtefeld, who painted the altar fresco and designed the exterior mosaic of St. George and the dragon. Mr. and Mrs. Kenneth Price were the artists for the Stations of the Cross.

Artist Erica Karawina (Mrs. Sidney Hsiao) has pioneered modern stained-glass design in Hawaii. Her little stained-glass altar cross made for the Sunday school of the Palolo Community Methodist Church was exhibited at the New York World Fair. Other minor yet striking windows were made for the chapel at the Salvation Army Waioli Cottages. Erica Karawina, who also designs stained glass set in concrete, has done major work for Our Lady of Sorrows Church in Wahiawa and has done Tree of Life designs for Wesley Memorial Methodist Church and the Manoa Valley United Church of Christ.

Although the Christian art in Hawaii is creative and cognizant of the Hawaiian setting, the religious art of the Orient is still traditional. There are artistic treasures of the past, such as the statue of Kannon in the Soto Mission Temple and the images of the ancient guardian gods in the Todaiji Temple. With pride, Japanese Buddhists tell of the art made in Japan, and the Chinese are ready to tell how their art came from Hong Kong or Canton before the Communists assumed control.

Although the Buddhist services and temple arrangements reflect contact with Western life, with hymns sung in European-scaled music accompanied by electric organs, there has been almost no Westernization of Buddhist sculpture or painting. Mr. Fritz Abplanalp carved a massive head of Buddha which was exhibited at the entrance of the Hawaiian Pavilion at the Seattle World Fair, but the lack of symbolical characteristics of the traditional Buddha brought adverse comment. The vitality of the Oriental faiths in Hawaii and the tremendous creativity of artists with Oriental ancestry has not yet produced art for the temples, although an indication of what may be in the future occasionally appears in art exhibitions.

Tseng Yu-Ho's artistic reputation came from her Dsui paintings, syntheses, or collages of silk and paper. Her work shows the artistic future possible for Oriental art in Hawaii. The frescos of Filial Piety in the Chinese Manoa Cemetery are her chief contribution to Oriental religious art.

The interchange of ideas of Western and Oriental art is significant in Hawaii, but rarely shows in the art in religious structures. The Community Church of Honolulu in 1965 held an exhibit of religious art in Hawaii; it indicated that the artists are portraying a meaningful faith shaped by the interplay of cultures. Using a Western art concept, the altar screen of the Community Church, a wood carved Tree of Life, shows both Chinese and Hawaiian influences. It is the work of Hon Chew Hee.

33. The Religious Scene in Hawaii

Religion in Hawaii has diversity. That diversity ranges from the unvoiced conditioning remaining from Hawaii's ancient stone-age culture to modern "death of God" theology. A Pakistani student at the East-West Center bowing toward Mecca, a Zen disciple sitting in silence, an old Hawaiian woman placing an offering to Pele before a lava flow, the beating of a Chinese gong, the Jewish Passover responses remembering the exodus from Egypt of three thousand years ago, the speaking in tongues at a Pentecostal service, the Lord's Prayer in Samoan, and Christian ministers and priests representing every race on earth—all of these and a thousand more testify to that diversity.

Hawaii has produced a strange duality in the people who come to its shore. There is the desire to belong to Hawaii and there is the desire to belong to the culture of the home country. People as diverse as an Eskimo from Nome, a Swede from Upsala, an Armenian from Lebanon, and a Maori from New Zealand expressed their pleasure over living in Hawaii, yet within minutes they told with eagerness whence they had come. This need to belong to the past has been a source of the multiplicity of religious organization. Church Row at Kailua, Oahu, has Lutheran, Southern Baptist, Methodist, Christian, Northern Baptist, Presbyterian, and Episcopal Churches. The motivation in building these churches was to provide a church like the church which was attended on the mainland so that people would feel at home. This has been supported by the missionary nature of the churches.

The Reverend Richard Isler, director of the Honolulu Council of Churches in the 1950's, felt that this desire to relate to some mainland groups, especially if that group provided financial assistance, was a weakening influence in the religious life in Hawaii.

This desire to relate to a source does not end with the first generation. There are Buddhists who recognize the need to sever ties with the past and emphasize life in Hawaii, yet some Buddhist groups have remained stationary in membership while the new religious faiths, such as Tensho Kotai Jingu Kyo and the Church of World Messianity, have flourished.

Because of the pervasiveness of American culture, and the persistence of Japanese culture, the seeking for a relationship outside of Hawaii affects even the Hawaiians. The desire is not to belong to the source or to Hawaii as much as to belong to something which has meaning. The travel agent planning a trip to New England for a Chinese-Hawaiian was startled when told, "I want to go to Plymouth Rock where our forefathers landed." In the Nichiren Shoshu Sect, with its Soka Gakkai branch pledged to the moral renewal of Japan, one enthusiastic leader was a Hawaiian youth whose father had been stationed in Japan.

Hawaii has diversity and that diversity seeks meaning primarily in the past, in terms of a beginning in lands other than Hawaii. Yet the churches do seek for meaningful relationship to Hawaii. The Queen's Prayer may be sung in churches whose denominational contact with Hawaiians is slight. People may relate to the Hawaiian past with an antiquarian interest that frustrates people who feel the modern challenge of Hawaii. The Hawaii Council of Housing, sponsored by individual churches as well as by the Hawaii Council of Churches and the International Longshoremen's and Warehousemen's Union, is a significant effort by churches and labor to provide adequate housing for low-income groups in one of Honolulu's blighted areas. This is seeking for significance in modern Hawaii. Yet some of these same groups were content to let the equally blighted area of Leeward Oahu remain in the pattern of an ancient Hawaiian past.

Hawaii is a land of youth, where the average age is the lowest in the nation. The future of religion in Hawaii will depend on these young people. The religious leaders find an uncertainty among the youth. If the religious faiths emphasize the religious meanings of other lands and other times, they may lose the young people, whose knowledge is only of Hawaii. If the religious faiths place only local meanings first, they may lose young people attracted by influences as remote from Hawaii as the Beatles of Liverpool.

The answer is not a compromise but a thrust for the

future. What has the deepest meaning anywhere in the world will have the deepest meaning in Hawaii, and the opposite is equally true. What has the deepest meaning for humanity in Hawaii will have the deepest meaning for humanity throughout the world.

Does Hawaii have a meaning, a significance for the entire world? Is the religious diversity in Hawaii only an interesting oddity formed by historical forces, or have the religions of Hawaii a creative force that can flow back to their many sources to reshape the faiths of the earth?

As people whose religious faith may have originated far from Hawaii, and who accept the many-cultured aspects of Hawaii with sympathy and goodwill develop that peculiar loving quality called aloha, they have a major contribution to give to the religions of the world. Hawaii is just beginning to see that it is not just a receiver of the world's religions, but Hawaii, shaping, changing, deepening the concepts of love, goodwill, and brotherhood, can become a major creative power in religion.

If this seems absurd, then remember—Bethlehem was no more important than Hoonaunau, where Opukahaia began his pilgrimage to faith in Christ. Gethsemane is no more isolated than Kalawao, where Father Damien knew that love meant suffering even unto death. "Can any good come out of Nazareth?" could be echoed of any community in Hawaii where a new meaning, a new faith, and a new purpose has come.

Hawaii has much to give to the world, for in the midst of its diversity, its duality, and its contradictions, it has sought and has found, as Reverend James Kekela expressed it, "O ke aloha, oia ka mole o mea pono ame na mea ioaio a pau. Love is the root of all that is good and all that is true forever."

Glossary of Hawaiian Words

The similarity of Polynesian languages is evident in spite of the wide variety in spelling developed when the languages became written. Some Polynesian words are better known in Tahitian forms than in Hawaiian, so in a few cases the Hawaiian words are followed by the Tahitian equivalent.

Aha Paeaina: Annual Conference; lit., gathering of all islands.
akua: god, used of all divinities; in Christian usage, God
ala wai: way of water, canal
alii: chief; rank was by an intricate kapu system
aloha: love; good will; commonly used as a word of greeting
aumakua: family or ancestral gods or spirits

Halemaumau: active crater within the greater Kilauea Crater
haole: stranger; foreigner; now used for Caucasians
hapa haole: part Caucasian
Hawaii nei: this Hawaii; present-day Hawaii
heiau: place for ancient Hawaiian worship
Hewahewa: high priest in time of Kamehameha the Great
Hiiaka: sister of Pele

hoike: Sunday school rally

Hoku Ao Nani: Beautiful Star, name of hymn book

hopekahu: assistant pastor

hula: dance; religious or secular

Io: hawk; derivative, high god

Iolani: Hawk of Heaven; a name of King Kamehameha IV

kahili: a standard made of feathers; used as a symbol of high
rank

kahu: shepherd, i.e. pastor

kahuna: ancient Hawaiian priest; the religious ceremonies
conducted by the priest

kahuna nui: high priest

Kanaloa (Taneroa, Ta'aroa): god of the sea

Kane (Tane): god of life; in Hawaii, chief god

kapu: forbidden and taboo

kapua: a being that is able to change form

Kilauea: crater on the island of Hawaii or the volcanic com-
plex with many active craters

Ku (Tu): god of war.

kuhina nui: chief adviser; prime minister

kukui: candlenut; derivative, light

Kumulipo: Hawaiian creation chant

lanai: veranda or porch

lomilomi: form of massage used in healing

Lono: god of agriculture

luahine: aged woman

luna: foreman

maile: vine with fragrant leaves used in religious or other
    ceremonies
makahiki: year; festival of thanksgiving marking the end of the
    year
mana: power, especially the power which comes to a person or
    thing from a higher source
menehune: legendary Hawaiian dwarfs

ohana: family; derivative, family worship
ohelo: upland mountain berry sacred to Pele

palapala: writing; derivative, learning
Papa: Earth Mother
Pele: goddess of the volcano
pule: prayer

Ulu Mau: Hawaiian village near Kaneohe, Oahu
unihipili: spirits of the dead

Wakea: Sky Father

Index

0739